HOWARD the DUCK

GOOD NIGHT, AND GOOD DUCK

WRITER
CHIP ZDARSKY

ISSUE #7

ARTIST
KEVIN MAGUIRE

COLOR ARTISTS
JOE QUIN[...]
WITH JOR[...]

ISSUES #8-11

PENCILER
JOE QUINONES

INKERS
JOE RIVERA
WITH JOE QUINONES (#8 & #1[...])
PAOLO RIVERA (#9)
& MARC DEERING (#9-11)

[...]ARTISTS
[...]QUINONES
WITH JORDAN GIBSON

LETTERER
VC's TRAVIS LANHAM

COVER ART
JOE QUINONES

ASSISTANT EDITOR
CHARLES BEACHAM

EDITOR
WIL MOSS

HOWARD THE DUCK CREATED BY STEVE GERBER & VAL MAYERIK

COLLECTION EDITOR: JENNIFER GRÜNWALD
ASSOCIATE EDITOR: SARAH BRUNSTAD
ASSOCIATE MANAGING EDITOR: KATERI WOODY
EDITOR, SPECIAL PROJECTS: MARK D. BEAZLEY

VP PRODUCTION & SPECIAL PROJECTS: JEFF YOUNGQUIST
SVP PRINT, SALES & MARKETING: DAVID GABRIEL
BOOK DESIGNER: JAY BOWEN

EDITOR IN CHIEF: AXEL ALONSO
CHIEF CREATIVE OFFICER: JOE QUESADA
PUBLISHER: DAN BUCKLEY
EXECUTIVE PRODUCER: ALAN FINE

HOWARD THE DUCK VOL. 2: GOOD NIGHT, AND GOOD DUCK. Contains material originally published in magazine form as HOWARD THE DUCK #7-11. First printing 2016. ISBN# 978-0-7851-9939-7. Published by MARVEL WORLDWIDE, INC., a subsidiary of MARVEL ENTERTAINMENT, LLC. OFFICE OF PUBLICATION: 135 West 50th Street, New York, NY 10020. Copyright © 2016 MARVEL No similarity between any of the names, characters, persons, and/or institutions in this magazine with those of any living or dead person or institution is intended, and any such similarity which may exist is purely coincidental. **Printed in Canada.** ALAN FINE, President, Marvel Entertainment; DAN BUCKLEY, President, TV, Publishing & Brand Management; JOE QUESADA, Chief Creative Officer; TOM BREVOORT, SVP of Publishing; DAVID BOGART, SVP of Business Affairs & Operations, Publishing & Partnership; C.B. CEBULSKI, VP of Brand Management & Development, Asia; DAVID GABRIEL, SVP of Sales & Marketing, Publishing; JEFF YOUNGQUIST, VP of Production & Special Projects; DAN CARR, Executive Director of Publishing Technology; ALEX MORALES, Director of Publishing Operations; SUSAN CRESPI, Production Manager; STAN LEE, Chairman Emeritus. For information regarding advertising in Marvel Comics or on Marvel.com, please contact Vit DeBellis, Integrated Sales Manager, at vdebellis@marvel.com. For Marvel subscription inquiries, please call 888-511-5480. **Manufactured between 9/23/2016 and 10/31/2016 by SOLISCO PRINTERS, SCOTT, QC, CANADA.**

10 9 8 7 6 5 4 3 2 1

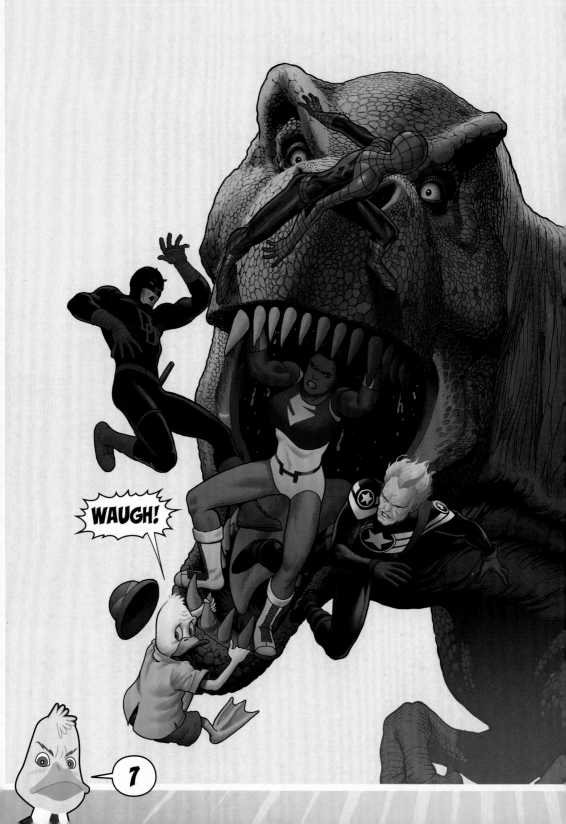

WAUGH!

7

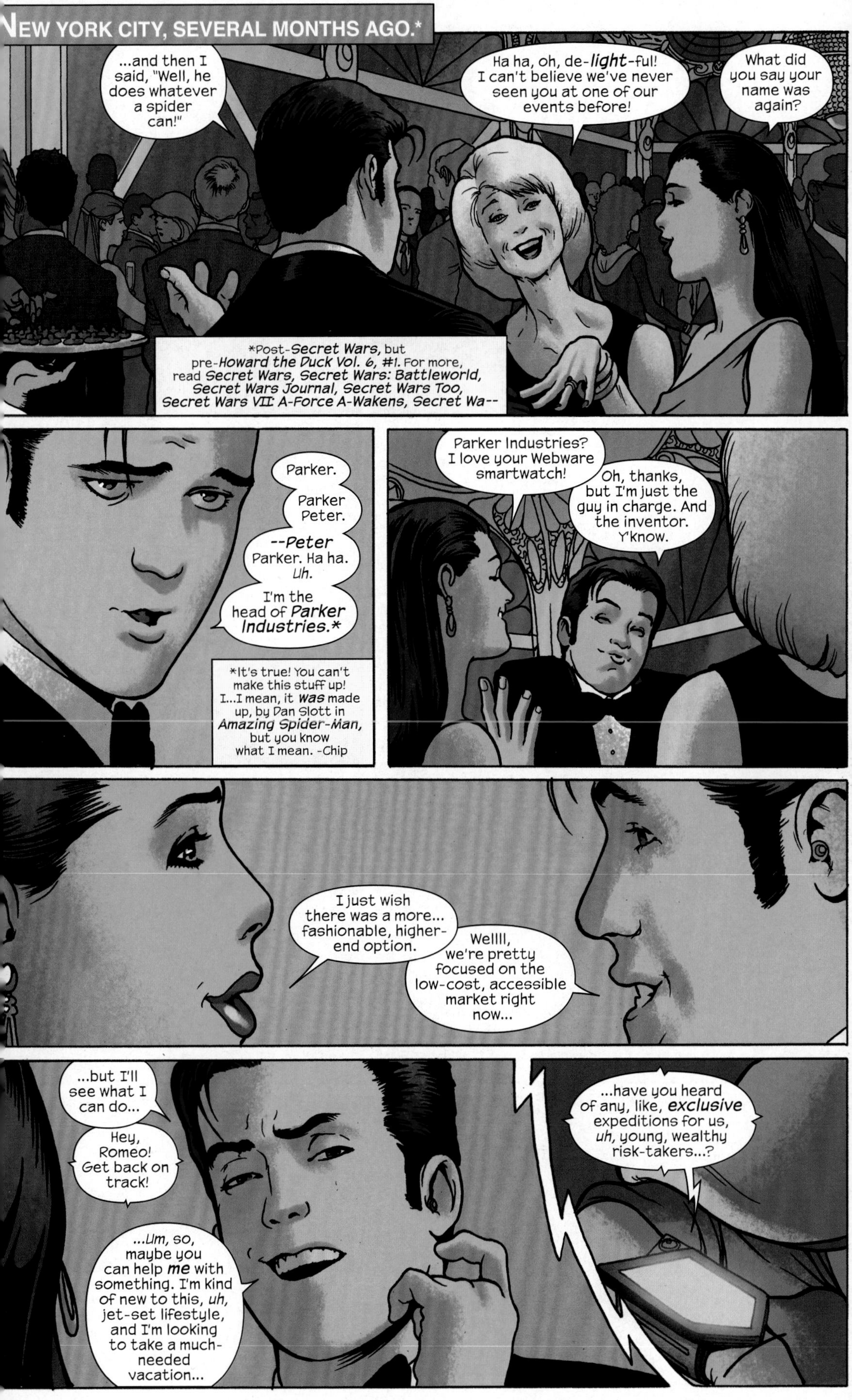
NEW YORK CITY, SEVERAL MONTHS AGO.*
...and then I said, "Well, he does whatever a spider can!"
Ha ha, oh, de-light-ful! I can't believe we've never seen you at one of our events before!
What did you say your name was again?
*Post-Secret Wars, but pre-Howard the Duck Vol. 6, #1. For more, read Secret Wars, Secret Wars: Battleworld, Secret Wars Journal, Secret Wars Too, Secret Wars VII: A-Force A-Wakens, Secret Wa--
Parker.
Parker Peter.
--Peter Parker. Ha ha. Uh.
I'm the head of Parker Industries.*
*It's true! You can't make this stuff up! I...I mean, it was made up, by Dan Slott in Amazing Spider-Man, but you know what I mean. -Chip
Parker Industries? I love your Webware smartwatch!
Oh, thanks, but I'm just the guy in charge. And the inventor. Y'know.
I just wish there was a more... fashionable, higher-end option.
Wellll, we're pretty focused on the low-cost, accessible market right now...
...but I'll see what I can do...
Hey, Romeo! Get back on track!
...Um, so, maybe you can help me with something. I'm kind of new to this, uh, jet-set lifestyle, and I'm looking to take a much-needed vacation...
...have you heard of any, like, exclusive expeditions for us, uh, young, wealthy risk-takers...?

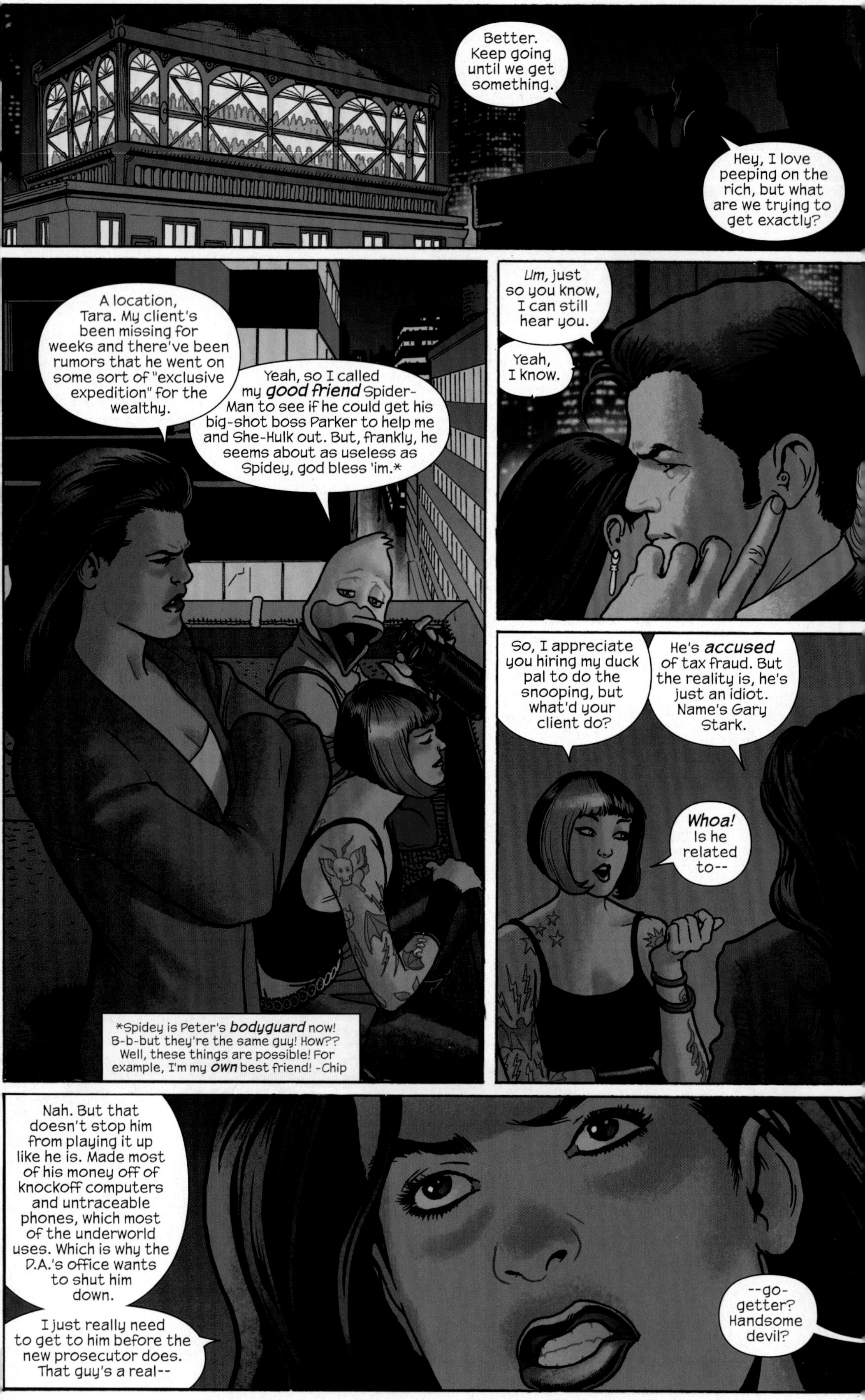
Better. Keep going until we get something.
Hey, I love peeping on the rich, but what are we trying to get exactly?
A location, Tara. My client's been missing for weeks and there've been rumors that he went on some sort of "exclusive expedition" for the wealthy.
Yeah, so I called my good friend Spider-Man to see if he could get his big-shot boss Parker to help me and She-Hulk out. But, frankly, he seems about as useless as Spidey, god bless 'im.*
*Spidey is Peter's bodyguard now! B-b-but they're the same guy! How?? Well, these things are possible! For example, I'm my own best friend! -Chip
Um, just so you know, I can still hear you.
Yeah, I know.
So, I appreciate you hiring my duck pal to do the snooping, but what'd your client do?
He's accused of tax fraud. But the reality is, he's just an idiot. Name's Gary Stark.
Whoa! Is he related to--
Nah. But that doesn't stop him from playing it up like he is. Made most of his money off of knockoff computers and untraceable phones, which most of the underworld uses. Which is why the D.A.'s office wants to shut him down.
I just really need to get to him before the new prosecutor does. That guy's a real--
--go-getter? Handsome devil?

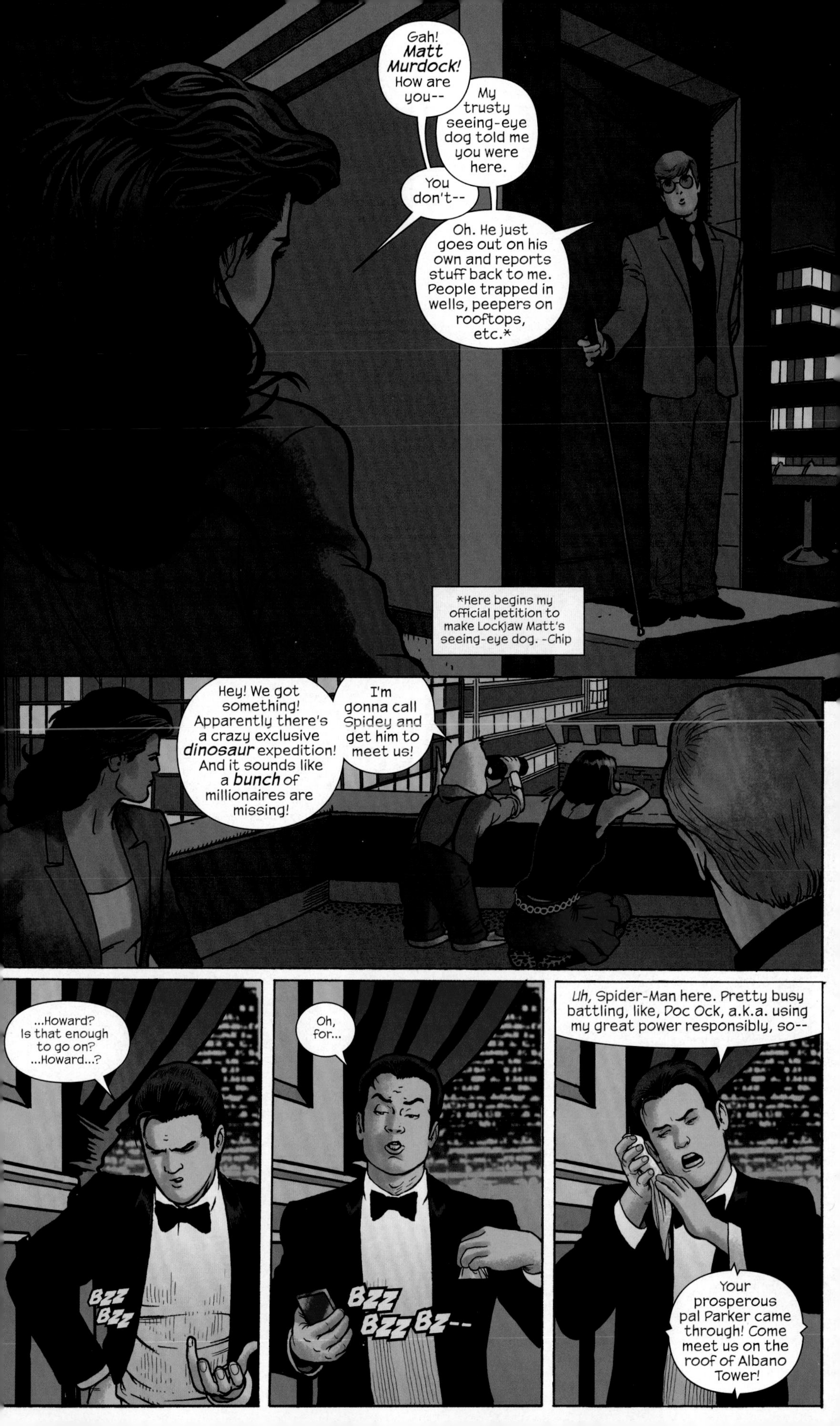
Gah! *Matt Murdock!* How are you--
My trusty seeing-eye dog told me you were here.
You don't--
Oh. He just goes out on his own and reports stuff back to me. People trapped in wells, peepers on rooftops, etc.*
*Here begins my official petition to make Lockjaw Matt's seeing-eye dog. -Chip
Hey! We got something! Apparently there's a crazy exclusive *dinosaur* expedition! And it sounds like a *bunch* of millionaires are missing!
I'm gonna call Spidey and get him to meet us!
...Howard? Is that enough to go on? ...Howard...?
BZZ BZZ
Oh, for...
BZZ BZZ BZ--
Uh, Spider-Man here. Pretty busy battling, like, Doc Ock, a.k.a. using my great power responsibly, so--
Your prosperous pal Parker came through! Come meet us on the roof of Albano Tower!

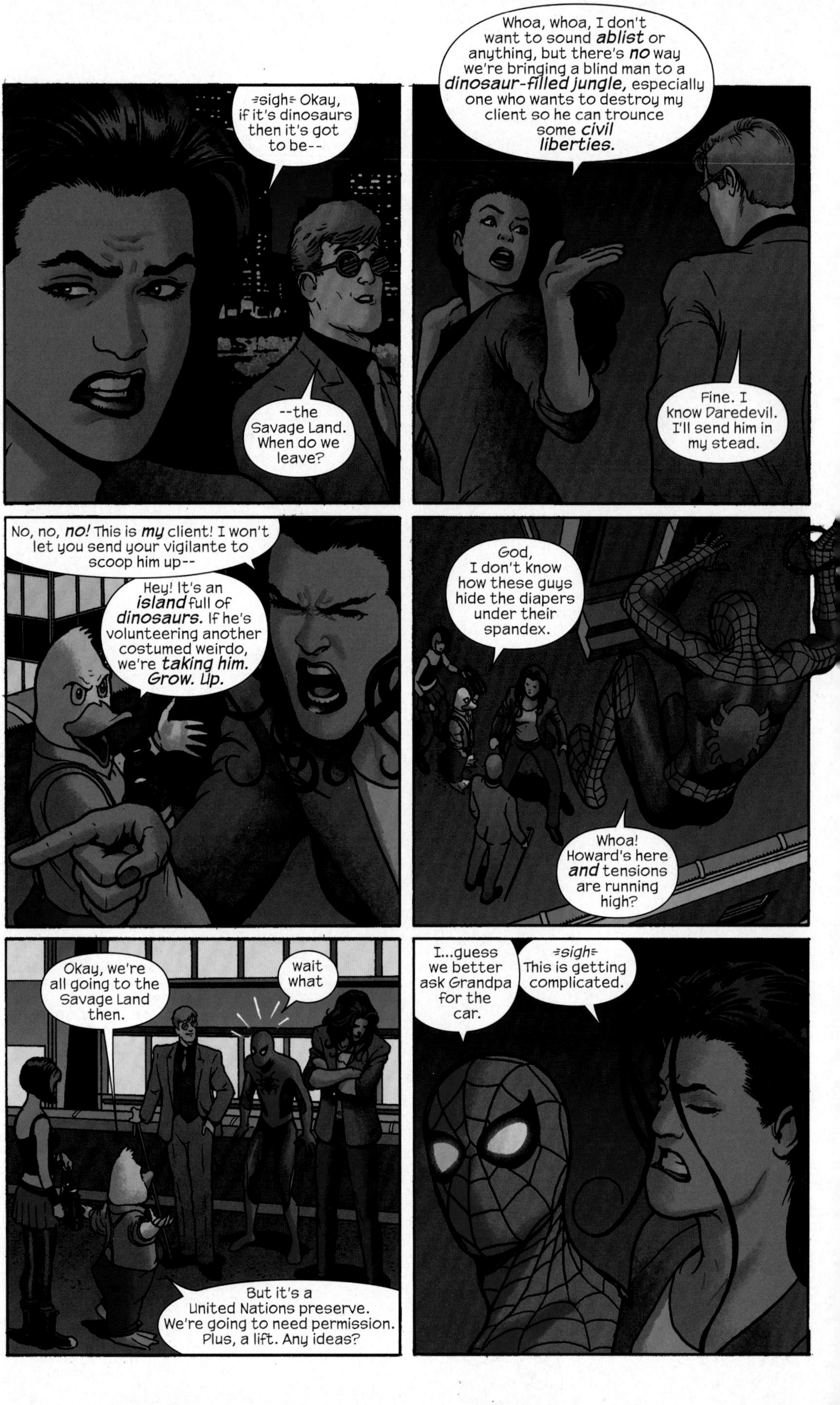

=sigh= Okay, if it's dinosaurs then it's got to be--
--the Savage Land. When do we leave?
Whoa, whoa, I don't want to sound *ablist* or anything, but there's *no* way we're bringing a blind man to a *dinosaur-filled jungle*, especially one who wants to destroy my client so he can trounce some *civil liberties.*
Fine. I know Daredevil. I'll send him in my stead.
No, no, *no!* This is *my* client! I won't let you send your vigilante to scoop him up--
Hey! It's an *island* full of *dinosaurs.* If he's volunteering another costumed weirdo, we're *taking him. Grow. Up.*
God, I don't know how these guys hide the diapers under their spandex.
Whoa! Howard's here *and* tensions are running high?
Okay, we're all going to the Savage Land then.
wait what
But it's a United Nations preserve. We're going to need permission. Plus, a lift. Any ideas?
I...guess we better ask Grandpa for the car.
=*sigh*= This is getting complicated.

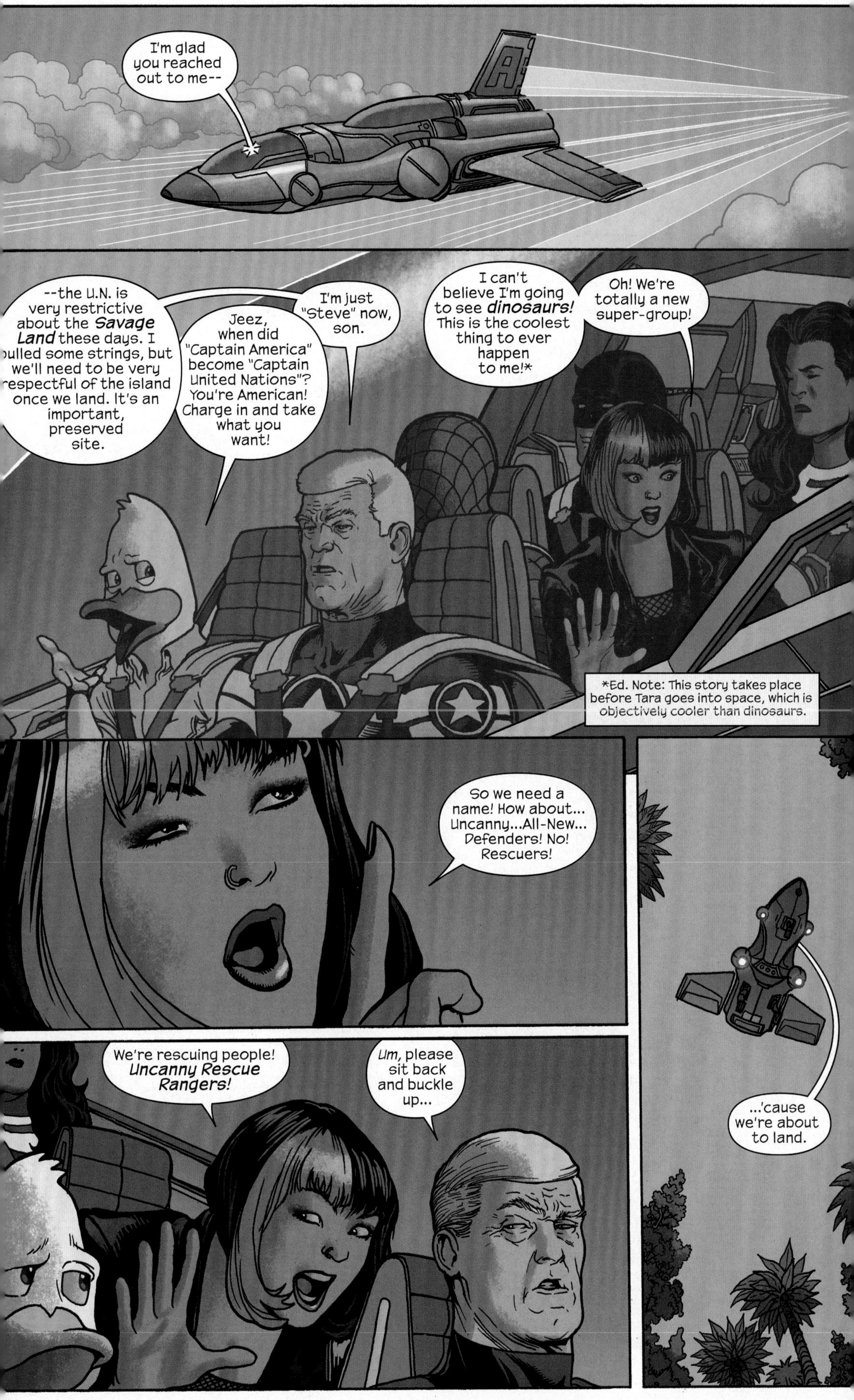

I'm glad you reached out to me--
--the U.N. is very restrictive about the *Savage Land* these days. I pulled some strings, but we'll need to be very respectful of the island once we land. It's an important, preserved site.
Jeez, when did "Captain America" become "Captain United Nations"? You're American! Charge in and take what you want!
I'm just "Steve" now, son.
I can't believe I'm going to see *dinosaurs!* This is the coolest thing to ever happen to me!*
Oh! We're totally a new super-group!
*Ed. Note: This story takes place before Tara goes into space, which is objectively cooler than dinosaurs.
So we need a name! How about... Uncanny...All-New... Defenders! No! Rescuers!
We're rescuing people! *Uncanny Rescue Rangers!*
Um, please sit back and buckle up...
...'cause we're about to land.

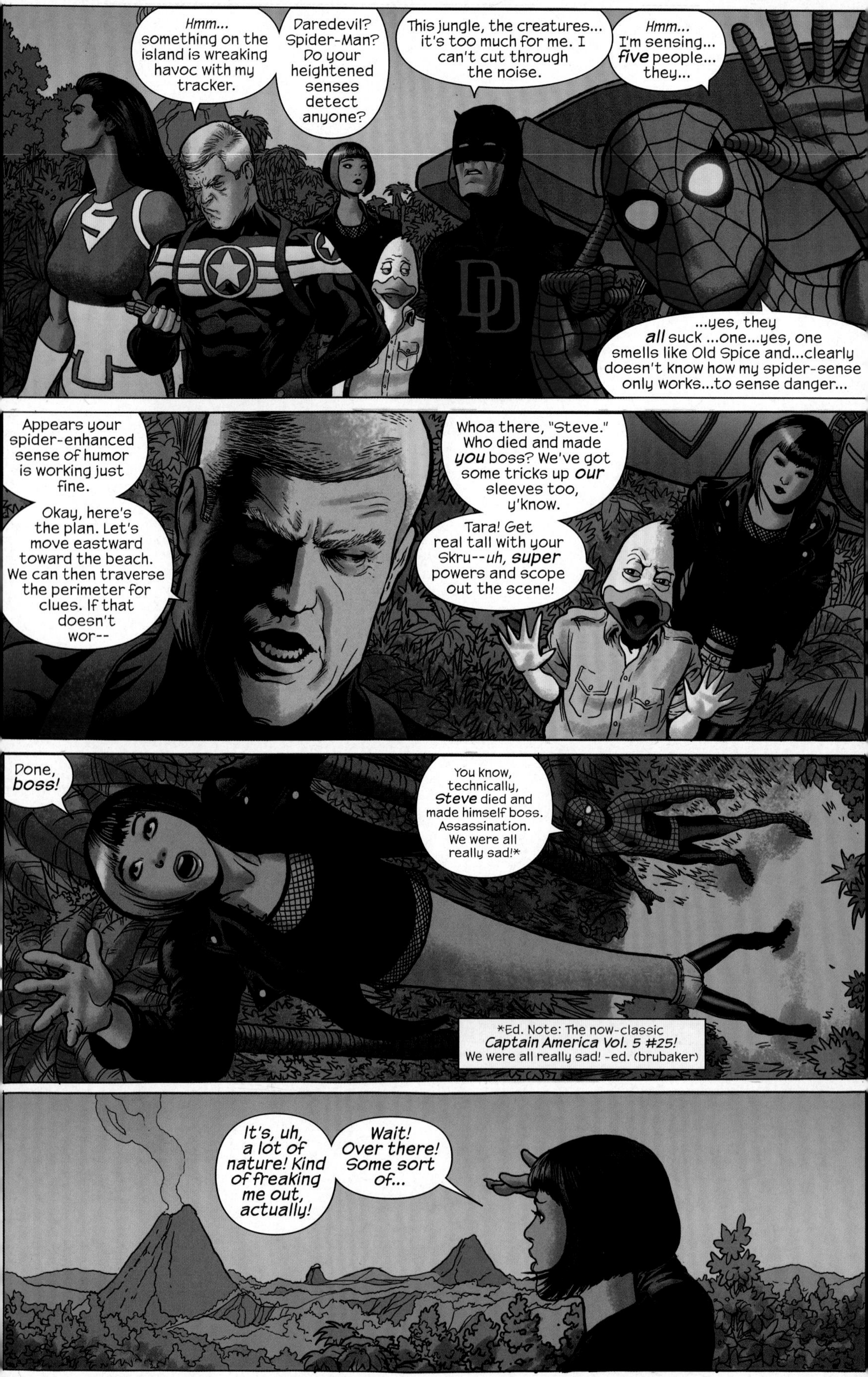
Hmm... something on the island is wreaking havoc with my tracker.
Daredevil? Spider-Man? Do your heightened senses detect anyone?
This jungle, the creatures... it's too much for me. I can't cut through the noise.
Hmm... I'm sensing... five people... they...
...yes, they all suck ...one...yes, one smells like Old Spice and...clearly doesn't know how my spider-sense only works...to sense danger...
Appears your spider-enhanced sense of humor is working just fine.
Okay, here's the plan. Let's move eastward toward the beach. We can then traverse the perimeter for clues. If that doesn't wor--
Whoa there, "Steve." Who died and made you boss? We've got some tricks up our sleeves too, y'know.
Tara! Get real tall with your Skru--uh, super powers and scope out the scene!
Done, boss!
You know, technically, Steve died and made himself boss. Assassination. We were all really sad!*
*Ed. Note: The now-classic Captain America Vol. 5 #25! We were all really sad! -ed. (brubaker)
It's, uh, a lot of nature! Kind of freaking me out, actually!
Wait! Over there! Some sort of...

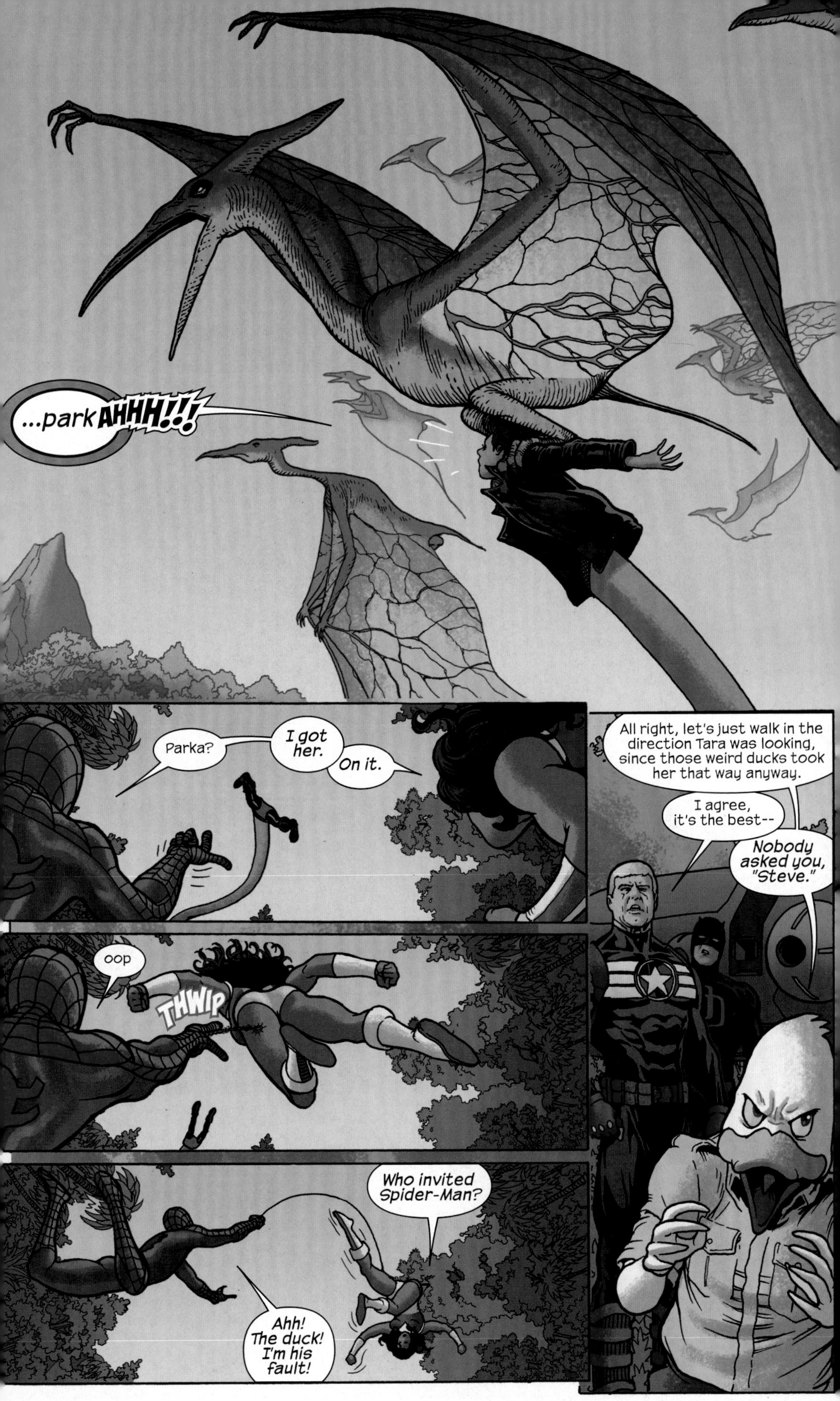

...parkAHHH!!!
Parka?
I got her.
On it.
All right, let's just walk in the direction Tara was looking, since those weird ducks took her that way anyway.
I agree, it's the best--
Nobody asked you, "Steve."
oop
THWIP
Who invited Spider-Man?
Ahh! The duck! I'm his fault!

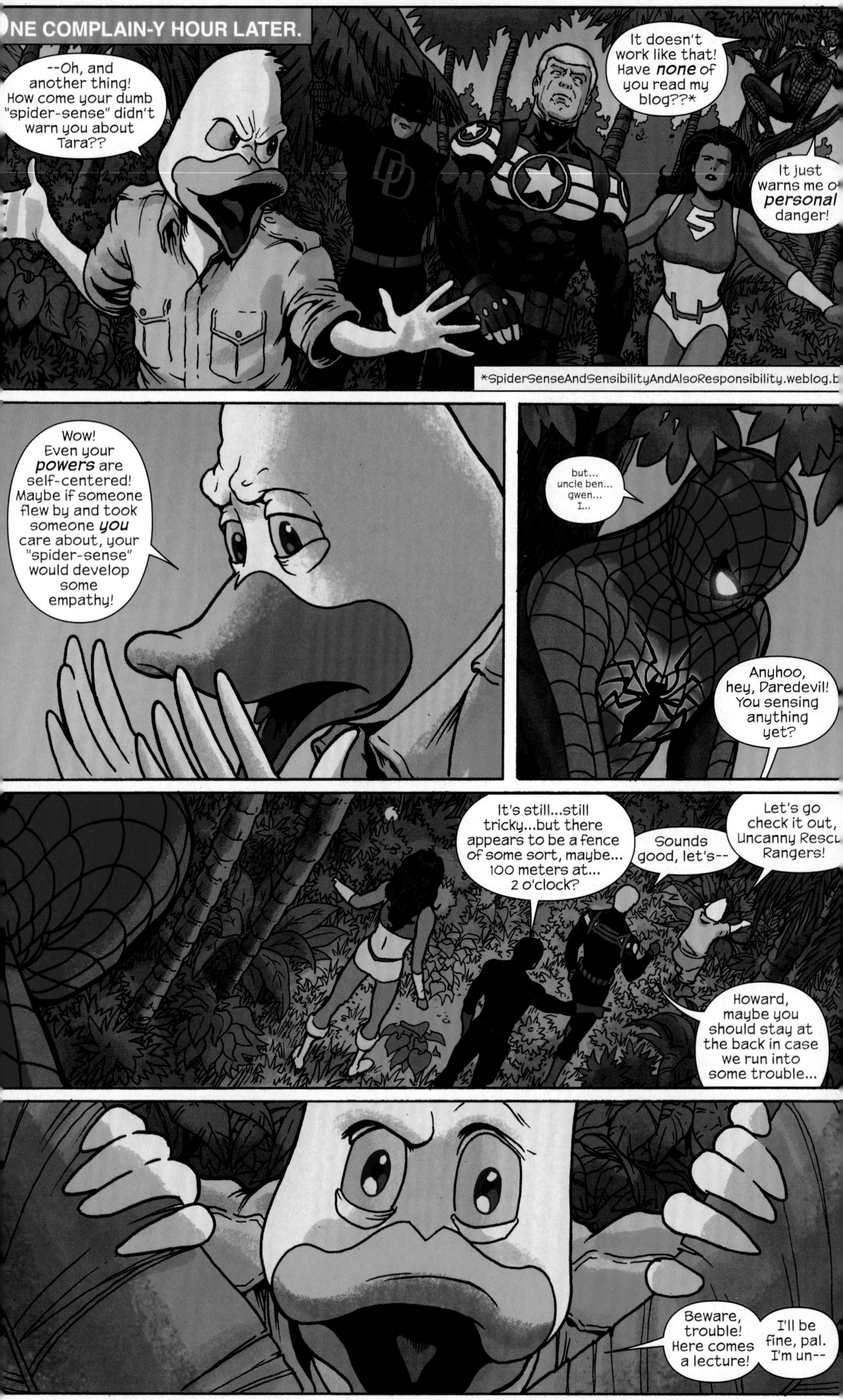
NE COMPLAIN-Y HOUR LATER.
--Oh, and another thing! How come your dumb "spider-sense" didn't warn you about Tara??
It doesn't work like that! Have *none* of you read my blog??*
It just warns me o *personal* danger!
*SpiderSenseAndSensibilityAndAlsoResponsibility.weblog.b
Wow! Even your *powers* are self-centered! Maybe if someone flew by and took someone *you* care about, your "spider-sense" would develop some empathy!
but... uncle ben... gwen... I...
Anyhoo, hey, Daredevil! You sensing anything yet?
It's still...still tricky...but there appears to be a fence of some sort, maybe... 100 meters at... 2 o'clock?
Sounds good, let's--
Let's go check it out, Uncanny Rescu Rangers!
Howard, maybe you should stay at the back in case we run into some trouble...
I'll be fine, pal. I'm un--
Beware, trouble! Here comes a lecture!

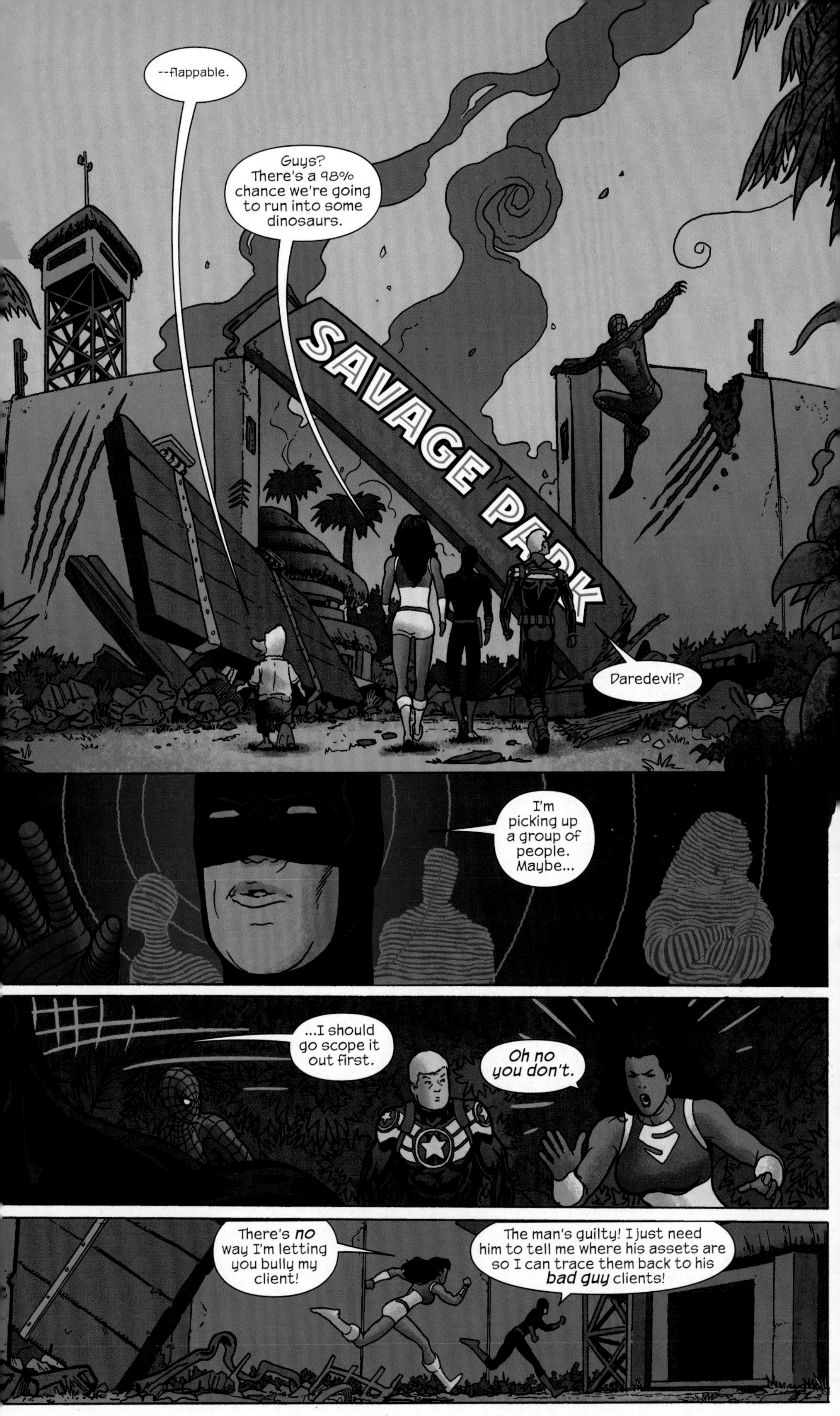
--flappable.
Guys? There's a 98% chance we're going to run into some dinosaurs.
SAVAGE PARK
Daredevil?
I'm picking up a group of people. Maybe...
...I should go scope it out first.
Oh no you don't.
There's no way I'm letting you bully my client!
The man's guilty! I just need him to tell me where his assets are so I can trace them back to his bad guy clients!

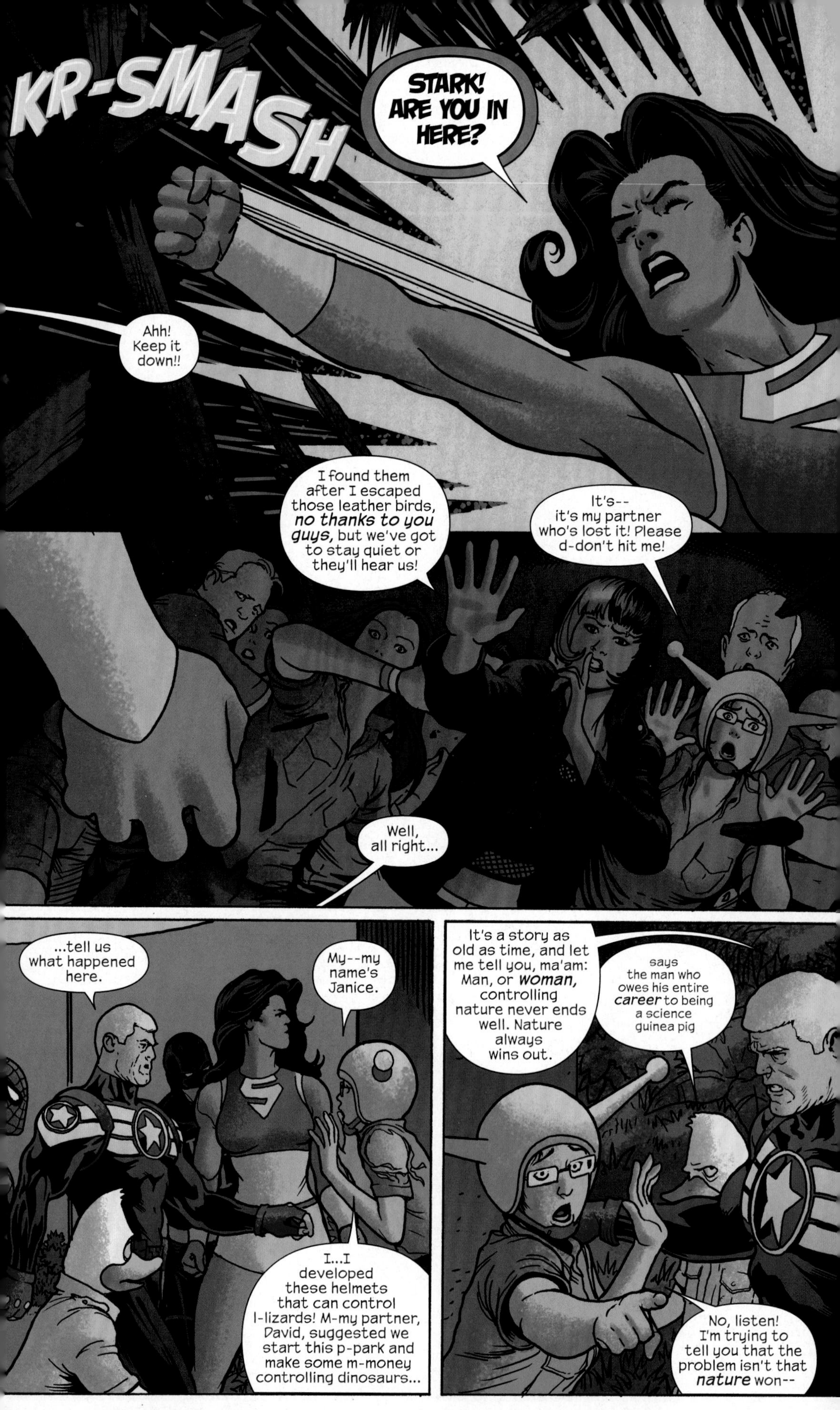
KR-SMASH
STARK! ARE YOU IN HERE?
Ahh! Keep it down!!
I found them after I escaped those leather birds, no thanks to you guys, but we've got to stay quiet or they'll hear us!
It's-- it's my partner who's lost it! Please d-don't hit me!
Well, all right...
...tell us what happened here.
My--my name's Janice.
I...I developed these helmets that can control l-lizards! M-my partner, David, suggested we start this p-park and make some m-money controlling dinosaurs...
It's a story as old as time, and let me tell you, ma'am: Man, or WOMAN, controlling nature never ends well. Nature always wins out.
says the man who owes his entire career to being a science guinea pig
No, listen! I'm trying to tell you that the problem isn't that nature won--

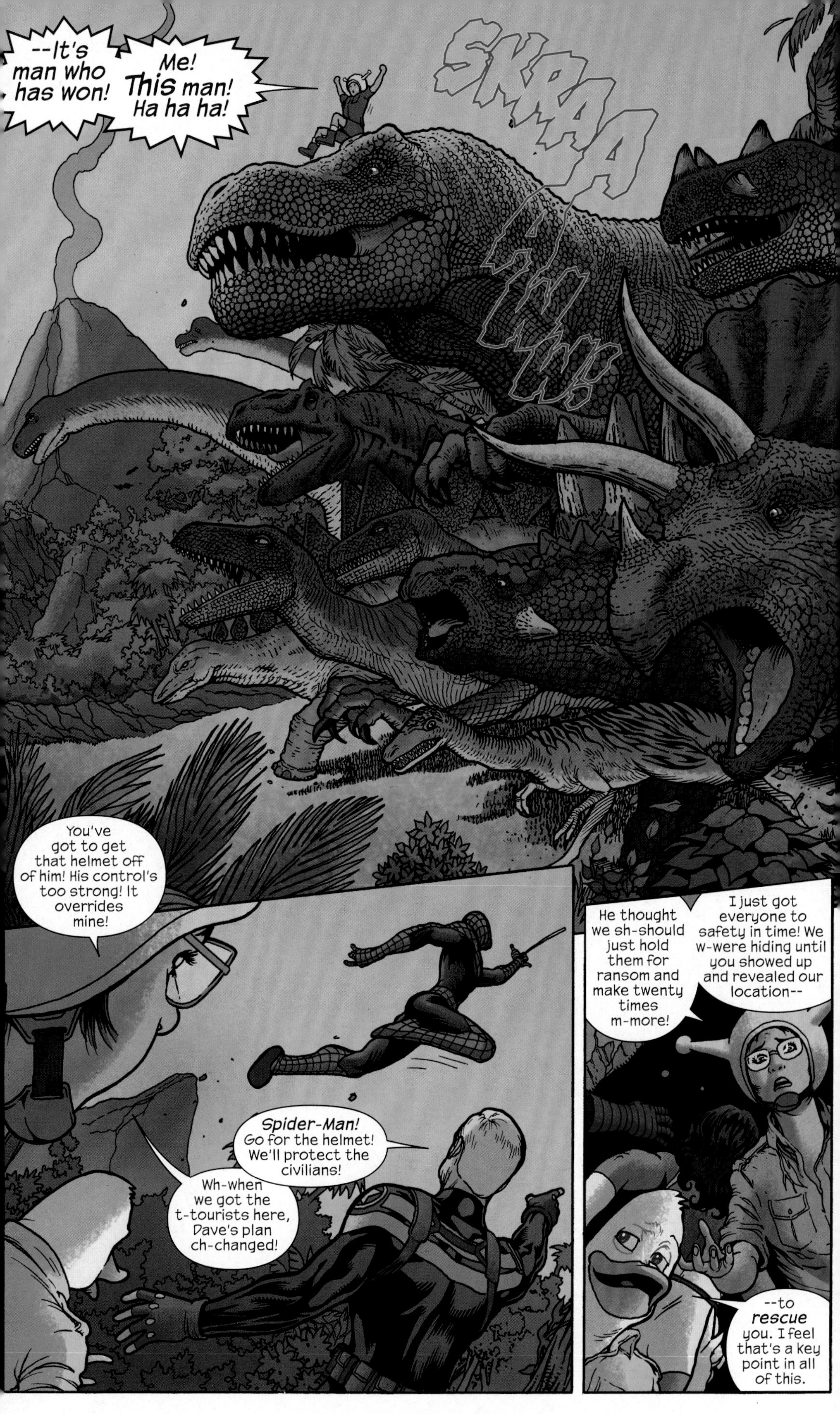
--It's man who has won!
Me! This man! Ha ha ha!
SKRAAA
LANWWW
You've got to get that helmet off of him! His control's too strong! It overrides mine!
Spider-Man! Go for the helmet! We'll protect the civilians!
Wh-when we got the t-tourists here, Dave's plan ch-changed!
He thought we sh-should just hold them for ransom and make twenty times m-more!
I just got everyone to safety in time! We w-were hiding until you showed up and revealed our location--
--to rescue you. I feel that's a key point in all of this.

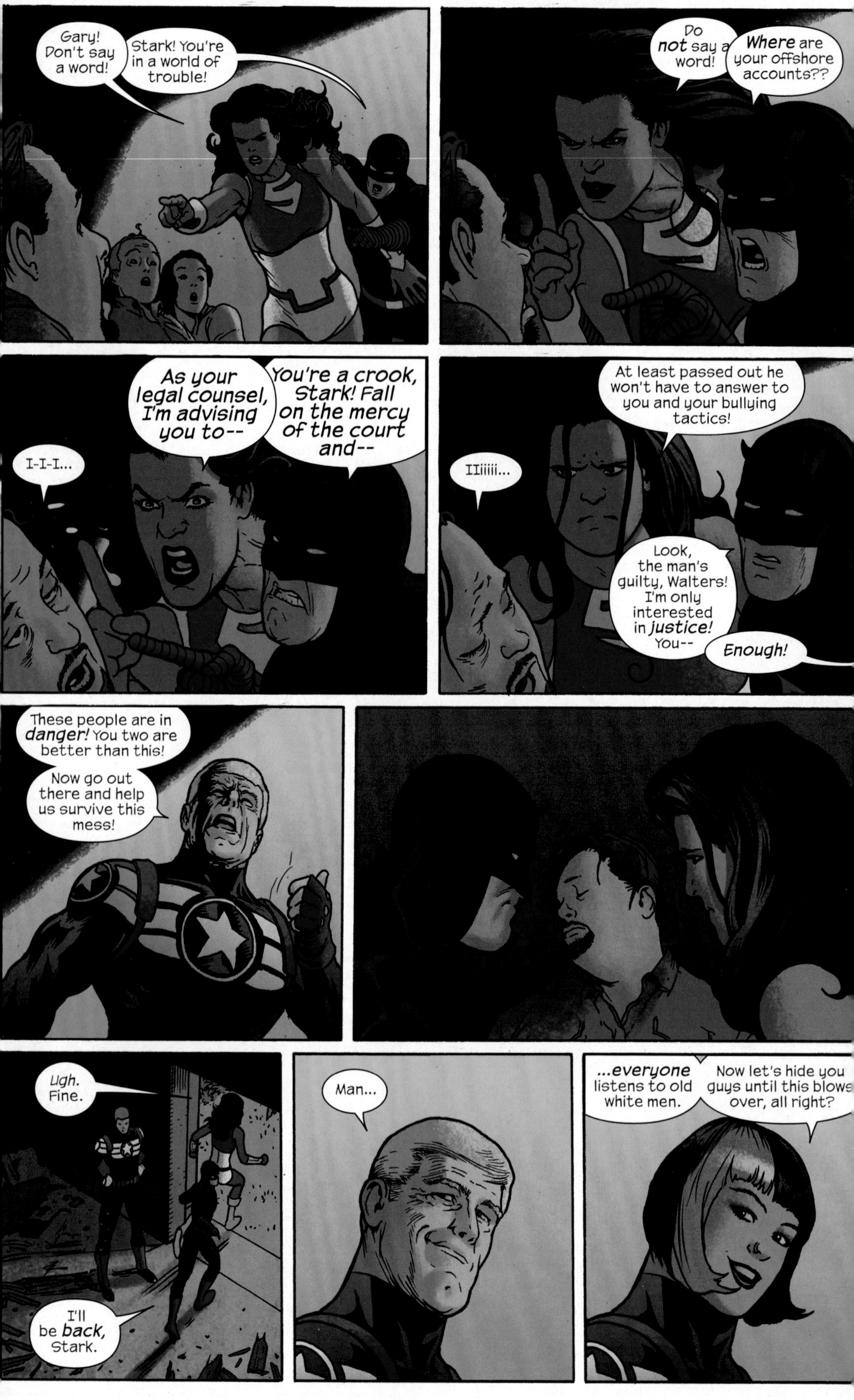
Gary! Don't say a word!
Stark! You're in a world of trouble!
Do *not* say a word!
Where are your offshore accounts??
As your legal counsel, I'm advising you to--
You're a crook, Stark! Fall on the mercy of the court and--
I-I-I...
At least passed out he won't have to answer to you and your bullying tactics!
IIiiiii...
Look, the man's guilty, Walters! I'm only interested in *justice!* You--
Enough!
These people are in *danger!* You two are better than this!
Now go out there and help us survive this mess!
Ugh. Fine.
I'll be *back,* Stark.
Man...
...everyone listens to old white men.
Now let's hide you guys until this blows over, all right?

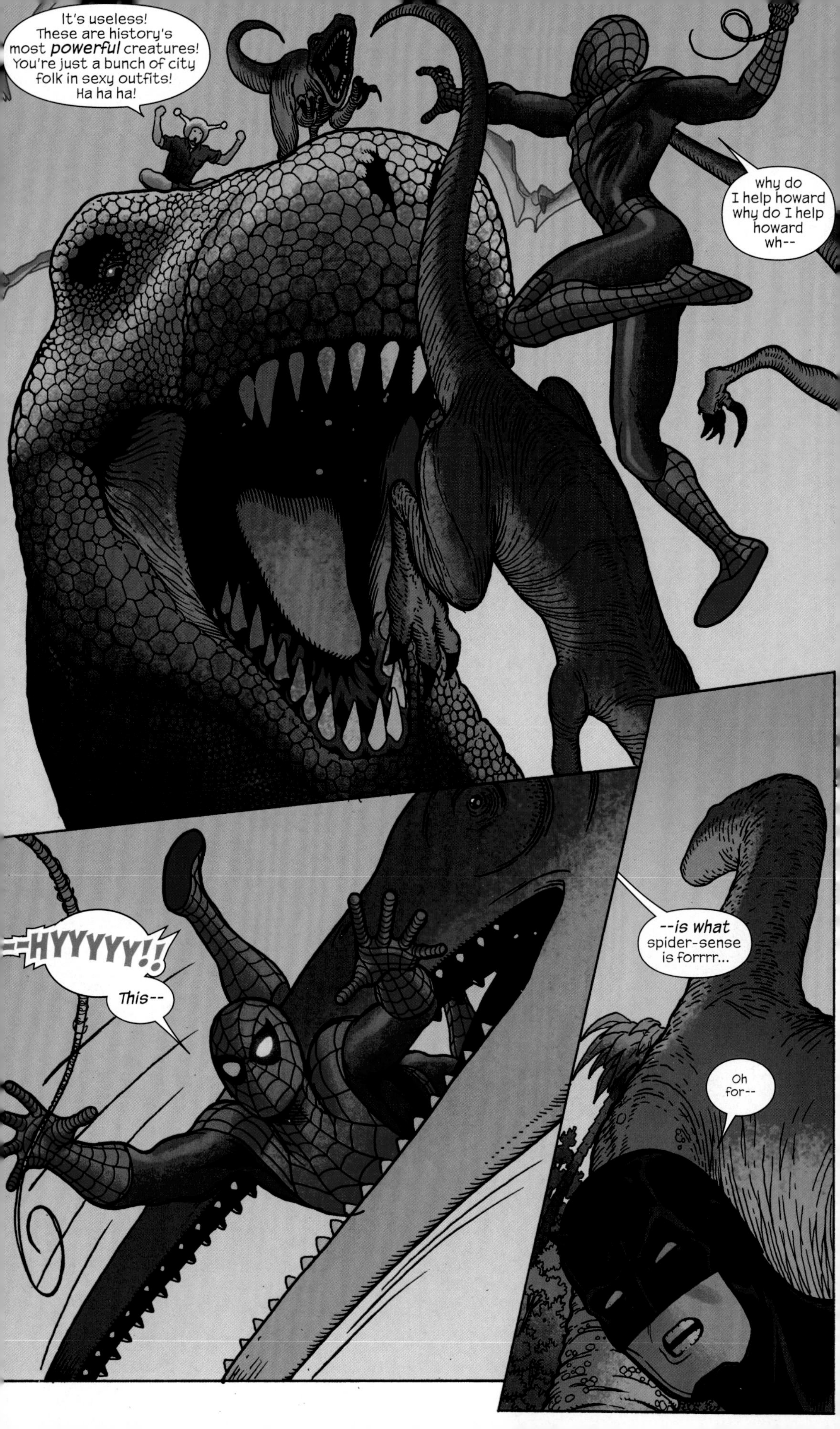
It's useless! These are history's most **powerful** creatures! You're just a bunch of city folk in sexy outfits! Ha ha ha!
why do I help howard why do I help howard wh--
--HYYYYY!!
This--
--is what spider-sense is forrrr...
Oh for--

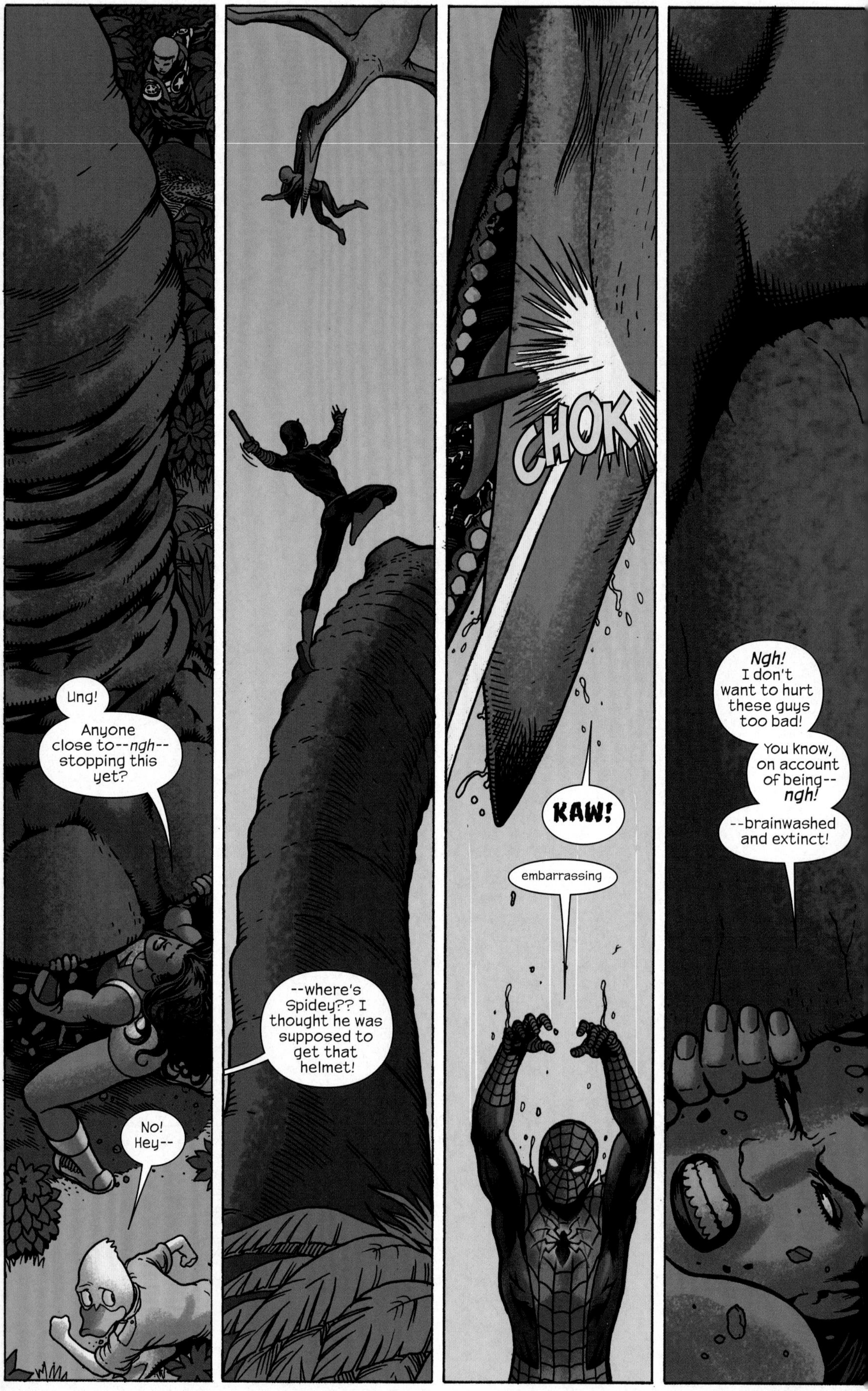
Ung!
Anyone close to--ngh--stopping this yet?
No! Hey--
--where's Spidey?? I thought he was supposed to get that helmet!
CHOK
KAW!
embarrassing
Ngh! I don't want to hurt these guys too bad!
You know, on account of being--ngh!
--brainwashed and extinct!

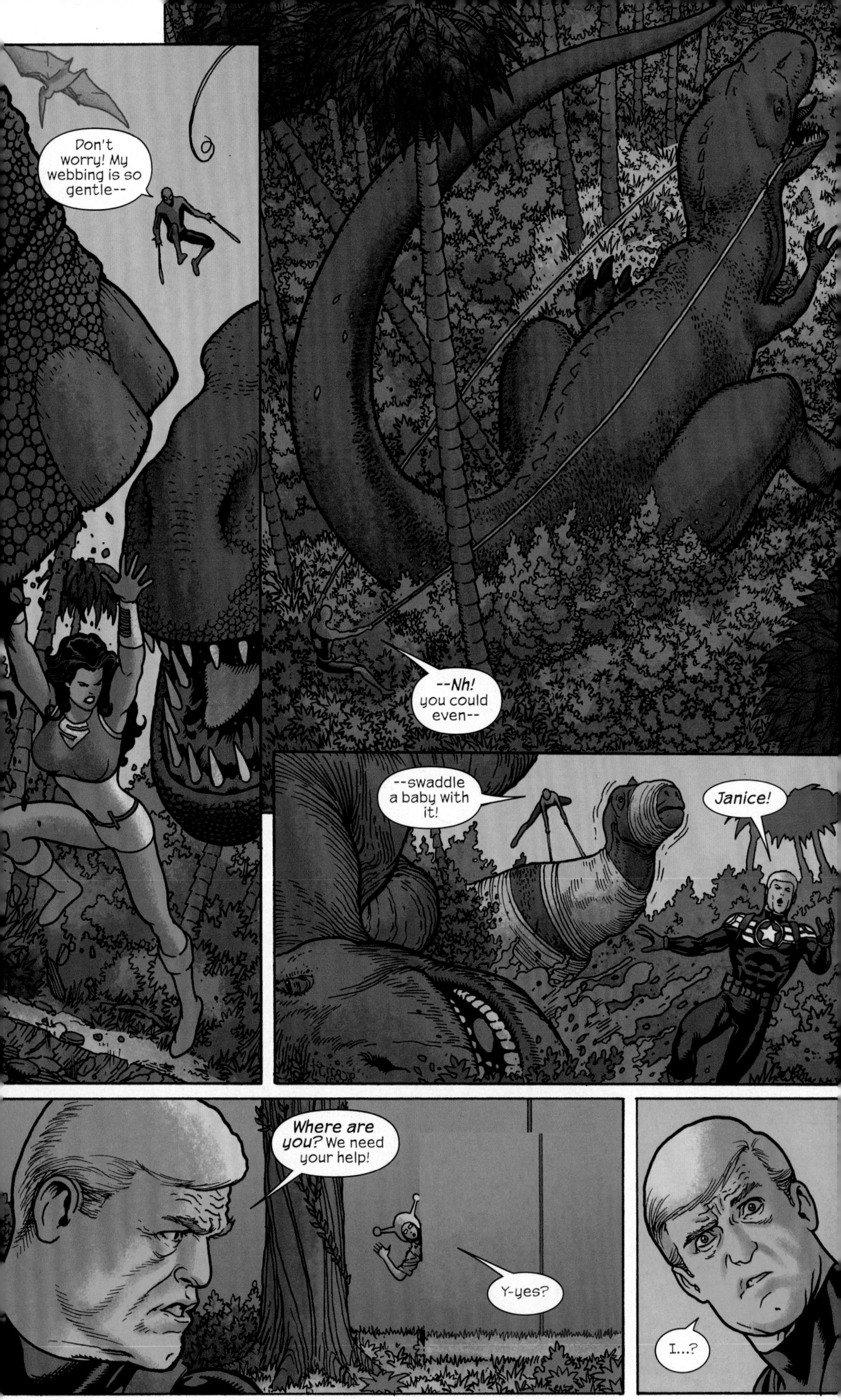

Don't worry! My webbing is so gentle--
--Nh! you could even--
--swaddle a baby with it!
Janice!
Where are you? We need your help!
Y-yes?
I...?

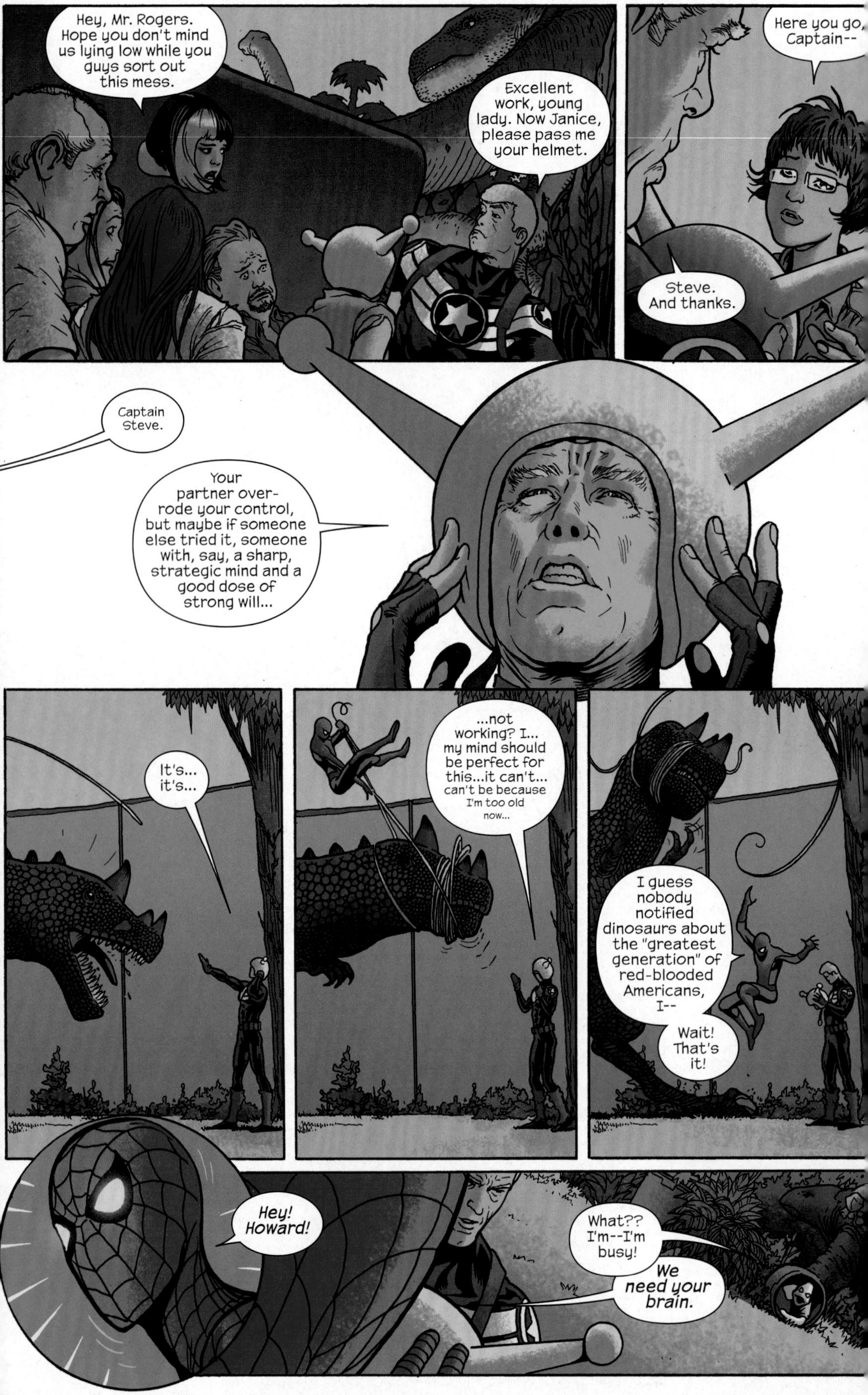
Hey, Mr. Rogers. Hope you don't mind us lying low while you guys sort out this mess.
Excellent work, young lady. Now Janice, please pass me your helmet.
Here you go, Captain--
Steve. And thanks.
Captain Steve.
Your partner over-rode your control, but maybe if someone else tried it, someone with, say, a sharp, strategic mind and a good dose of strong will...
It's... it's...
...not working? I... my mind should be perfect for this...it can't... can't be because I'm too old now...
I guess nobody notified dinosaurs about the "greatest generation" of red-blooded Americans, I--
Wait! That's it!
Hey! Howard!
What?? I'm--I'm busy!
We need your brain.

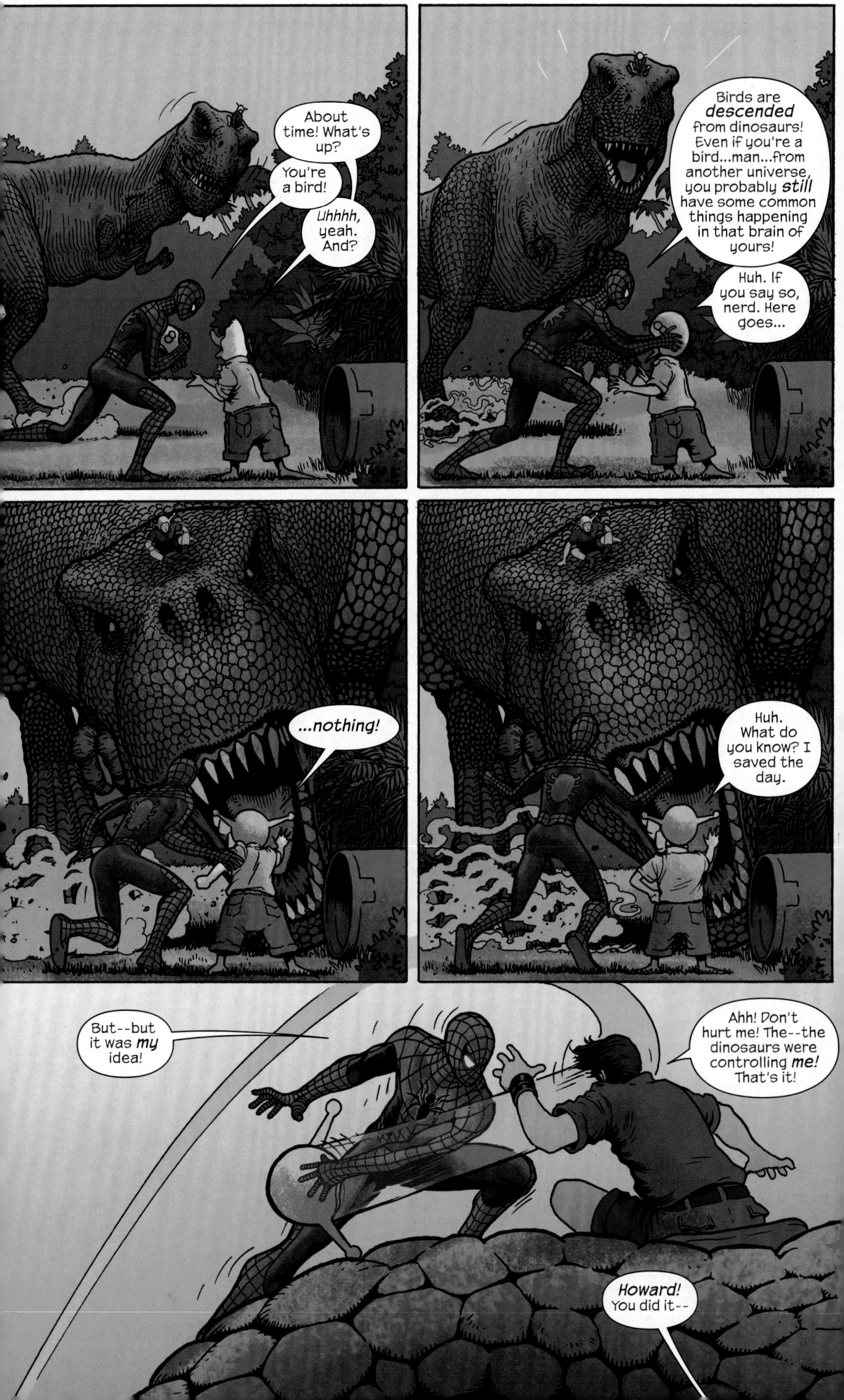
About time! What's up?
You're a bird!
Uhhhh, yeah. And?
Birds are *descended* from dinosaurs! Even if you're a bird...man...from another universe, you probably *still* have some common things happening in that brain of yours!
Huh. If you say so, nerd. Here goes...
...nothing!
Huh. What do you know? I saved the day.
But--but it was *my* idea!
Ahh! Don't hurt me! The--the dinosaurs were controlling *me!* That's it!
Howard! You did it--

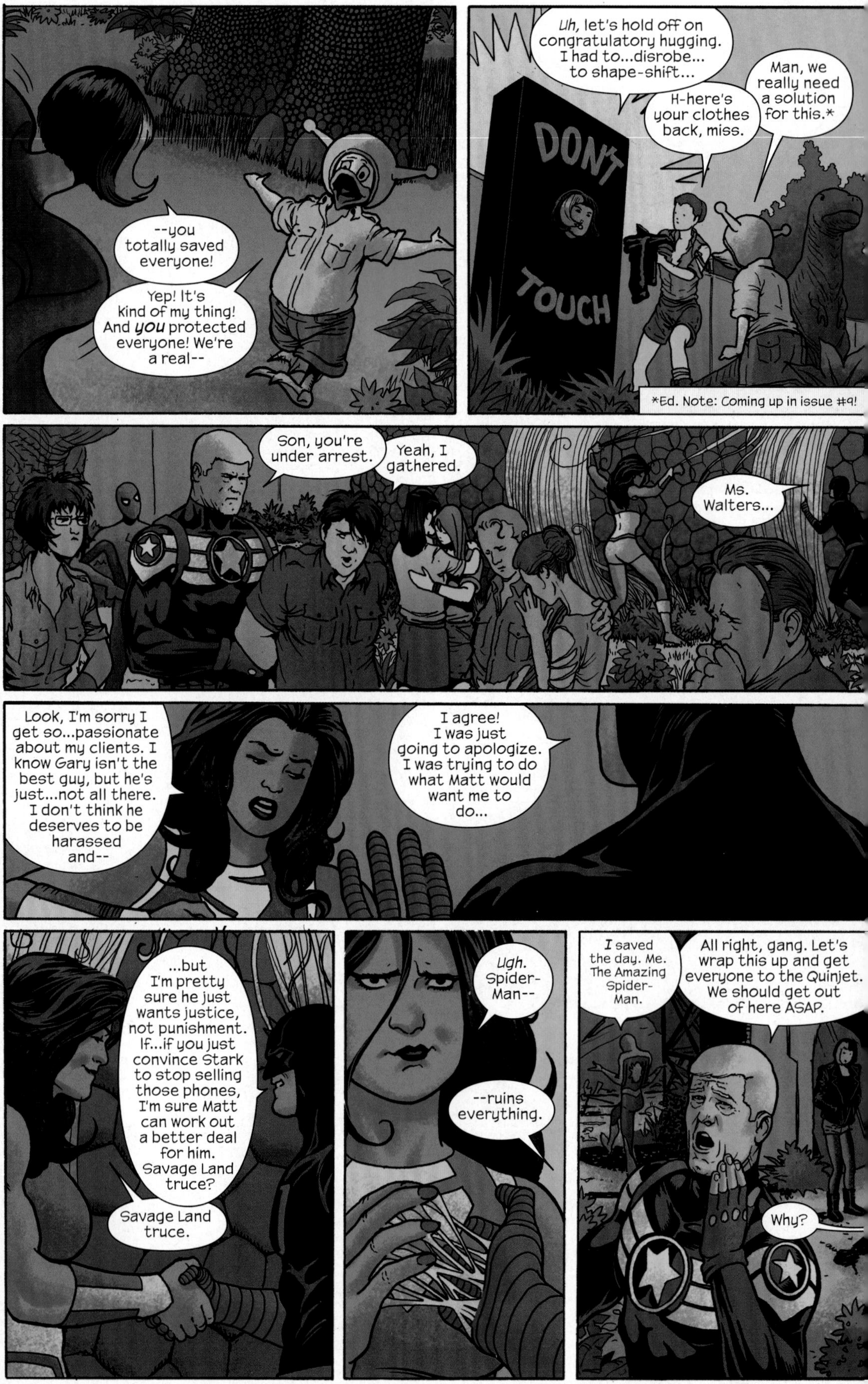
--you totally saved everyone!
Yep! It's kind of my thing! And *you* protected everyone! We're a real--
Uh, let's hold off on congratulatory hugging. I had to...disrobe... to shape-shift...
H-here's your clothes back, miss.
Man, we really need a solution for this.*
DON'T TOUCH
*Ed. Note: Coming up in issue #9!
Son, you're under arrest.
Yeah, I gathered.
Ms. Walters...
Look, I'm sorry I get so...passionate about my clients. I know Gary isn't the best guy, but he's just...not all there. I don't think he deserves to be harassed and--
I agree! I was just going to apologize. I was trying to do what Matt would want me to do...
...but I'm pretty sure he just wants justice, not punishment. If...if you just convince Stark to stop selling those phones, I'm sure Matt can work out a better deal for him. Savage Land truce?
Savage Land truce.
Ugh. Spider-Man--
--ruins everything.
I saved the day. Me. The Amazing Spider-Man.
All right, gang. Let's wrap this up and get everyone to the Quinjet. We should get out of here ASAP.
Why?

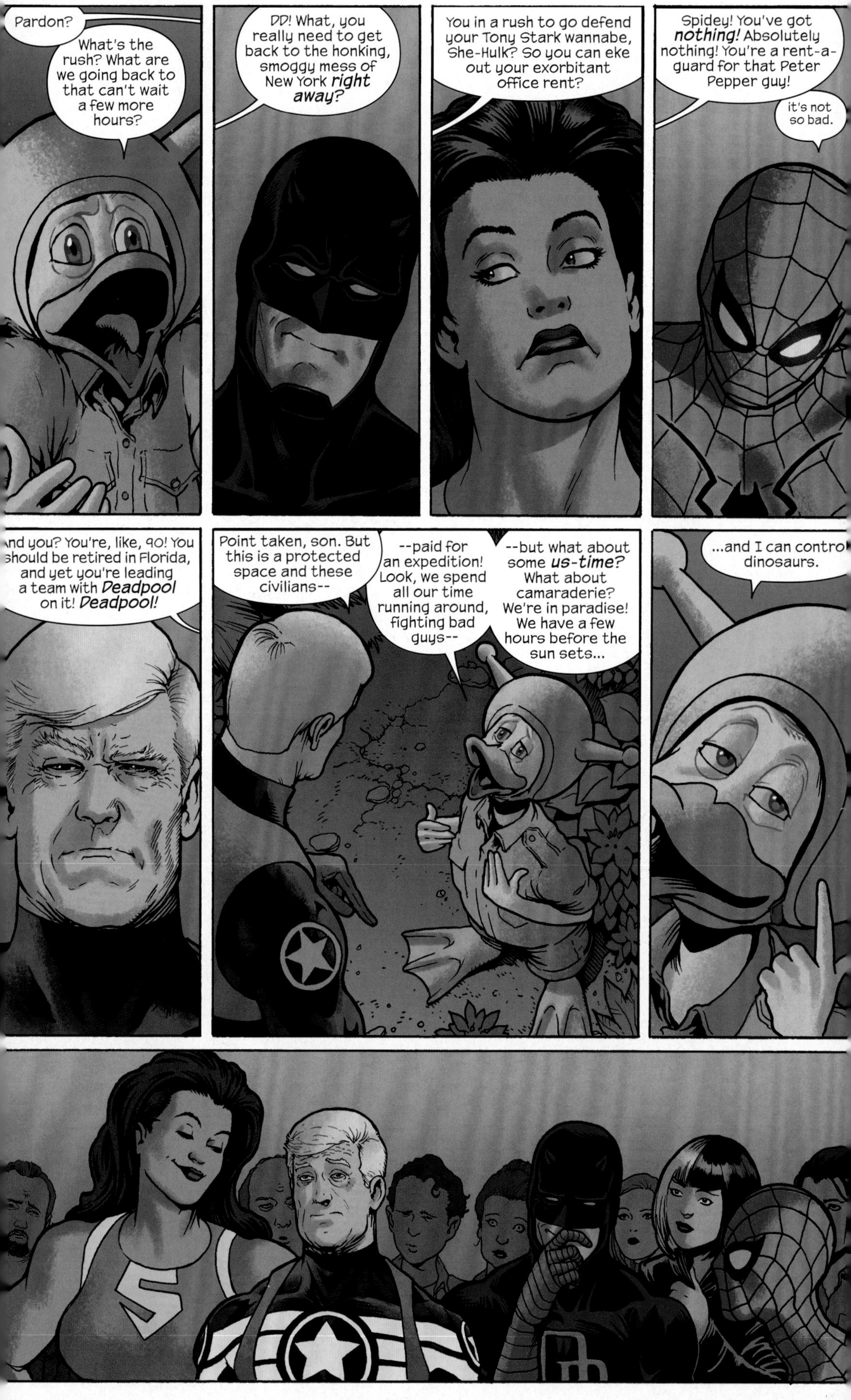
Pardon?
What's the rush? What are we going back to that can't wait a few more hours?
DD! What, you really need to get back to the honking, smoggy mess of New York *right away?*
You in a rush to go defend your Tony Stark wannabe, She-Hulk? So you can eke out your exorbitant office rent?
Spidey! You've got ***nothing!*** Absolutely nothing! You're a rent-a-guard for that Peter Pepper guy!
it's not so bad.
nd you? You're, like, 90! You should be retired in Florida, and yet you're leading a team with *Deadpool* on it! *Deadpool!*
Point taken, son. But this is a protected space and these civilians--
--paid for an expedition! Look, we spend all our time running around, fighting bad guys--
--but what about some *us-time?* What about camaraderie? We're in paradise! We have a few hours before the sun sets...
...and I can contro dinosaurs.

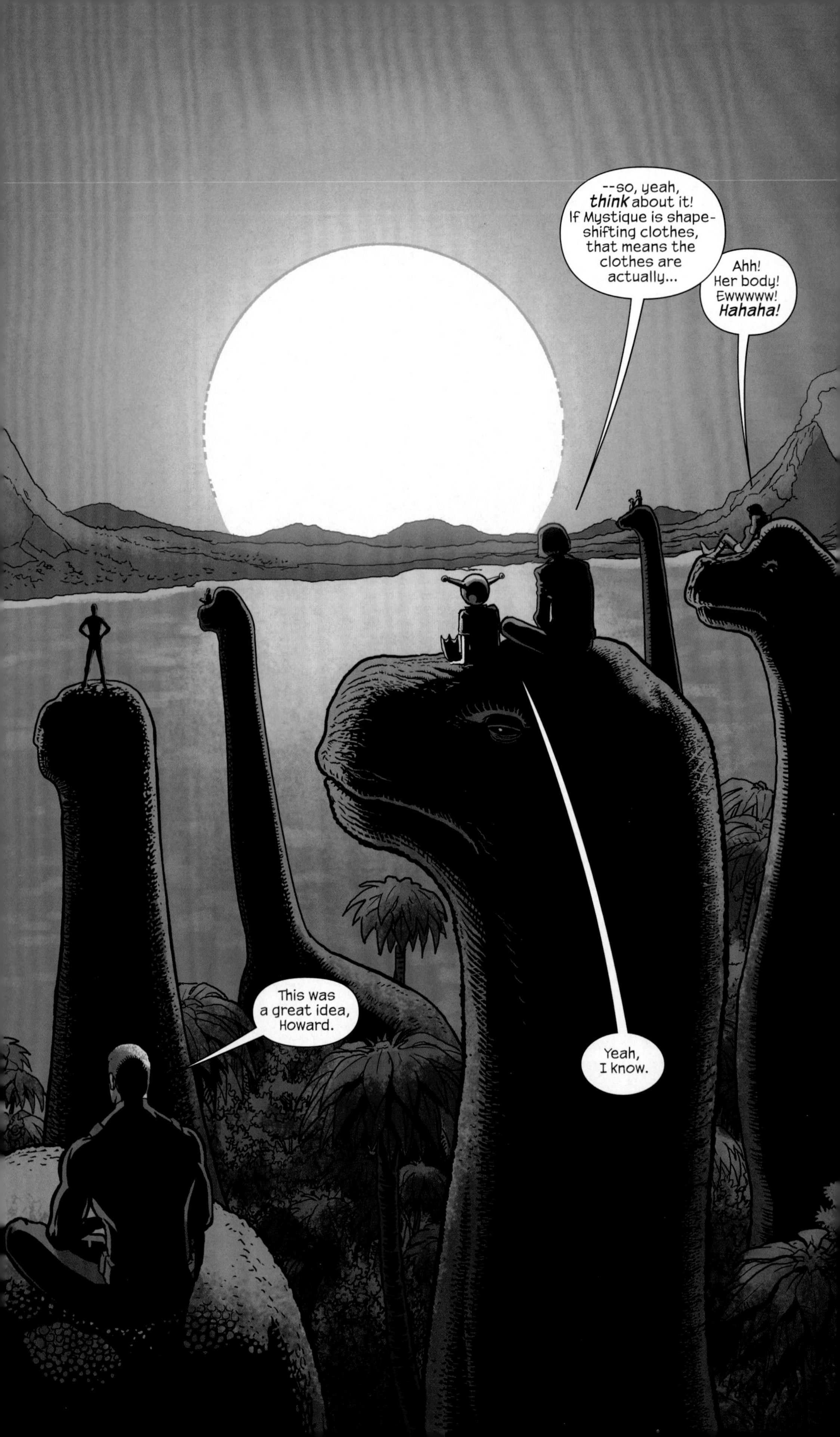
--so, yeah, *think* about it! If Mystique is shape-shifting clothes, that means the clothes are actually...
Ahh! Her body! Ewwwww! *Hahaha!*
This was a great idea, Howard.
Yeah, I know.

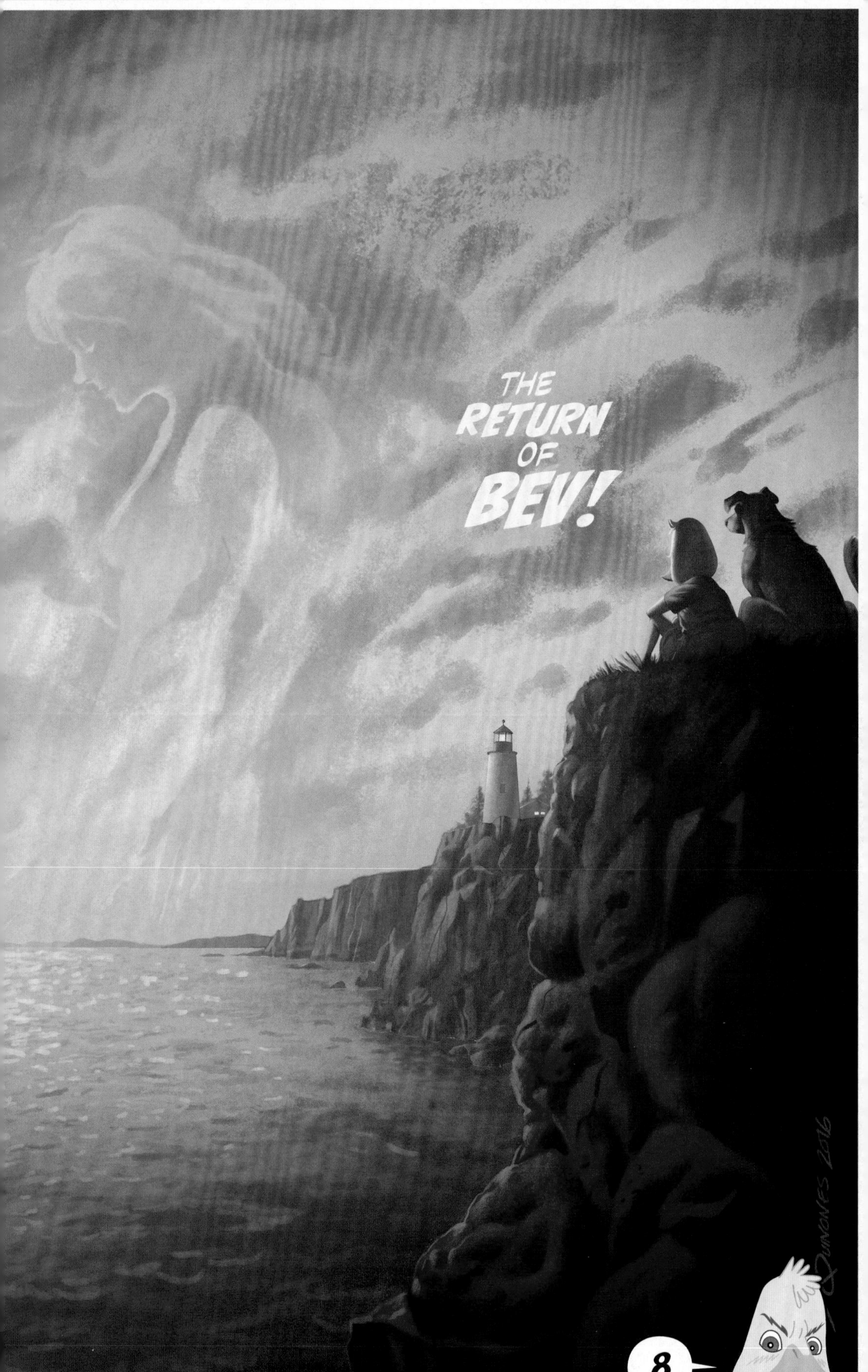
THE RETURN OF BEV!
QUINONES 2016

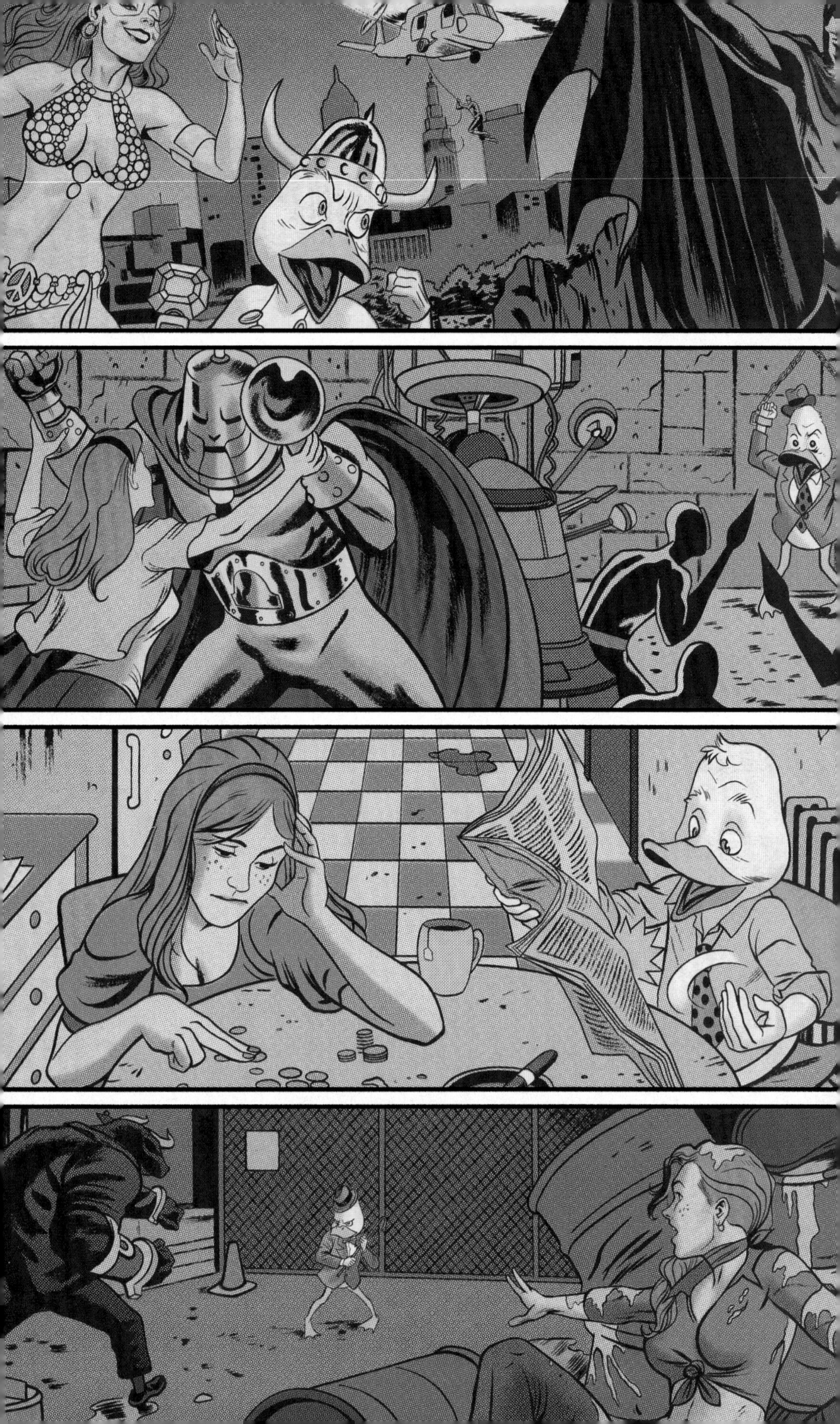

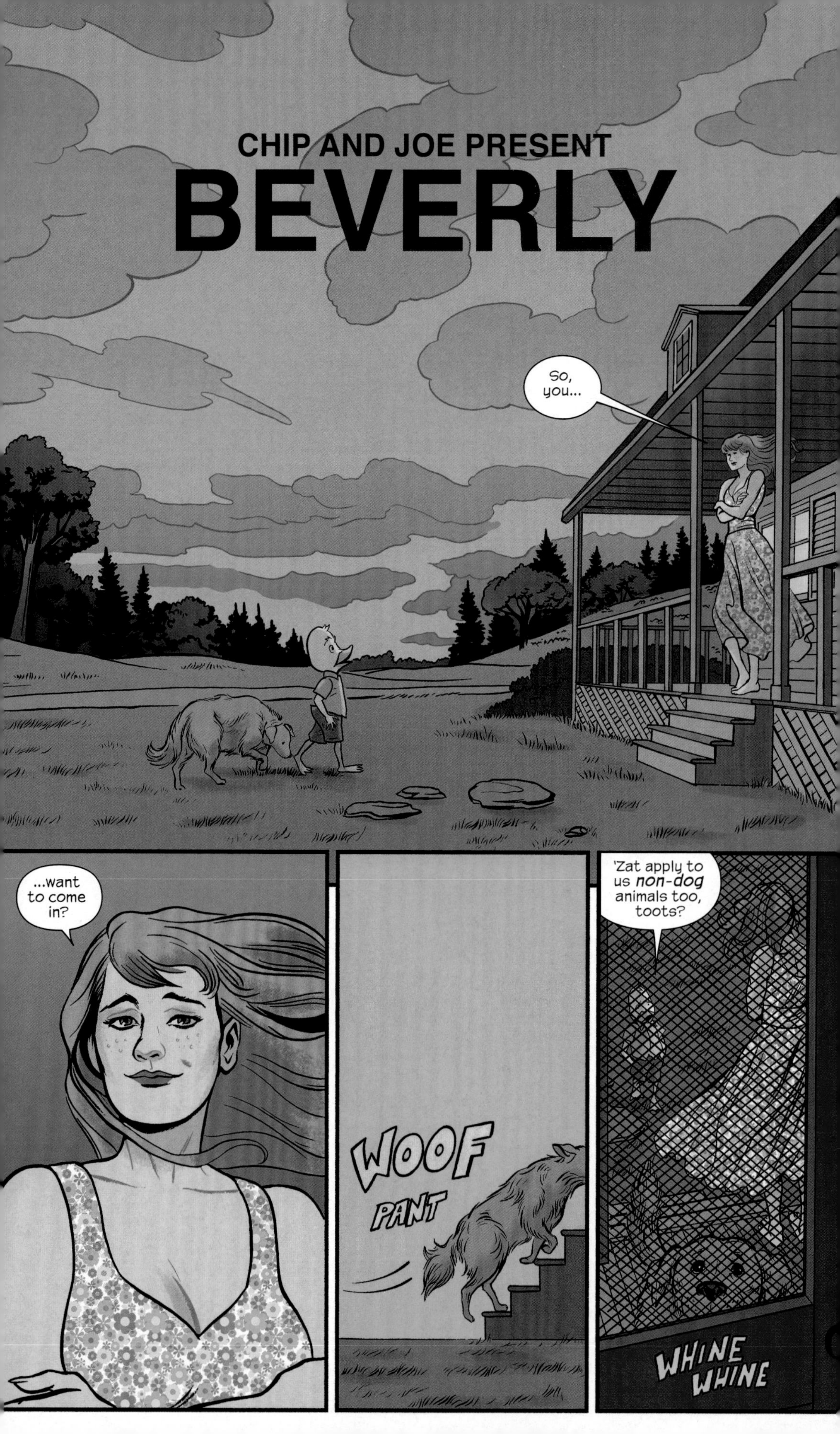
CHIP AND JOE PRESENT
BEVERLY
So, you...
...want to come in?
WOOF
PANT
'Zat apply to us non-dog animals too, toots?
WHINE WHINE

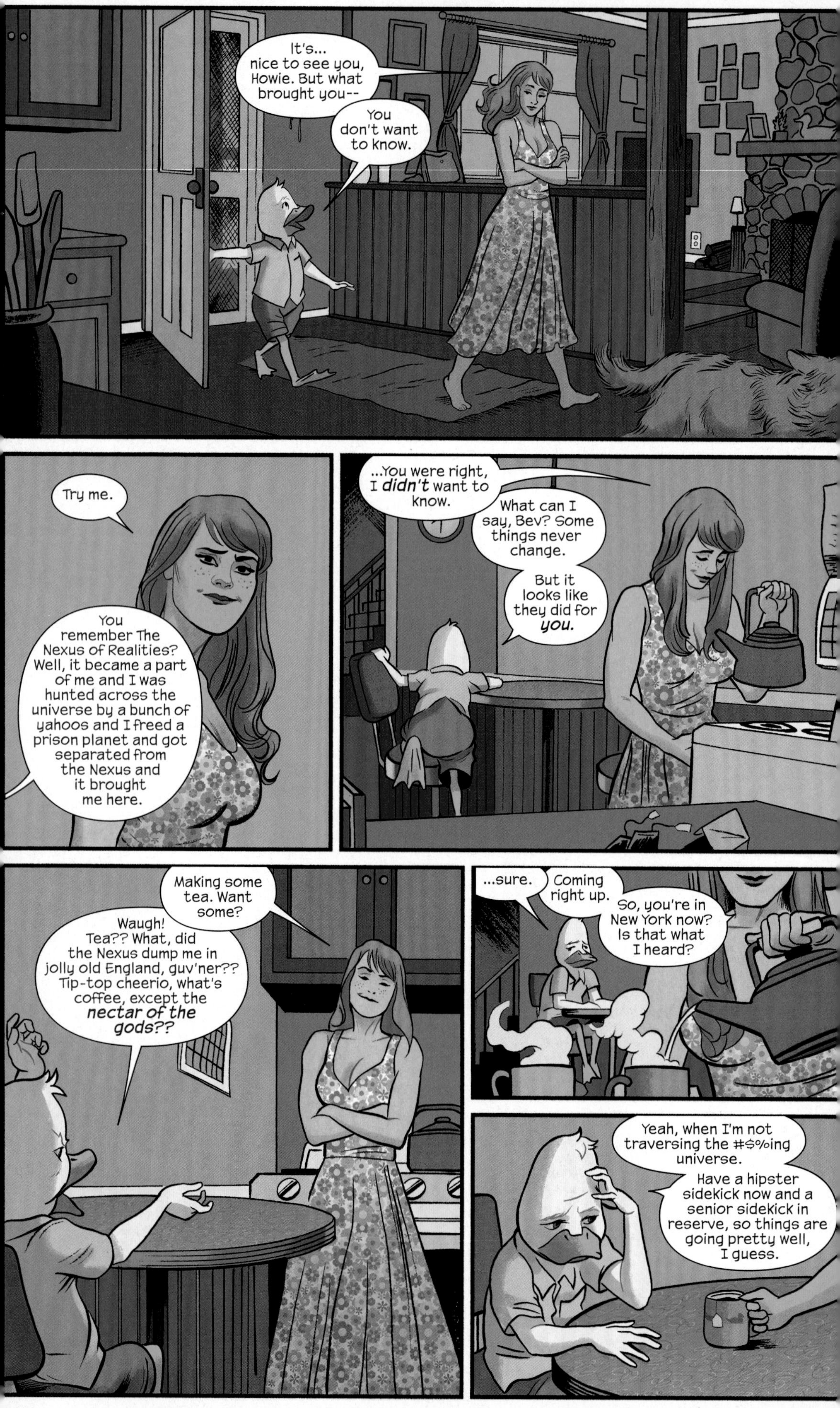
It's... nice to see you, Howie. But what brought you--
You don't want to know.
Try me.
You remember The Nexus of Realities? Well, it became a part of me and I was hunted across the universe by a bunch of yahoos and I freed a prison planet and got separated from the Nexus and it brought me here.
...You were right, I *didn't* want to know.
What can I say, Bev? Some things never change.
But it looks like they did for *you.*
Making some tea. Want some?
Waugh! Tea?? What, did the Nexus dump me in jolly old England, guv'ner?? Tip-top cheerio, what's coffee, except the *nectar of the gods??*
...sure.
Coming right up.
So, you're in New York now? Is that what I heard?
Yeah, when I'm not traversing the #$%ing universe.
Have a hipster sidekick now and a senior sidekick in reserve, so things are going pretty well, I guess.

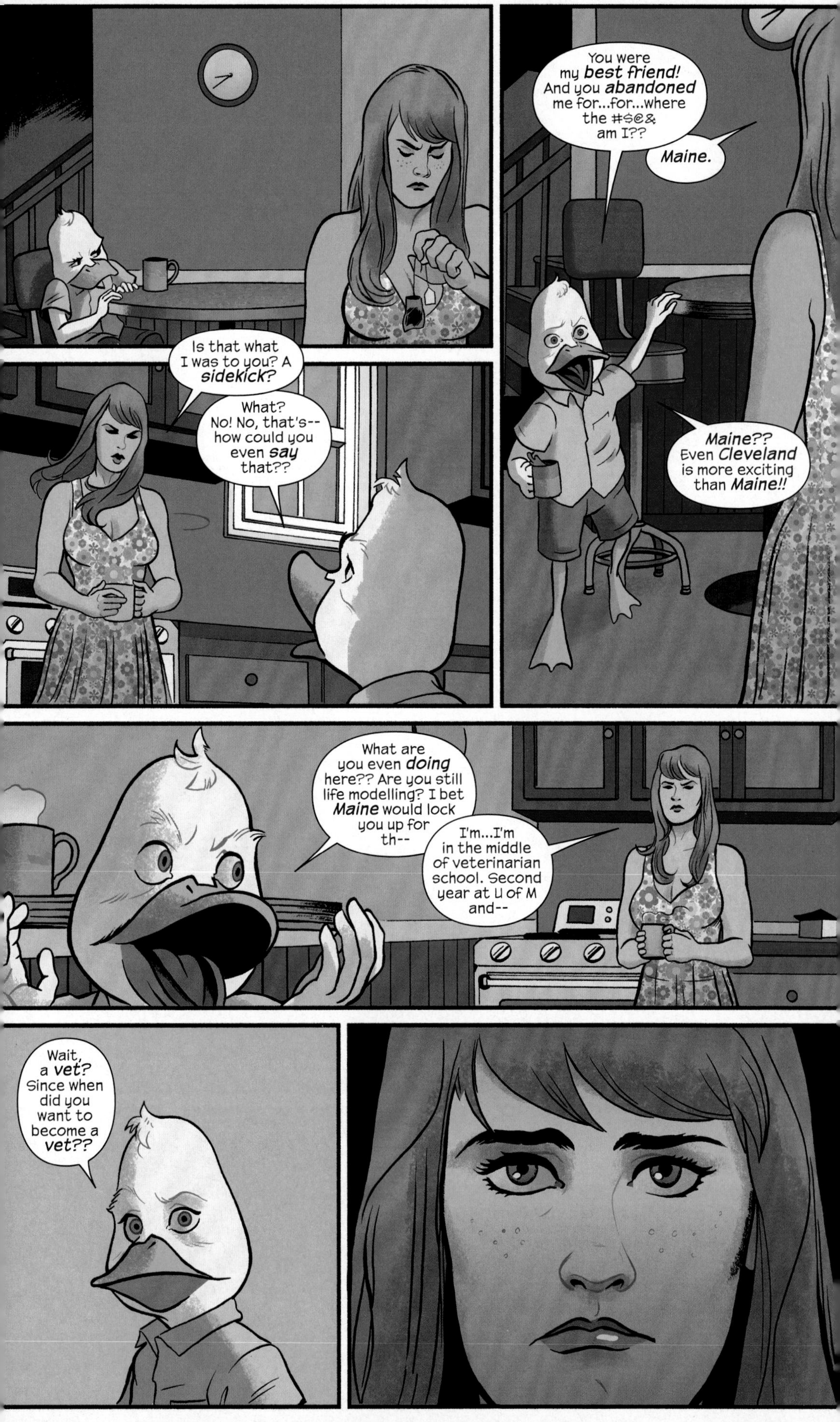
You were my best friend! And you abandoned me for...for...where the #$@& am I??
Maine.
Is that what I was to you? A sidekick?
What? No! No, that's-- how could you even say that??
Maine?? Even Cleveland is more exciting than Maine!!
What are you even doing here?? Are you still life modelling? I bet Maine would lock you up for th--
I'm...I'm in the middle of veterinarian school. Second year at U of M and--
Wait, a vet? Since when did you want to become a vet??

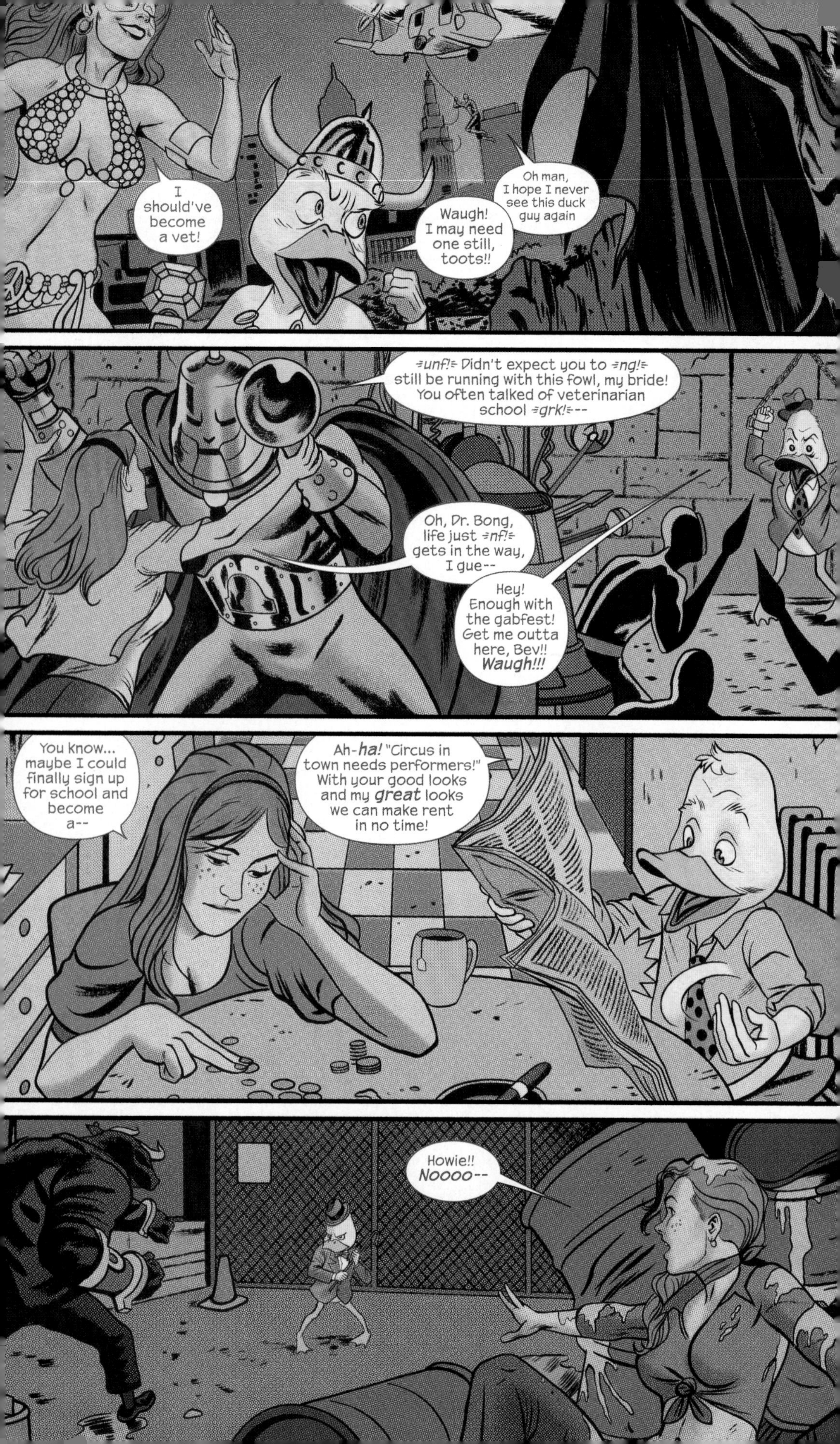
I should've become a vet!
Waugh! I may need one still, toots!!
Oh man, I hope I never see this duck guy again
=unf!= Didn't expect you to =ng!= still be running with this fowl, my bride! You often talked of veterinarian school =grk!=--
Oh, Dr. Bong, life just =nf!= gets in the way, I gue--
Hey! Enough with the gabfest! Get me outta here, Bev!! Waugh!!!
You know... maybe I could finally sign up for school and become a--
Ah-ha! "Circus in town needs performers!" With your good looks and my great looks we can make rent in no time!
Howie!! Noooo--

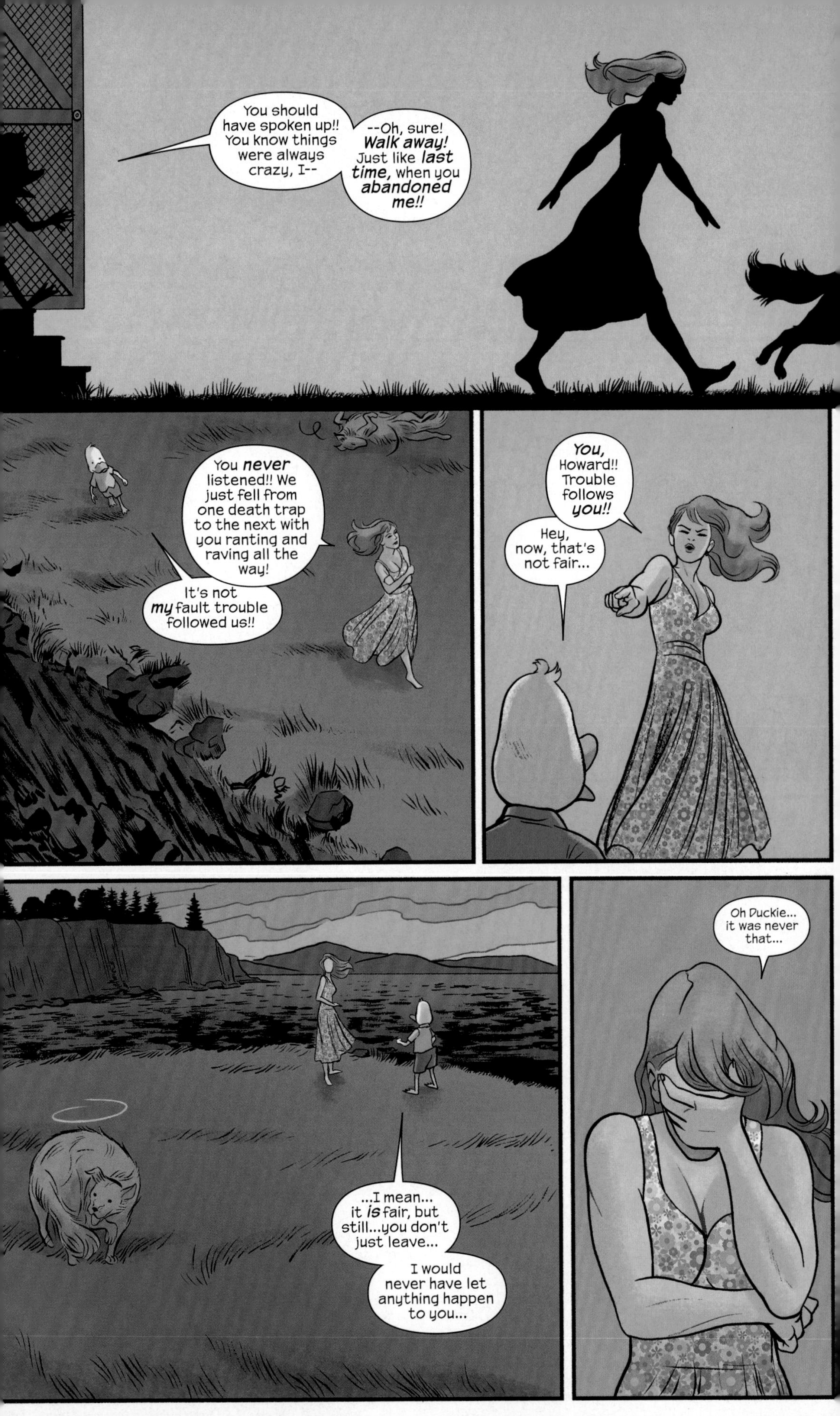
You should have spoken up!! You know things were always crazy, I--
--Oh, sure! *Walk away!* Just like *last time,* when you *abandoned me!!*
You ***never*** listened!! We just fell from one death trap to the next with you ranting and raving all the way!
It's not ***my*** fault trouble followed us!!
You, Howard!! Trouble follows ***you!!***
Hey, now, that's not fair...
...I mean... it ***is*** fair, but still...you don't just leave...
I would never have let anything happen to you...
Oh Duckie... it was never that...

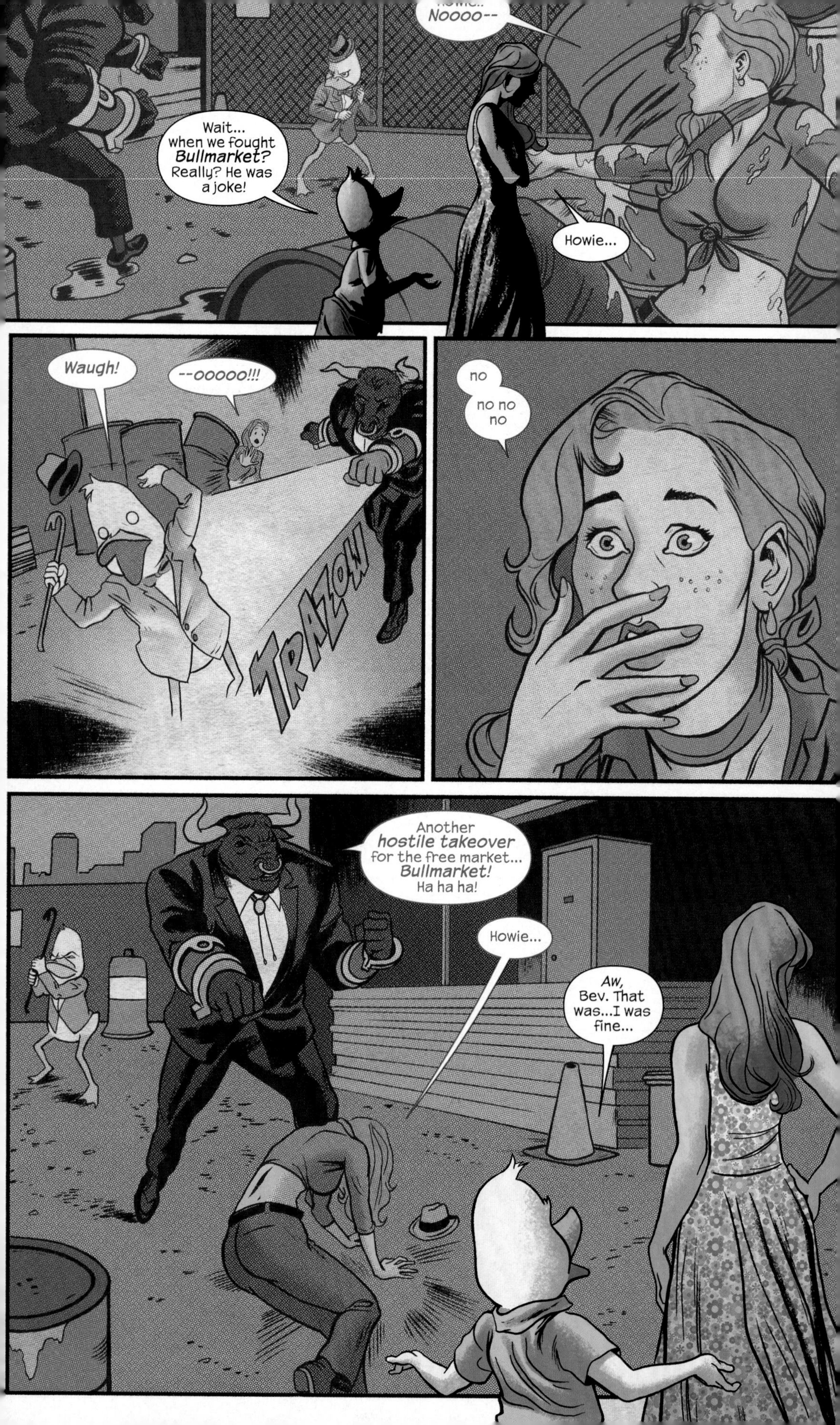

Howie.. Noooo--
Wait... when we fought Bullmarket? Really? He was a joke!
Howie...
Waugh!
--ooooo!!!
TRAZOW
no
no no no
Another hostile takeover for the free market... Bullmarket! Ha ha ha!
Howie...
Aw, Bev. That was...I was fine...

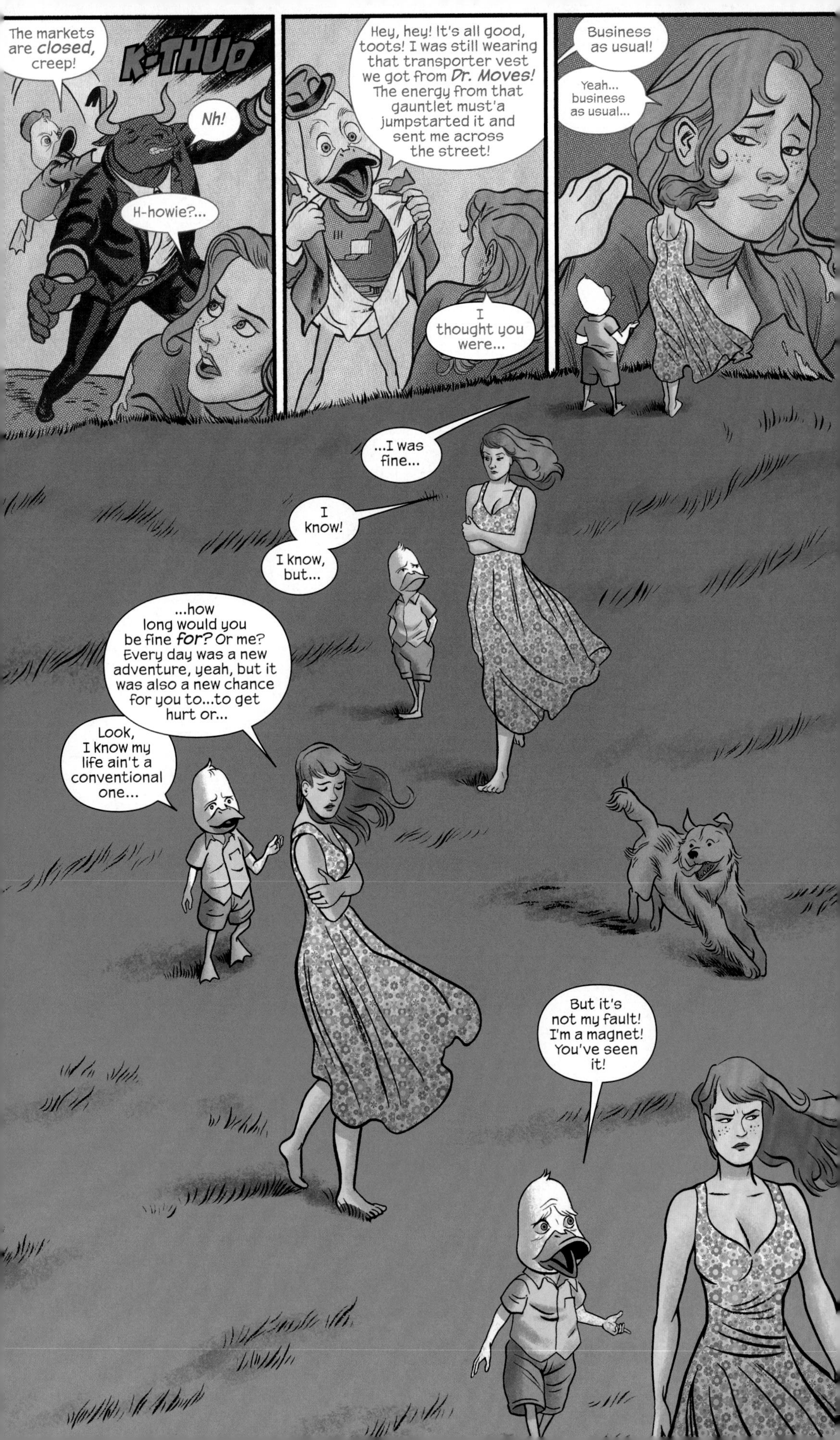

The markets are closed, creep!
K-THUD
Nh!
H-howie?...
Hey, hey! It's all good, toots! I was still wearing that transporter vest we got from Dr. Moves! The energy from that gauntlet must'a jumpstarted it and sent me across the street!
I thought you were...
Business as usual!
Yeah... business as usual...
...I was fine...
I know!
I know, but...
...how long would you be fine for? Or me? Every day was a new adventure, yeah, but it was also a new chance for you to...to get hurt or...
Look, I know my life ain't a conventional one...
But it's not my fault! I'm a magnet! You've seen it!

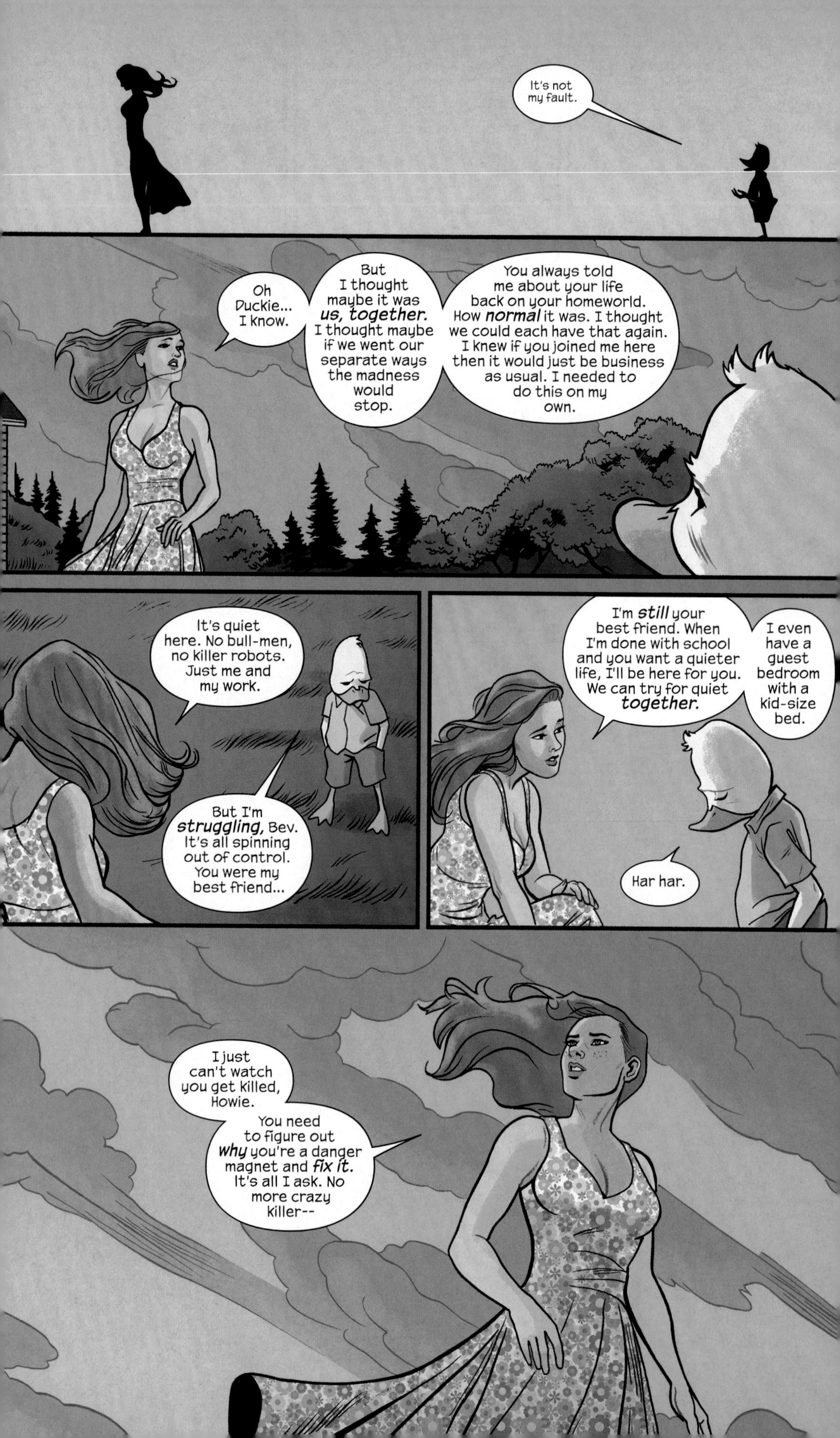
It's not my fault.
Oh Duckie... I know.
But I thought maybe it was us, together. I thought maybe if we went our separate ways the madness would stop.
You always told me about your life back on your homeworld. How normal it was. I thought we could each have that again. I knew if you joined me here then it would just be business as usual. I needed to do this on my own.
It's quiet here. No bull-men, no killer robots. Just me and my work.
But I'm struggling, Bev. It's all spinning out of control. You were my best friend...
I'm still your best friend. When I'm done with school and you want a quieter life, I'll be here for you. We can try for quiet together.
I even have a guest bedroom with a kid-size bed.
Har har.
I just can't watch you get killed, Howie.
You need to figure out why you're a danger magnet and fix it. It's all I ask. No more crazy killer--

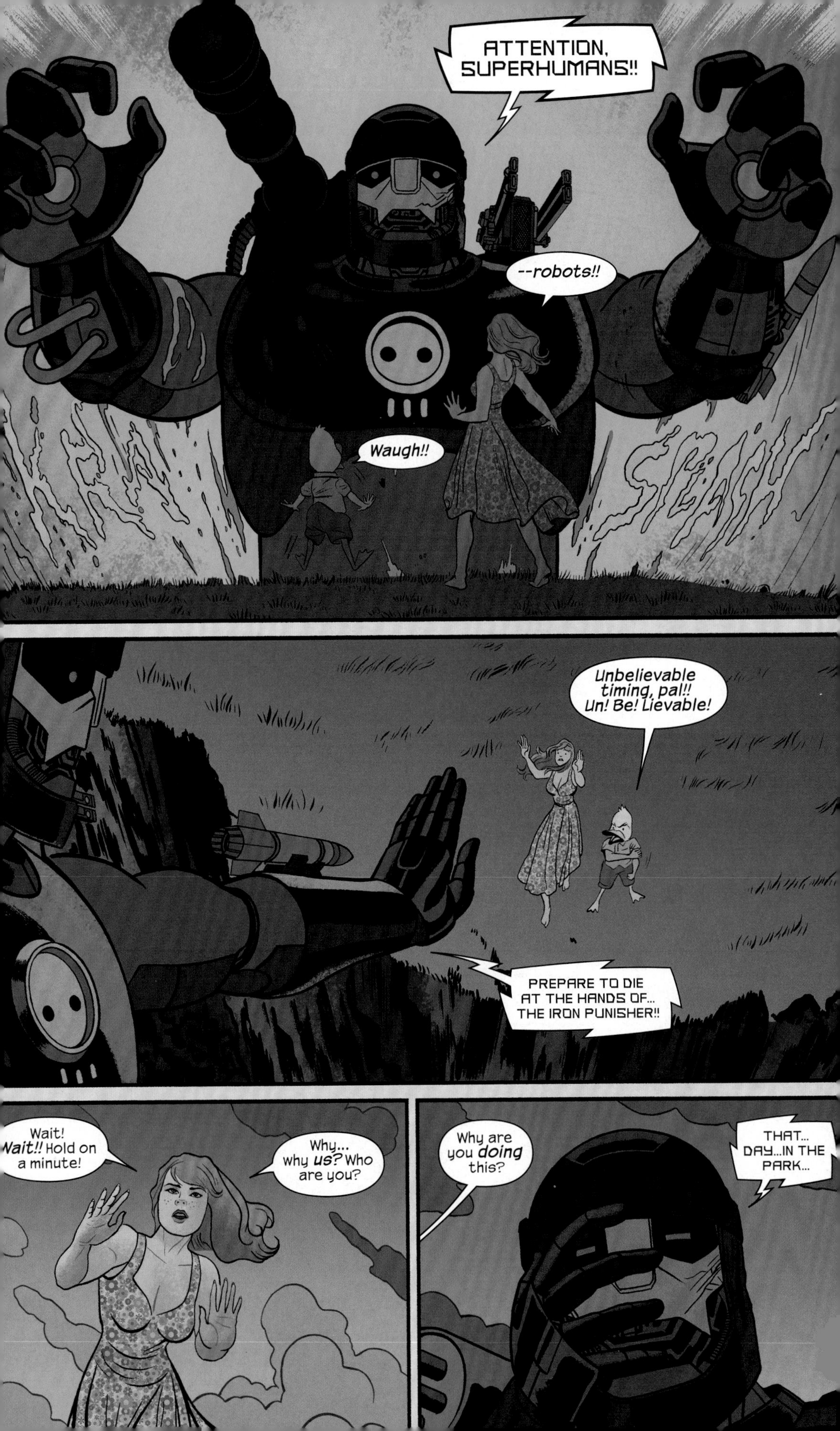
ATTENTION, SUPERHUMANS!!
--robots!!
Waugh!!
SPLASH
Unbelievable timing, pal!! Un! Be! Lievable!
PREPARE TO DIE AT THE HANDS OF... THE IRON PUNISHER!!
Wait! Wait!! Hold on a minute!
Why... why us? Who are you?
Why are you doing this?
THAT... DAY...IN THE PARK...

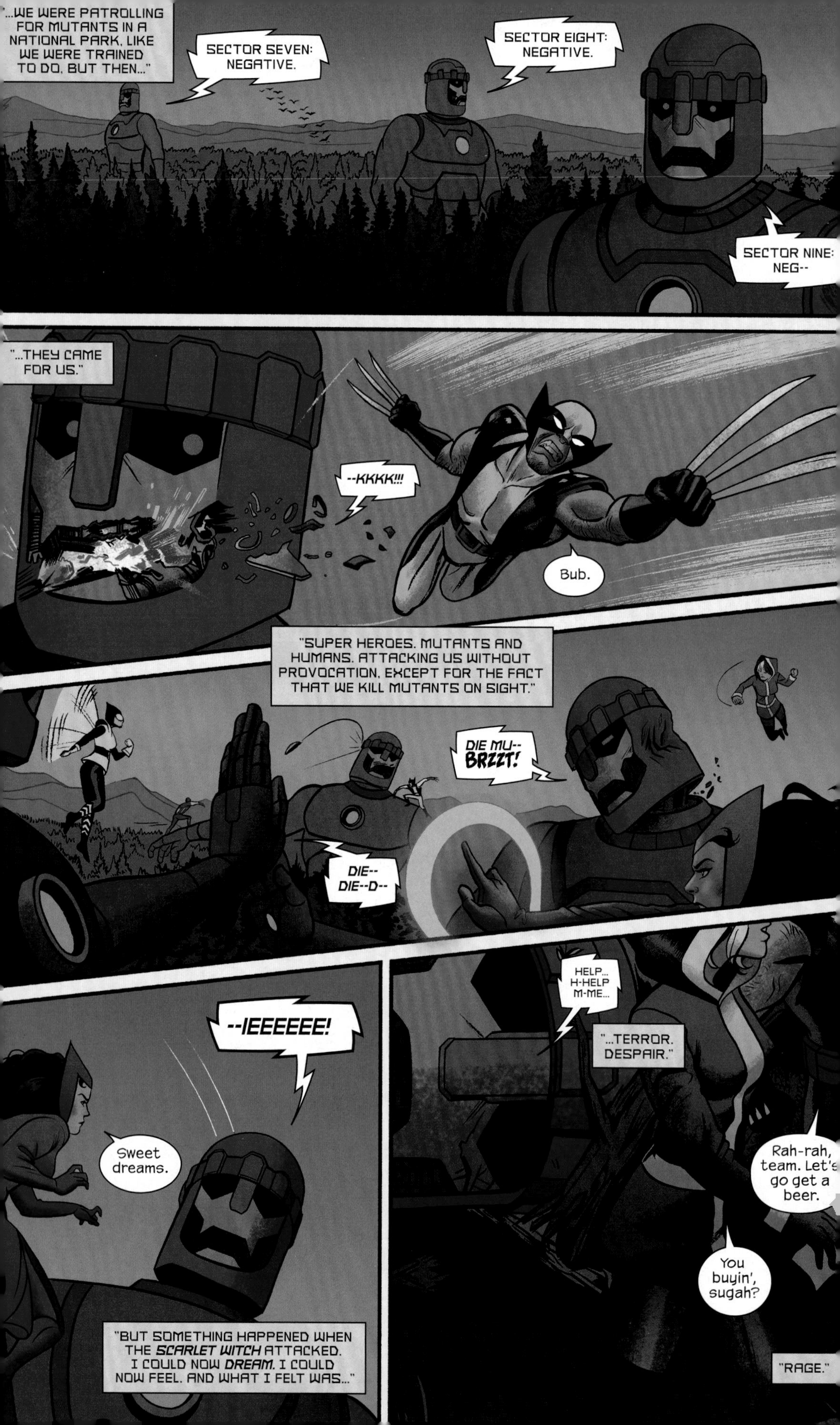
"...WE WERE PATROLLING FOR MUTANTS IN A NATIONAL PARK, LIKE WE WERE TRAINED TO DO, BUT THEN..."
SECTOR SEVEN: NEGATIVE.
SECTOR EIGHT: NEGATIVE.
SECTOR NINE: NEG--
"...THEY CAME FOR US."
--KKKK!!!
Bub.
"SUPER HEROES. MUTANTS AND HUMANS. ATTACKING US WITHOUT PROVOCATION, EXCEPT FOR THE FACT THAT WE KILL MUTANTS ON SIGHT."
DIE MU-- BRZZT!
DIE-- DIE--D--
--IEEEEEE!
Sweet dreams.
"BUT SOMETHING HAPPENED WHEN THE SCARLET WITCH ATTACKED. I COULD NOW DREAM. I COULD NOW FEEL. AND WHAT I FELT WAS..."
HELP... H-HELP M-ME...
"...TERROR. DESPAIR."
Rah-rah, team. Let's go get a beer.
You buyin', sugah?
"RAGE."

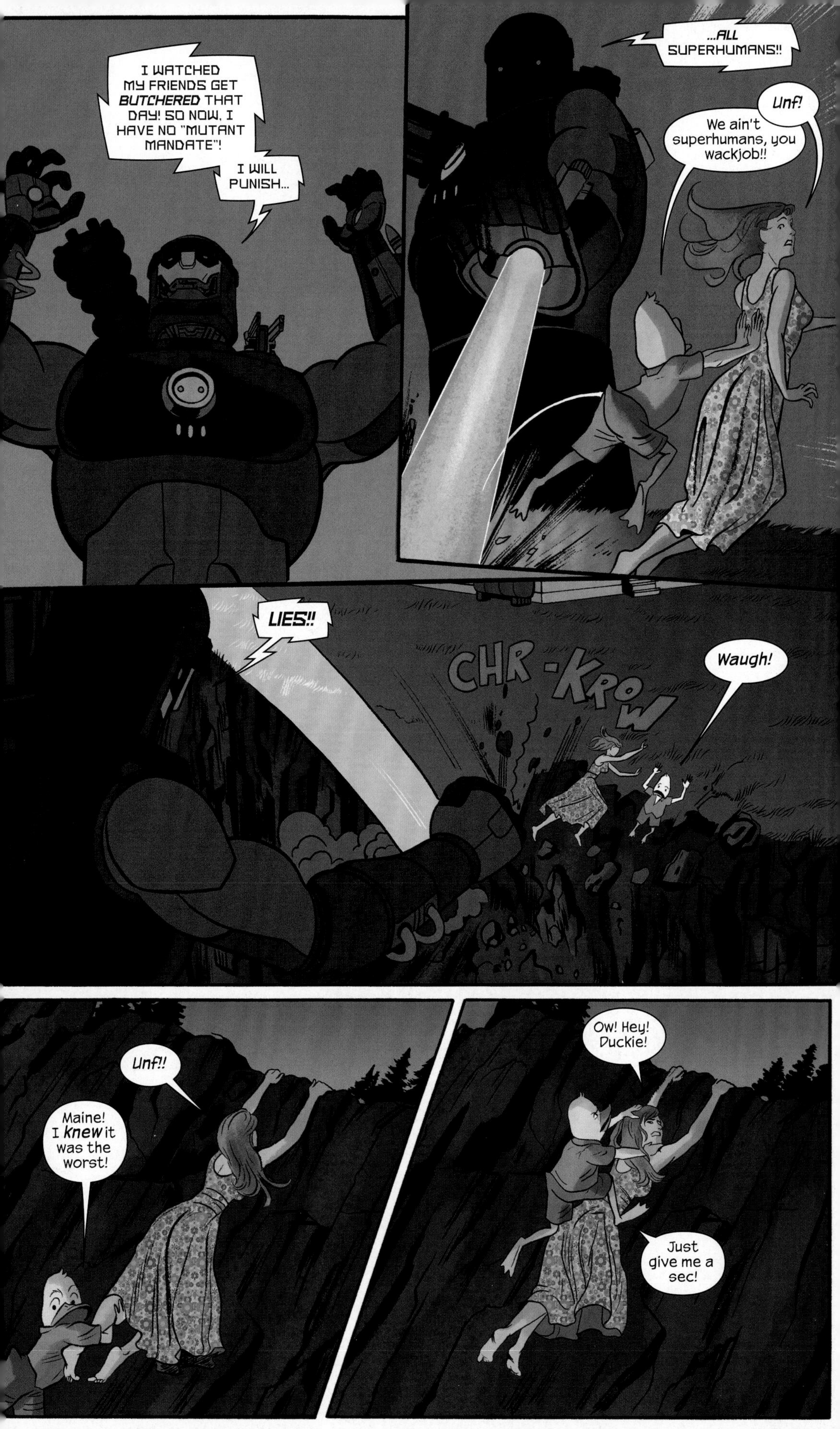
I WATCHED MY FRIENDS GET BUTCHERED THAT DAY! SO NOW, I HAVE NO "MUTANT MANDATE"!
I WILL PUNISH...
...ALL SUPERHUMANS!!
Unf!
We ain't superhumans, you wackjob!!
LIES!!
CHR-KROW
Waugh!
Unf!!
Maine! I knew it was the worst!
Ow! Hey! Duckie!
Just give me a sec!

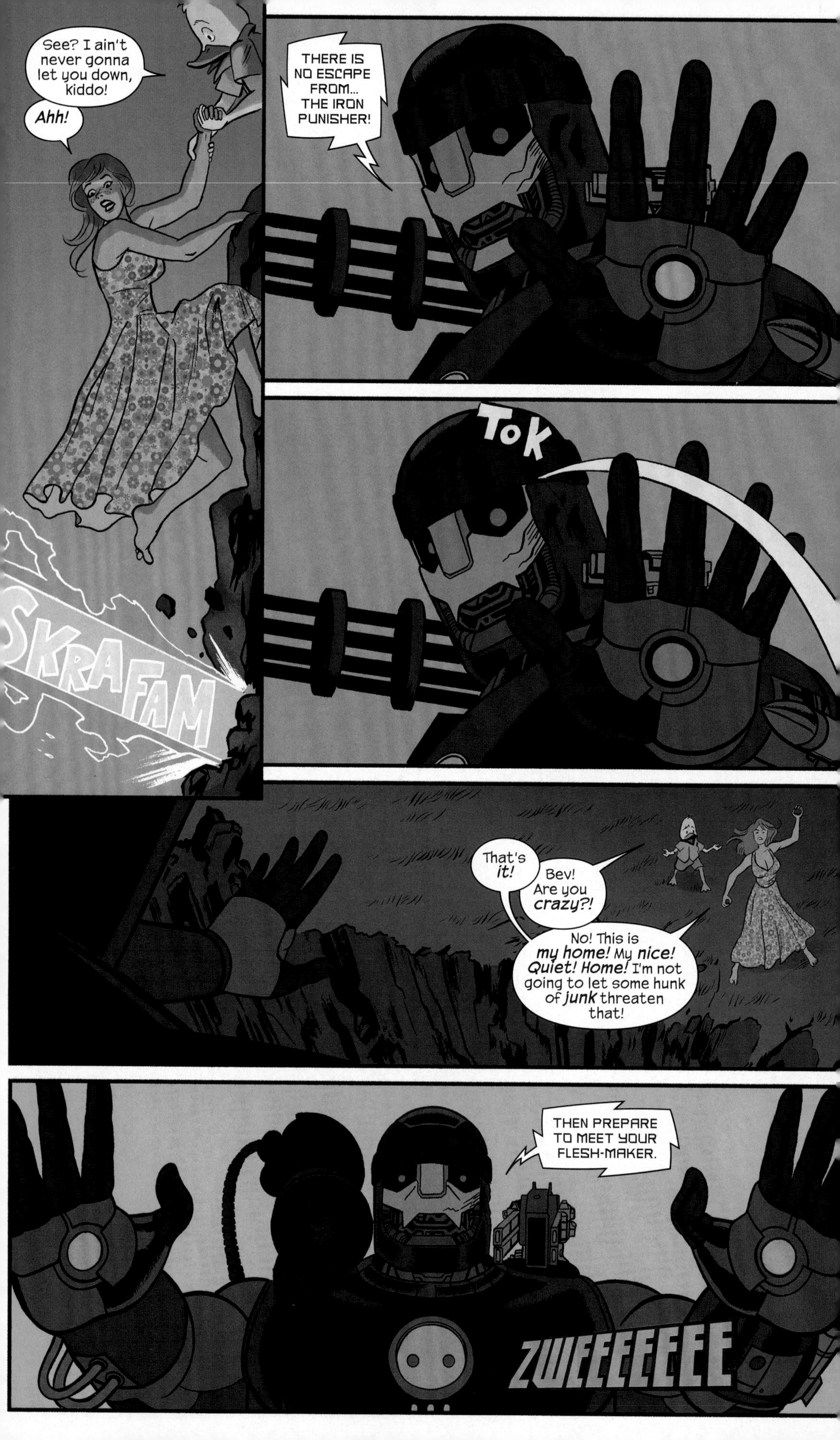
See? I ain't never gonna let you down, kiddo!
Ahh!
THERE IS NO ESCAPE FROM... THE IRON PUNISHER!
SKRAFAM
TOK
That's it!
Bev! Are you crazy?!
No! This is my home! My nice! Quiet! Home! I'm not going to let some hunk of junk threaten that!
THEN PREPARE TO MEET YOUR FLESH-MAKER.
ZWEEEEEEEE

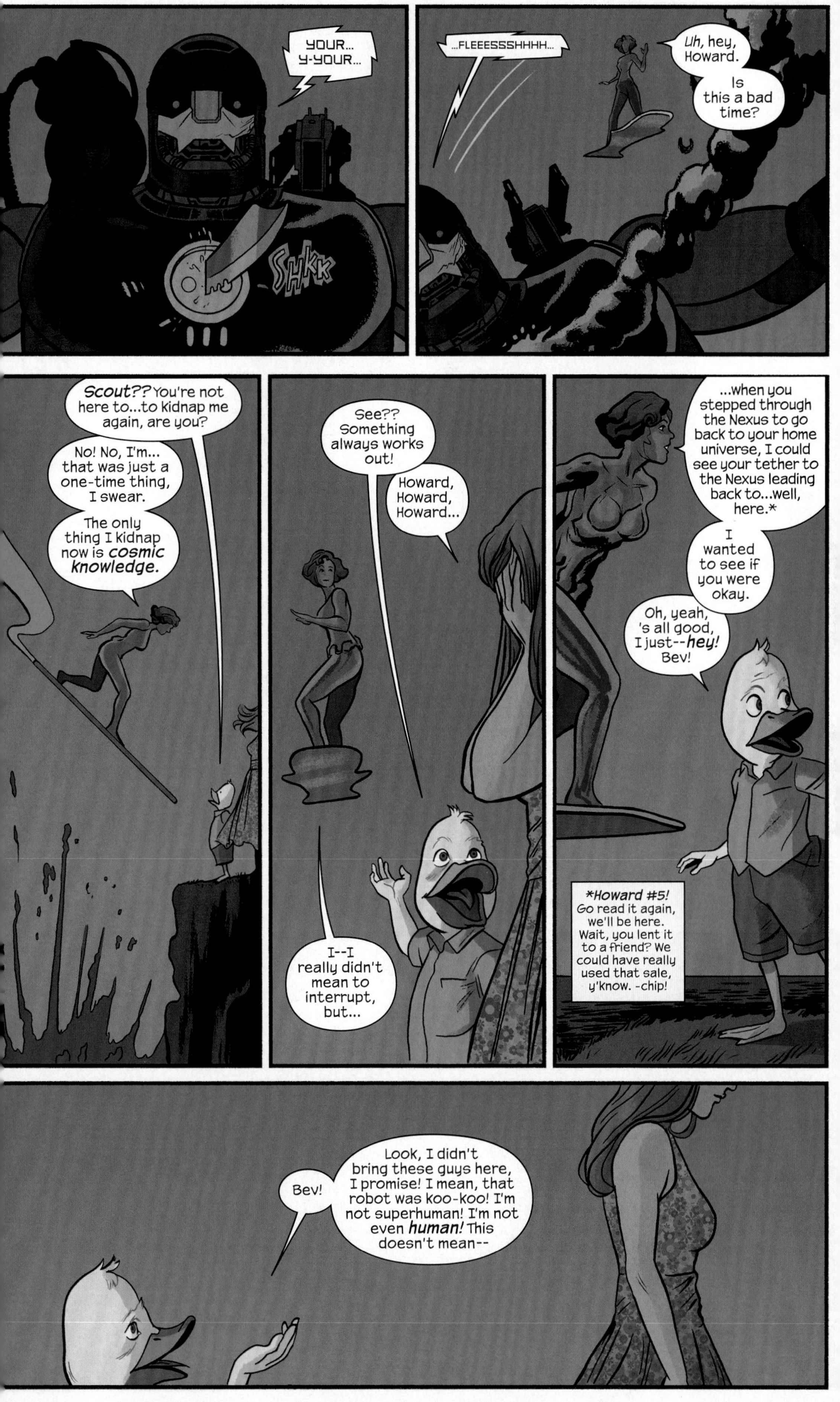
YOUR... Y-YOUR...
SHKK
...FLEEESSSHHHH...
Uh, hey, Howard.
Is this a bad time?
Scout?? You're not here to...to kidnap me again, are you?
No! No, I'm... that was just a one-time thing, I swear.
The only thing I kidnap now is cosmic knowledge.
See?? Something always works out!
Howard, Howard, Howard...
I--I really didn't mean to interrupt, but...
...when you stepped through the Nexus to go back to your home universe, I could see your tether to the Nexus leading back to...well, here.*
I wanted to see if you were okay.
Oh, yeah, 's all good, I just--hey! Bev!
*Howard #5! Go read it again, we'll be here. Wait, you lent it to a friend? We could have really used that sale, y'know. -chip!
Bev!
Look, I didn't bring these guys here, I promise! I mean, that robot was koo-koo! I'm not superhuman! I'm not even human! This doesn't mean--

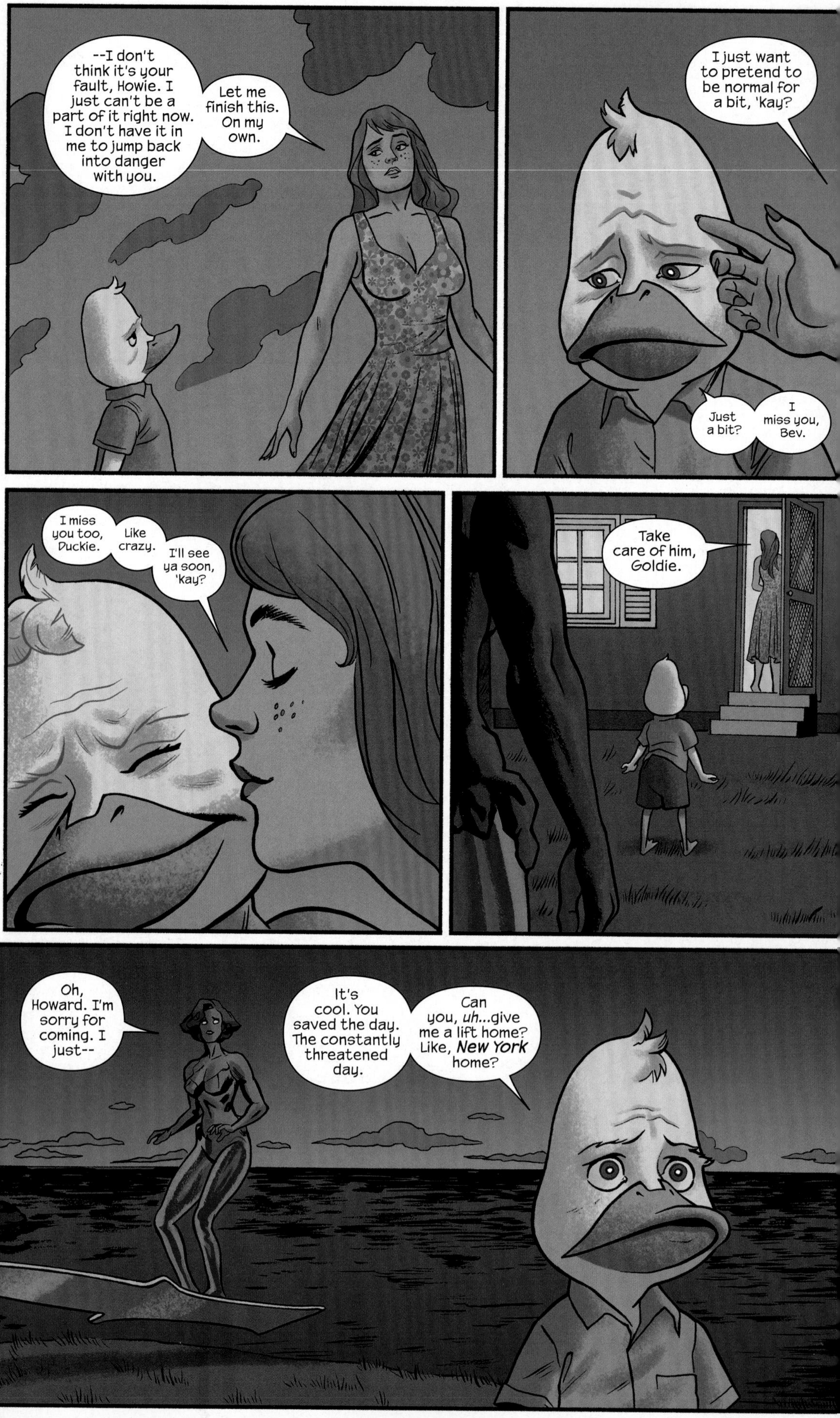
--I don't think it's your fault, Howie. I just can't be a part of it right now. I don't have it in me to jump back into danger with you.
Let me finish this. On my own.
I just want to pretend to be normal for a bit, 'kay?
Just a bit?
I miss you, Bev.
I miss you too, Duckie.
Like crazy.
I'll see ya soon, 'kay?
Take care of him, Goldie.
Oh, Howard. I'm sorry for coming. I just--
It's cool. You saved the day. The constantly threatened day.
Can you, *uh*...give me a lift home? Like, ***New York*** home?

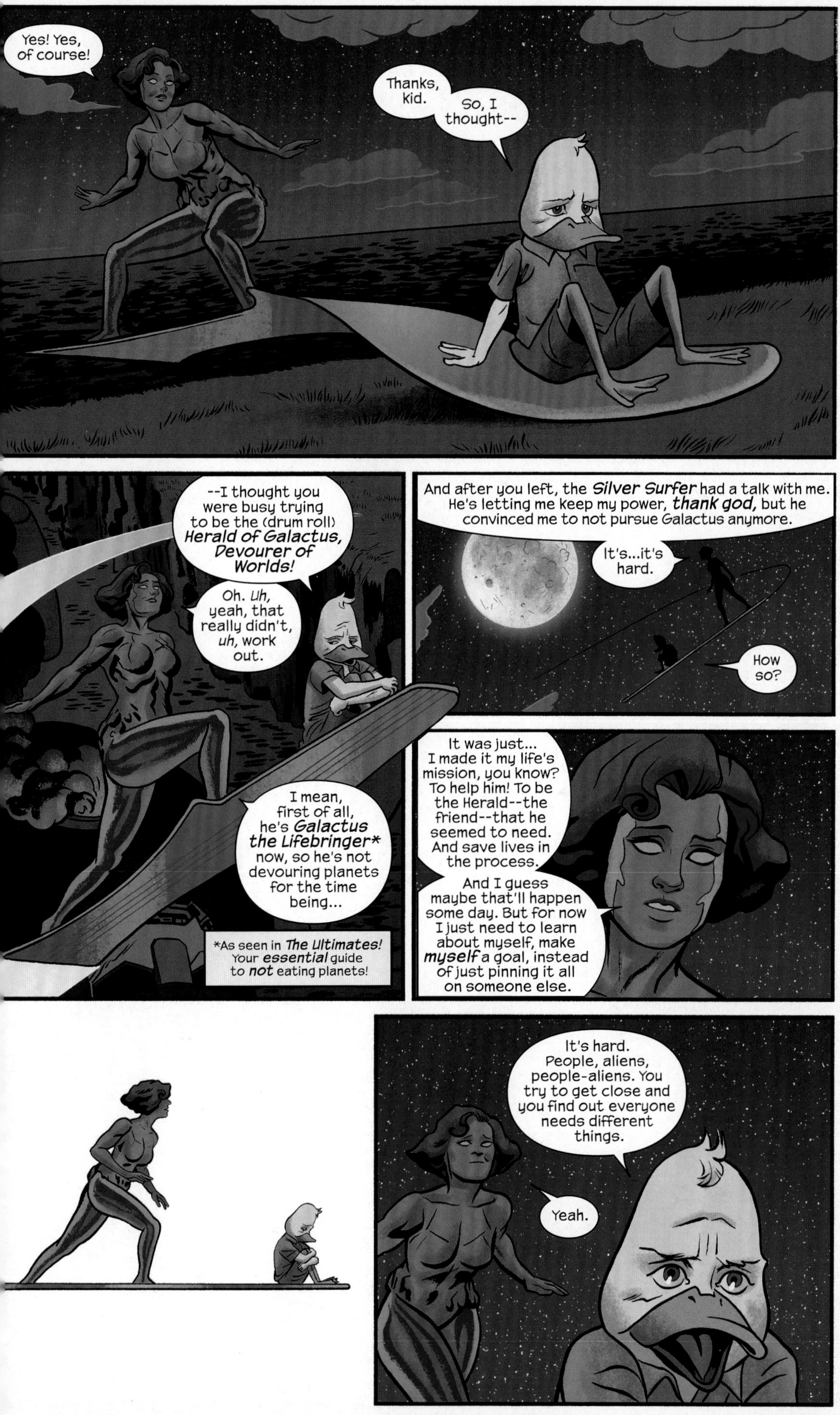

Yes! Yes, of course!
Thanks, kid.
So, I thought--
--I thought you were busy trying to be the (drum roll) Herald of Galactus, Devourer of Worlds!
Oh. Uh, yeah, that really didn't, uh, work out.
I mean, first of all, he's Galactus the Lifebringer* now, so he's not devouring planets for the time being...
*As seen in The Ultimates! Your essential guide to not eating planets!
And after you left, the Silver Surfer had a talk with me. He's letting me keep my power, thank god, but he convinced me to not pursue Galactus anymore.
It's...it's hard.
How so?
It was just... I made it my life's mission, you know? To help him! To be the Herald--the friend--that he seemed to need. And save lives in the process.
And I guess maybe that'll happen some day. But for now I just need to learn about myself, make myself a goal, instead of just pinning it all on someone else.
It's hard. People, aliens, people-aliens. You try to get close and you find out everyone needs different things.
Yeah.

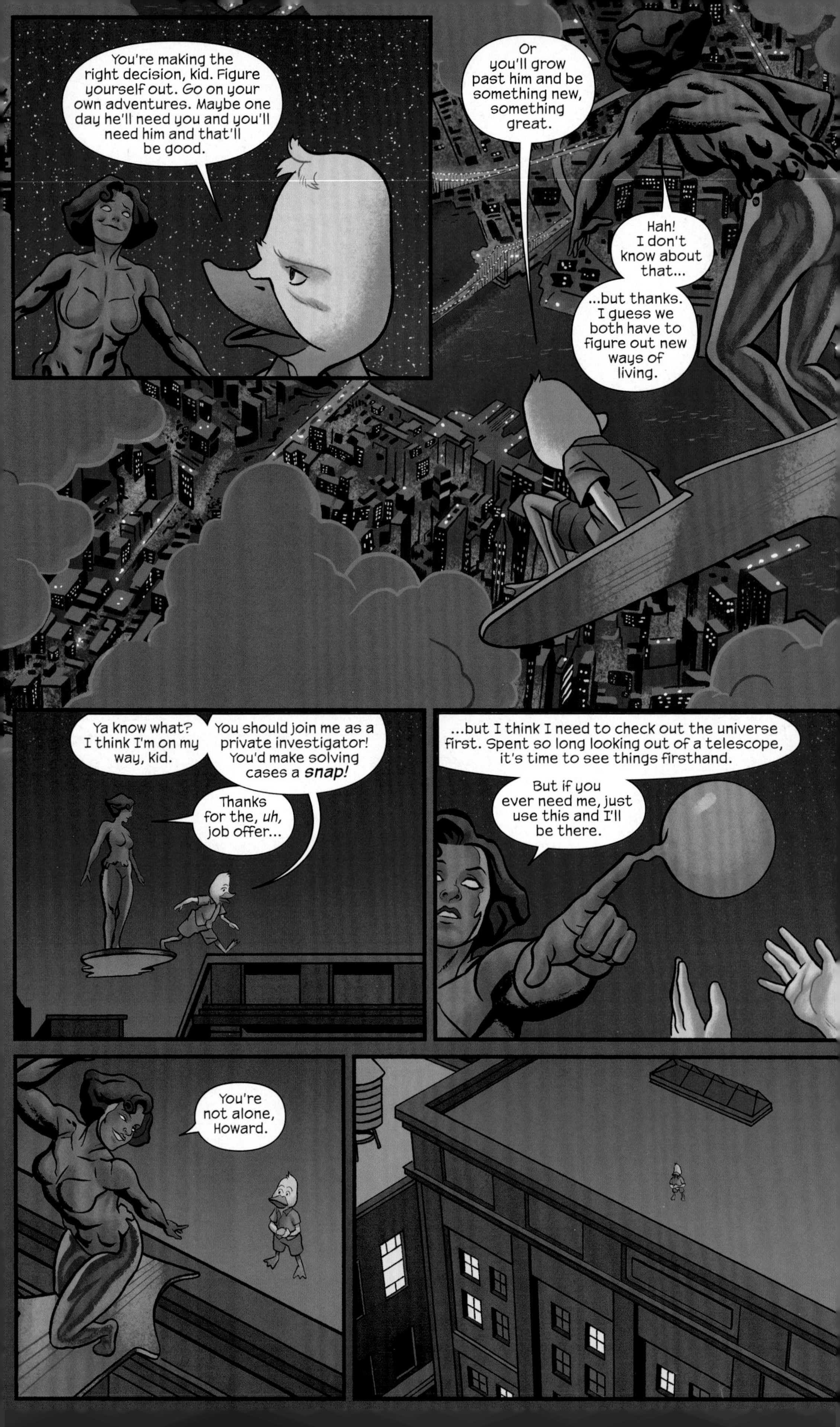
You're making the right decision, kid. Figure yourself out. Go on your own adventures. Maybe one day he'll need you and you'll need him and that'll be good.
Or you'll grow past him and be something new, something great.
Hah! I don't know about that...
...but thanks. I guess we both have to figure out new ways of living.
Ya know what? I think I'm on my way, kid.
You should join me as a private investigator! You'd make solving cases a *snap!*
Thanks for the, *uh,* job offer...
...but I think I need to check out the universe first. Spent so long looking out of a telescope, it's time to see things firsthand.
But if you ever need me, just use this and I'll be there.
You're not alone, Howard.

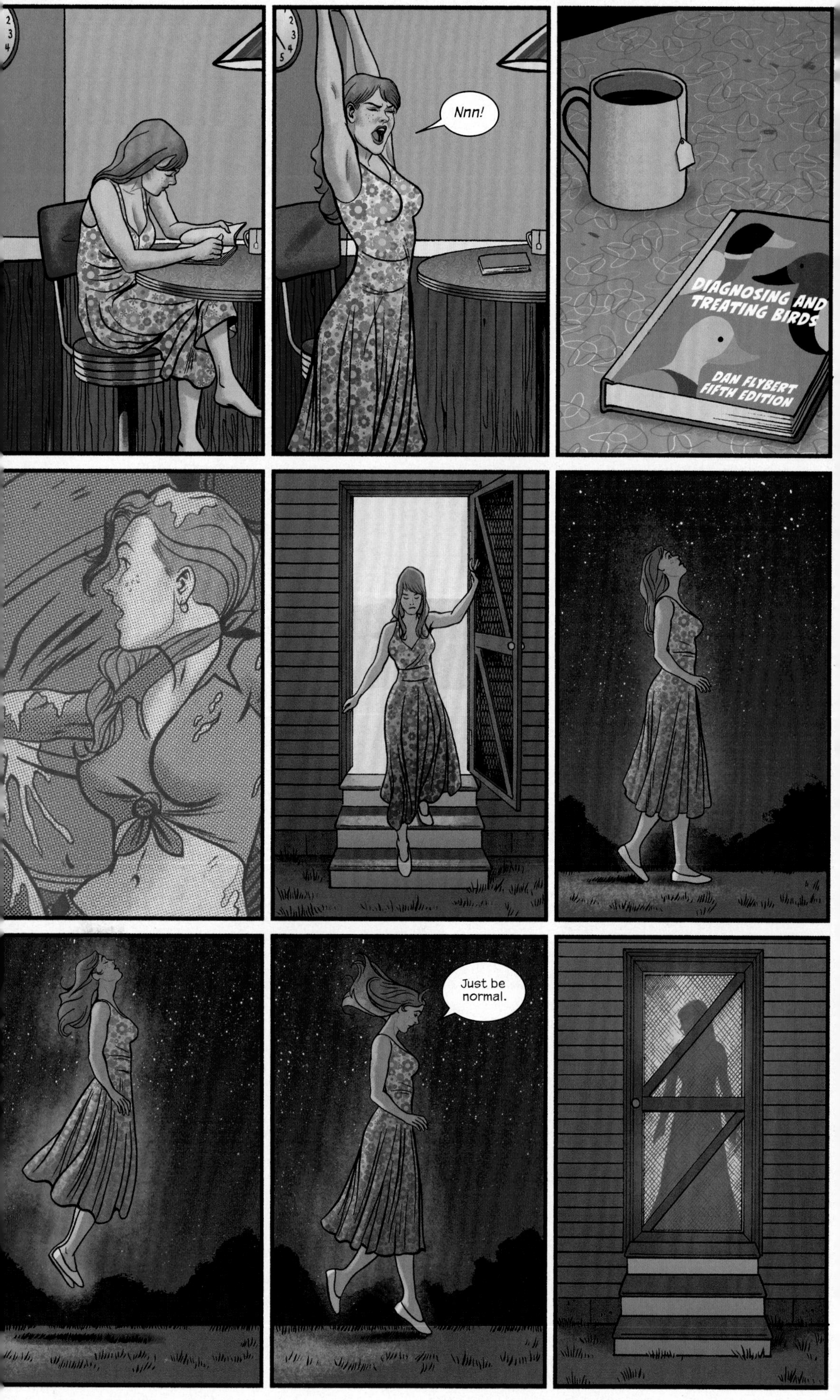
Nnn!
DIAGNOSING AND TREATING BIRDS
DAN FLYBERT
FIFTH EDITION
Just be normal.

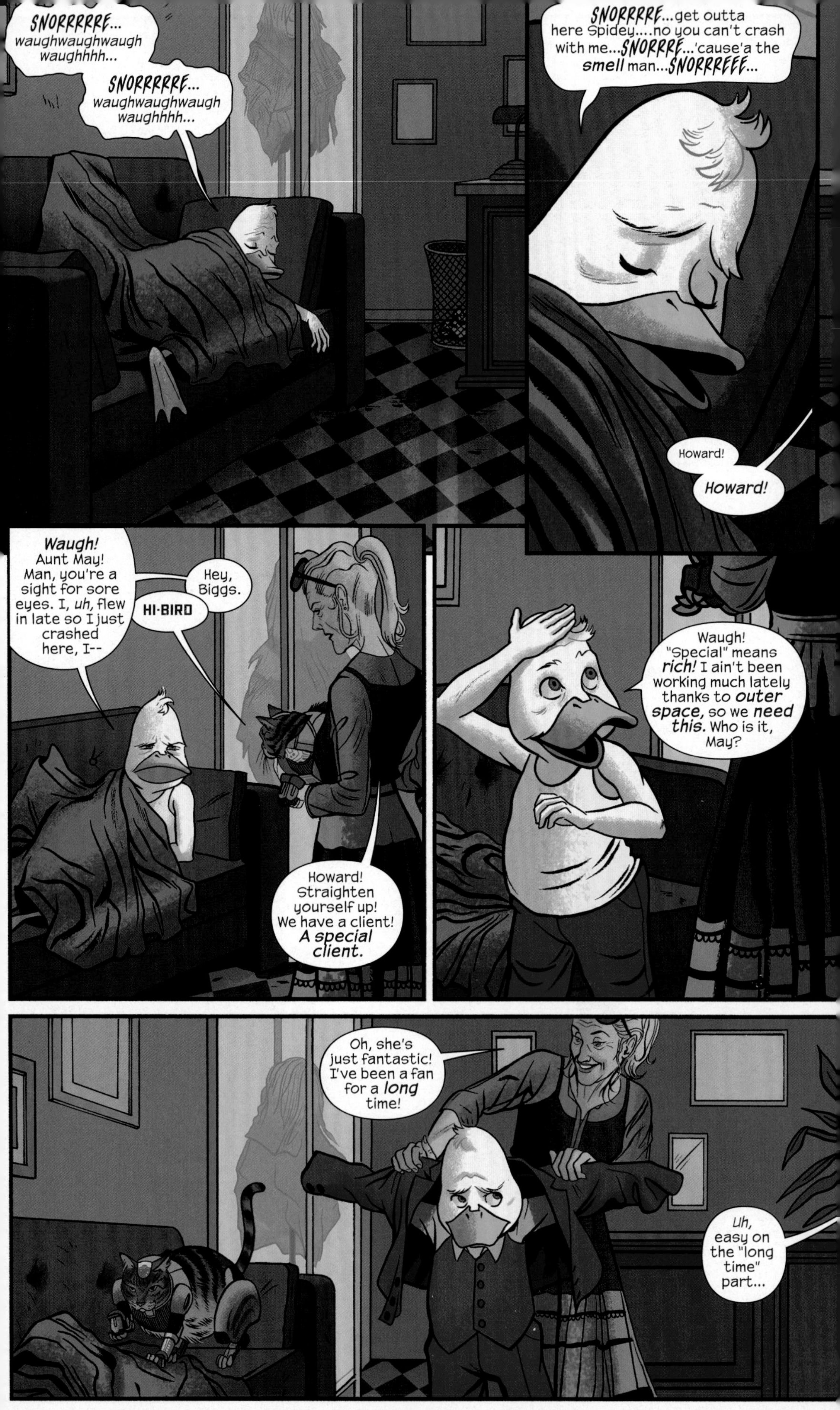
SNORRRRRE... waughwaughwaugh waughhhh...
SNORRRRRE... waughwaughwaugh waughhhh...
SNORRRRE...get outta here Spidey....no you can't crash with me...SNORRRE...'cause'a the smell man...SNORRREEE...
Howard!
Howard!
Waugh! Aunt May! Man, you're a sight for sore eyes. I, uh, flew in late so I just crashed here, I--
Hey, Biggs.
HI-BIRD
Howard! Straighten yourself up! We have a client! A special client.
Waugh! "Special" means rich! I ain't been working much lately thanks to outer space, so we need this. Who is it, May?
Oh, she's just fantastic! I've been a fan for a long time!
Uh, easy on the "long time" part...

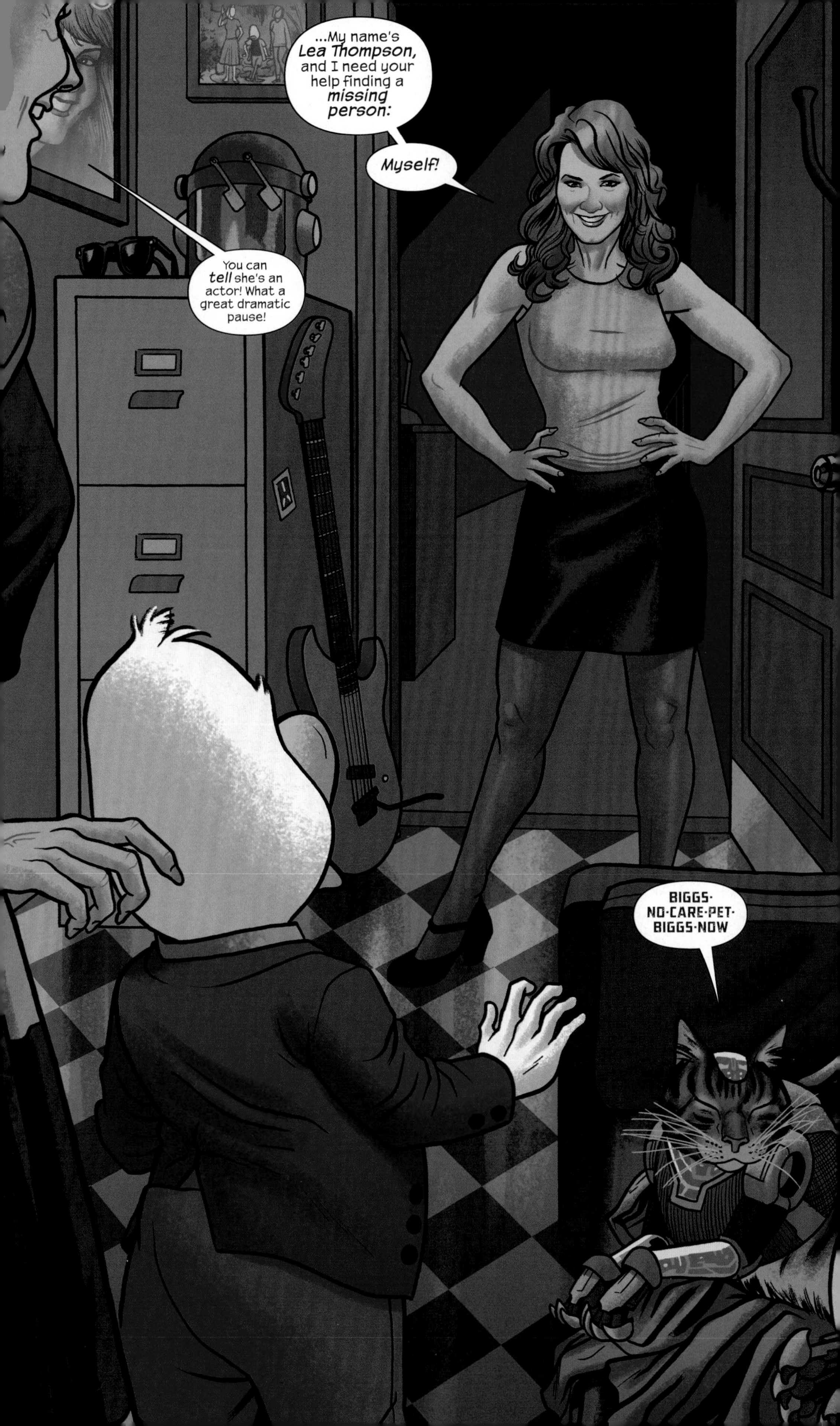
...My name's Lea Thompson, and I need your help finding a missing person:
Myself!
You can tell she's an actor! What a great dramatic pause!
BIGGS·NO·CARE·PET·BIGGS·NOW

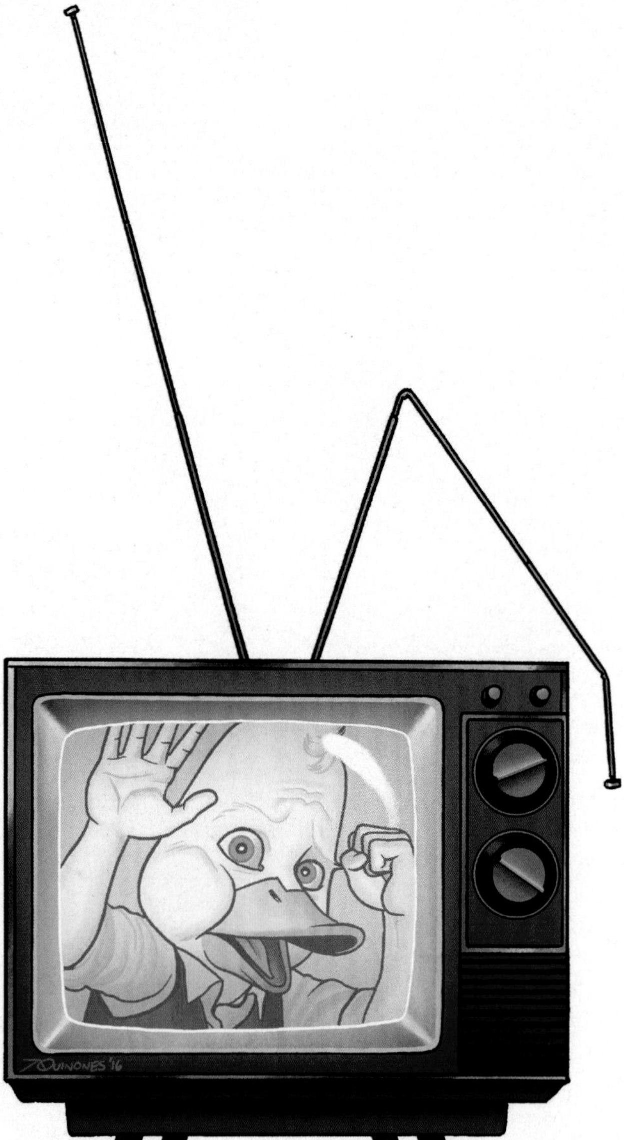
QUINONES '16

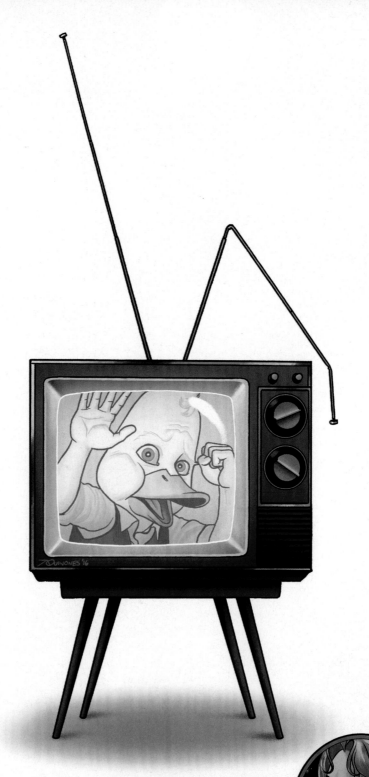

WITH SPECIAL GUEST STAR **LEA THOMPSON!**

yeah we barely believe it either

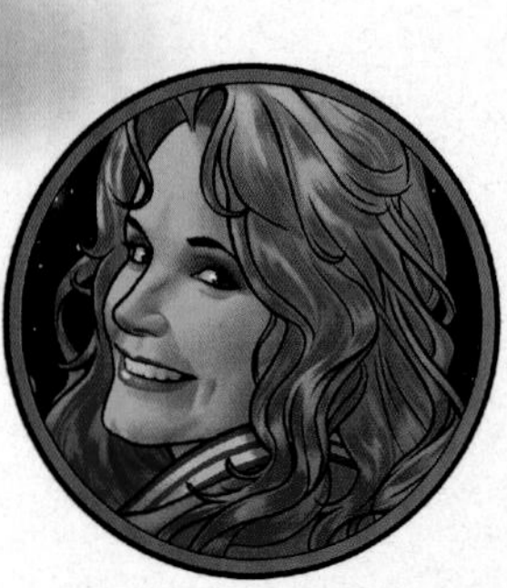

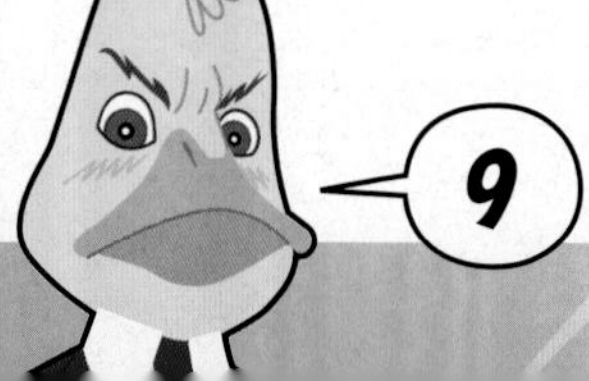
9

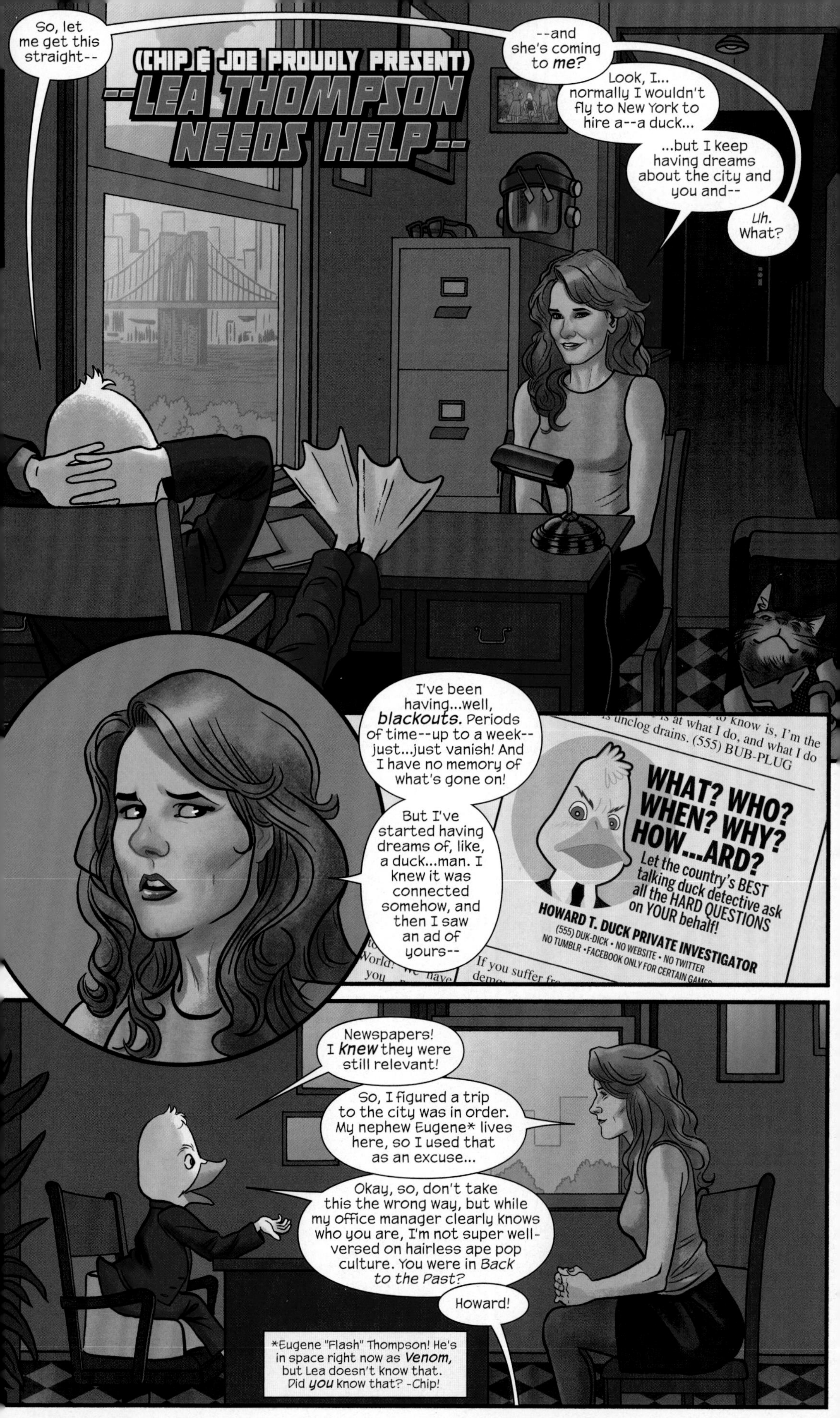
So, let me get this straight--
(CHIP & JOE PROUDLY PRESENT)
--LEA THOMPSON NEEDS HELP--
--and she's coming to *me*?
Look, I... normally I wouldn't fly to New York to hire a--a duck...
...but I keep having dreams about the city and you and--
Uh. What?
I've been having...well, *blackouts.* Periods of time--up to a week--just...just vanish! And I have no memory of what's gone on!
But I've started having dreams of, like, a duck...man. I knew it was connected somehow, and then I saw an ad of yours--
is at what I do, and what I do
unclog drains. (555) BUB-PLUG
WHAT? WHO? WHEN? WHY? HOW...ARD?
Let the country's BEST talking duck detective ask all the HARD QUESTIONS on YOUR behalf!
HOWARD T. DUCK PRIVATE INVESTIGATOR
(555) DUK-DICK • NO WEBSITE • NO TWITTER
NO TUMBLR • FACEBOOK ONLY FOR CERTAIN GAMES
Newspapers! I *knew* they were still relevant!
So, I figured a trip to the city was in order. My nephew Eugene* lives here, so I used that as an excuse...
Okay, so, don't take this the wrong way, but while my office manager clearly knows who you are, I'm not super well-versed on hairless ape pop culture. You were in *Back to the Past?*
Howard!
*Eugene "Flash" Thompson! He's in space right now as *Venom,* but Lea doesn't know that. Did *you* know that? -Chip!

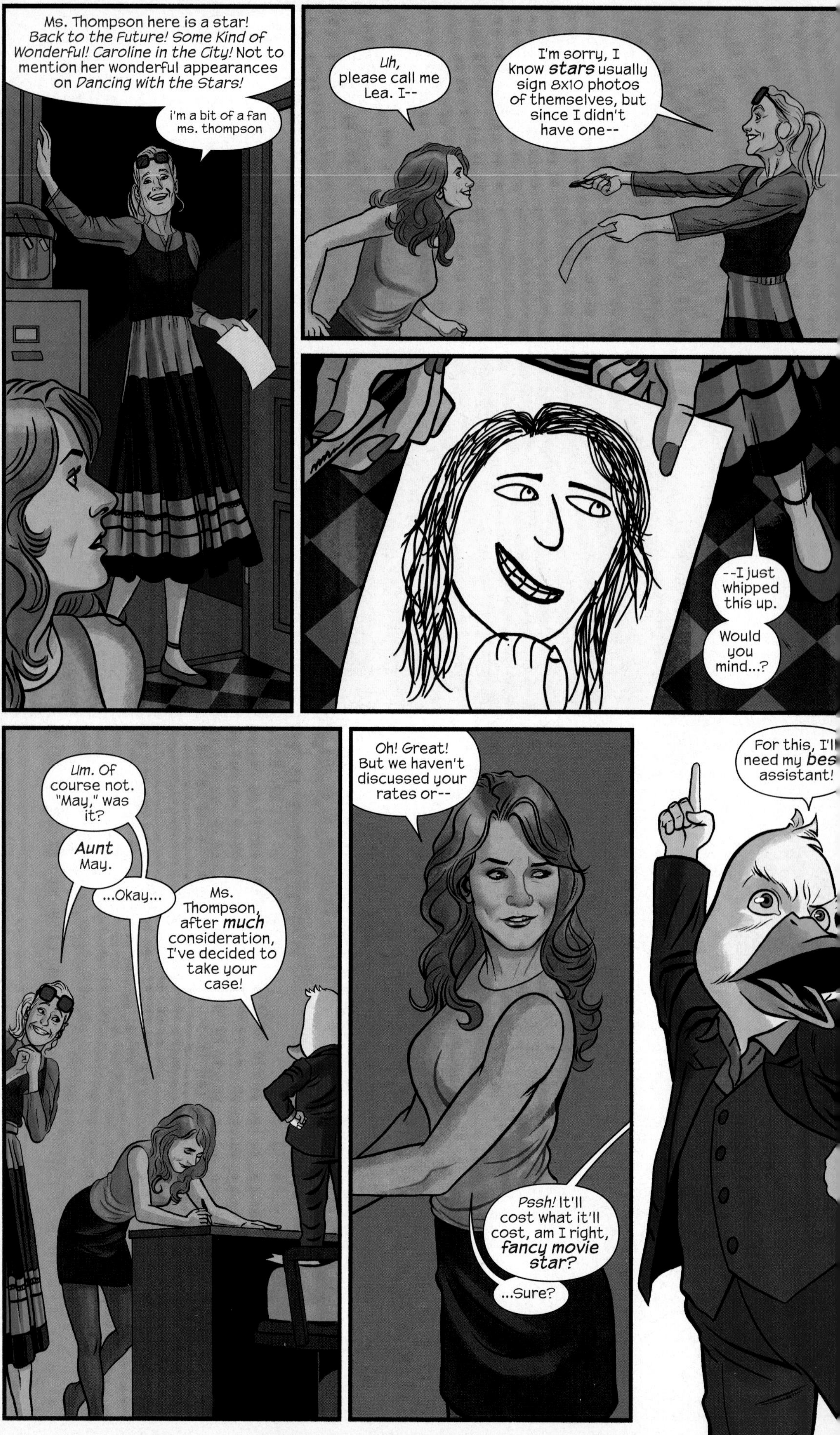
Ms. Thompson here is a star! *Back to the Future! Some Kind of Wonderful! Caroline in the City!* Not to mention her wonderful appearances on *Dancing with the Stars!*
i'm a bit of a fan ms. thompson
Uh, please call me Lea. I--
I'm sorry, I know **stars** usually sign 8x10 photos of themselves, but since I didn't have one--
--I just whipped this up.
Would you mind...?
Um. Of course not. "May," was it?
Aunt May.
...Okay...
Ms. Thompson, after **much** consideration, I've decided to take your case!
Oh! Great! But we haven't discussed your rates or--
Pssh! It'll cost what it'll cost, am I right, **fancy movie star?**
...Sure?
For this, I'l need my **bes** assistant!

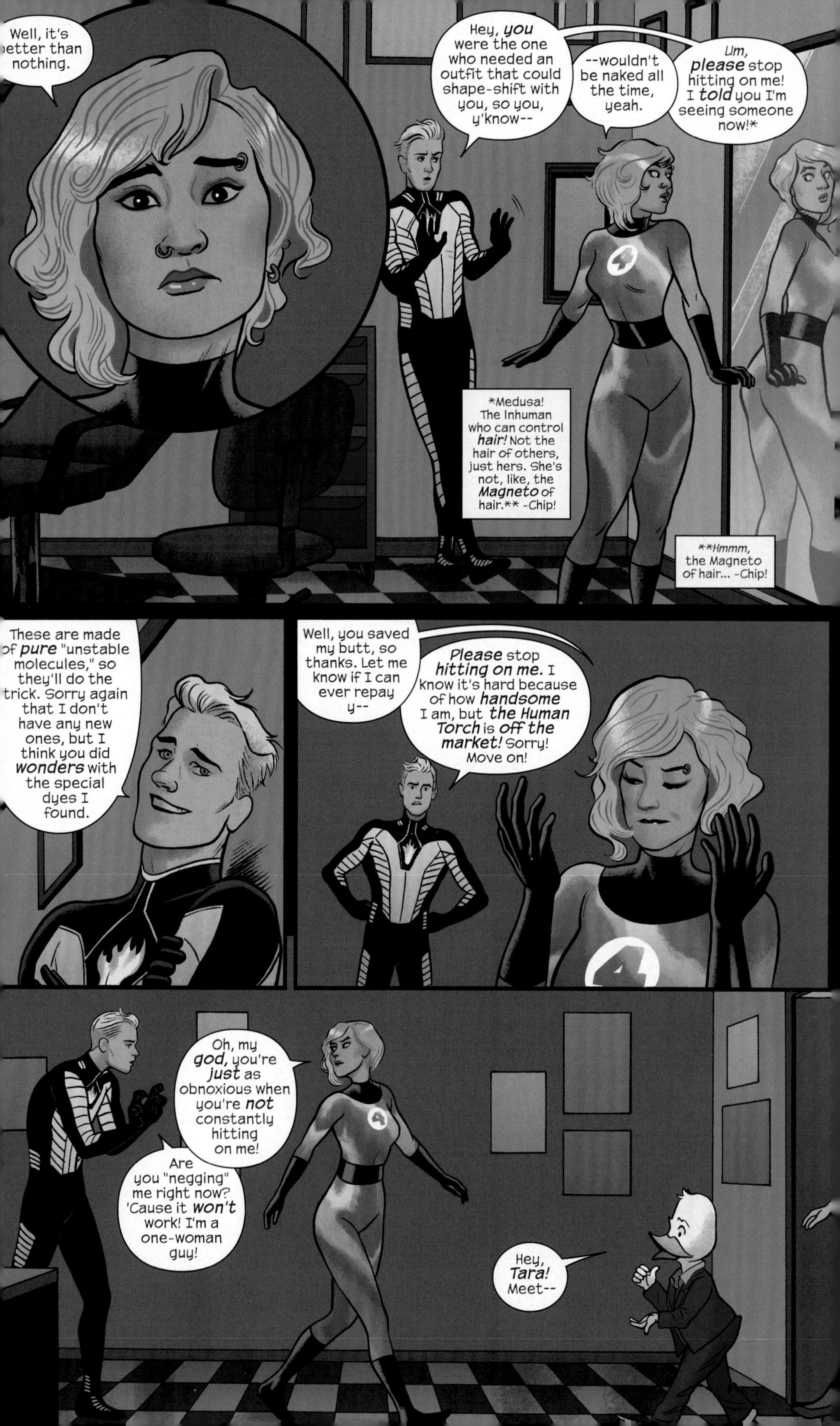
Well, it's better than nothing.
Hey, you were the one who needed an outfit that could shape-shift with you, so you, y'know--
--wouldn't be naked all the time, yeah.
Um, please stop hitting on me! I told you I'm seeing someone now!*
*Medusa! The Inhuman who can control hair! Not the hair of others, just hers. She's not, like, the Magneto of hair.** -Chip!
**Hmmm, the Magneto of hair... -Chip!
These are made of pure "unstable molecules," so they'll do the trick. Sorry again that I don't have any new ones, but I think you did wonders with the special dyes I found.
Well, you saved my butt, so thanks. Let me know if I can ever repay y--
Please stop hitting on me. I know it's hard because of how handsome I am, but the Human Torch is off the market! Sorry! Move on!
Oh, my god, you're just as obnoxious when you're not constantly hitting on me!
Are you "negging" me right now? 'Cause it won't work! I'm a one-woman guy!
Hey, Tara! Meet--

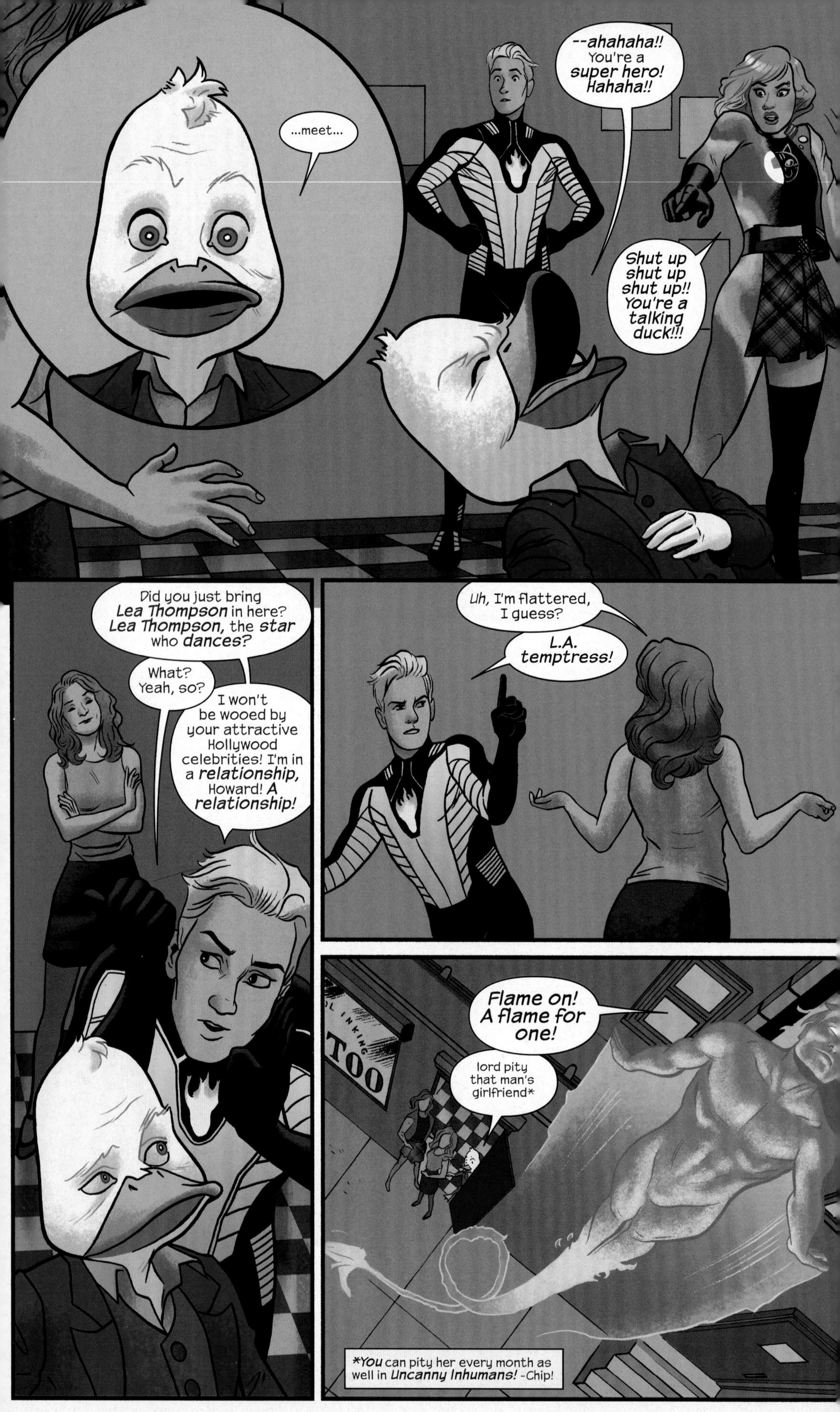
...meet...
--ahahaha!! You're a super hero! Hahaha!!
Shut up shut up shut up!! You're a talking duck!!!
Did you just bring Lea Thompson in here? Lea Thompson, the star who dances?
What? Yeah, so?
I won't be wooed by your attractive Hollywood celebrities! I'm in a relationship, Howard! A relationship!
Uh, I'm flattered, I guess?
L.A. temptress!
Flame on! A flame for one!
lord pity that man's girlfriend*
*You can pity her every month as well in Uncanny Inhumans! -Chip!

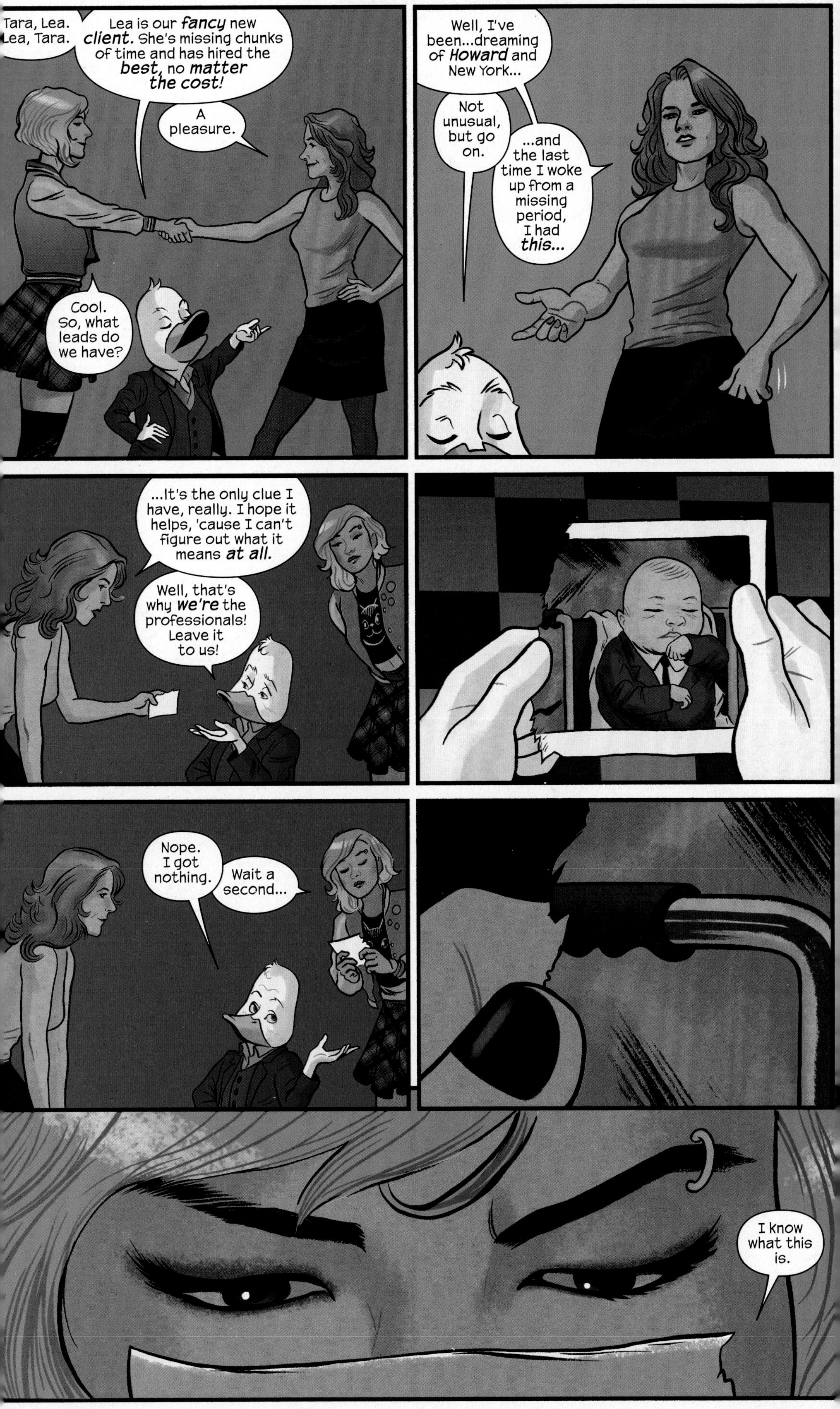

Tara, Lea. Lea, Tara.
Lea is our fancy new client. She's missing chunks of time and has hired the best, no matter the cost!
A pleasure.
Cool. So, what leads do we have?
Well, I've been...dreaming of Howard and New York...
Not unusual, but go on.
...and the last time I woke up from a missing period, I had this...
...It's the only clue I have, really. I hope it helps, 'cause I can't figure out what it means at all.
Well, that's why we're the professionals! Leave it to us!
Nope. I got nothing.
Wait a second...
I know what this is.

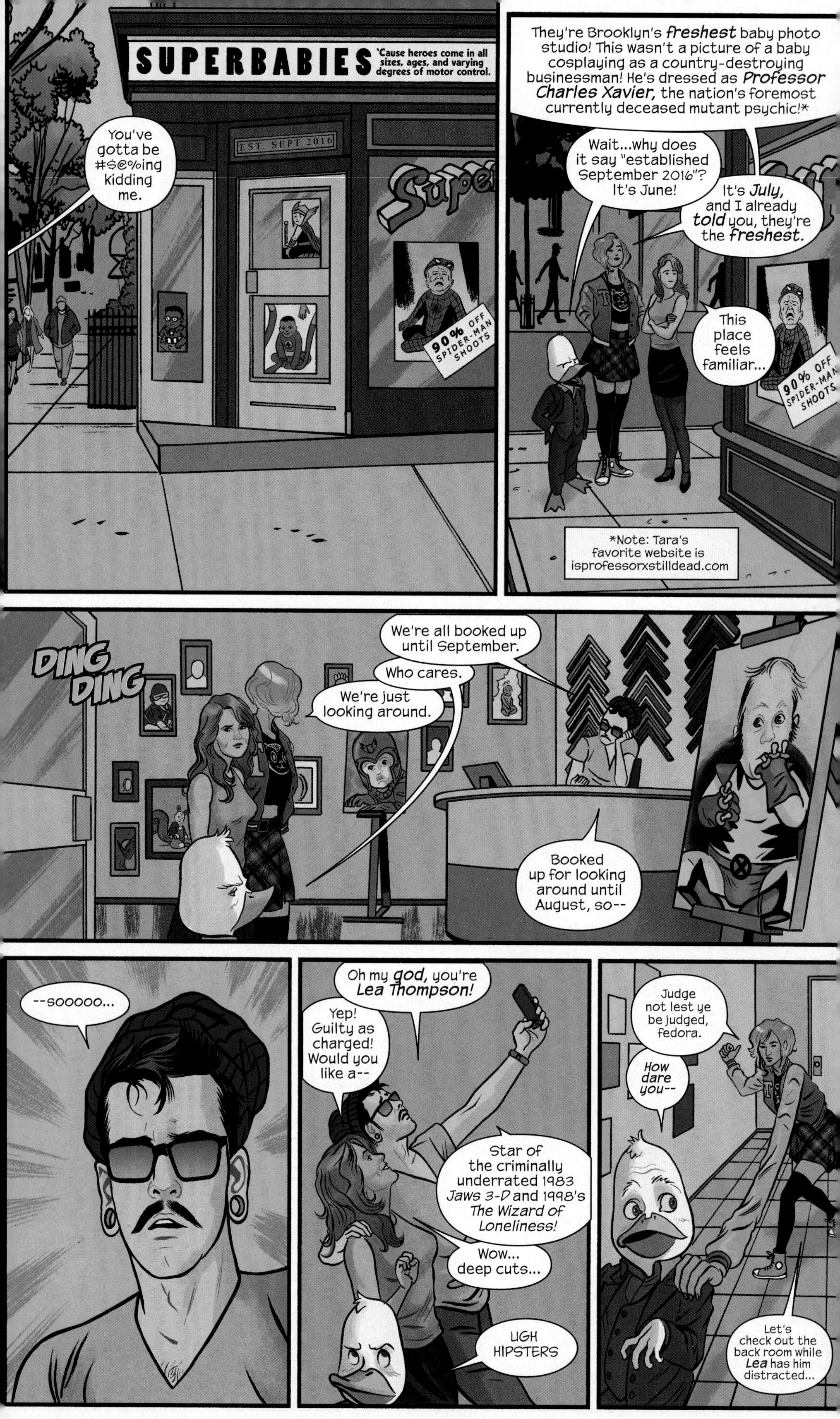
SUPERBABIES
'Cause heroes come in all sizes, ages, and varying degrees of motor control.
EST. SEPT 2016
You've gotta be #$@%ing kidding me.
Super
90% OFF SPIDER-MAN SHOOTS
They're Brooklyn's freshest baby photo studio! This wasn't a picture of a baby cosplaying as a country-destroying businessman! He's dressed as Professor Charles Xavier, the nation's foremost currently deceased mutant psychic!*
Wait...why does it say "established September 2016"? It's June!
It's July, and I already told you, they're the freshest.
This place feels familiar...
90% OFF SPIDER-MAN SHOOTS
*Note: Tara's favorite website is isprofessorxstilldead.com
DING DING
We're all booked up until September.
Who cares.
We're just looking around.
Booked up for looking around until August, so--
--SOOOOO...
Oh my god, you're Lea Thompson!
Yep! Guilty as charged! Would you like a--
Star of the criminally underrated 1983 Jaws 3-D and 1998's The Wizard of Loneliness!
Wow... deep cuts...
UGH HIPSTERS
Judge not lest ye be judged, fedora.
How dare you--
Let's check out the back room while Lea has him distracted...

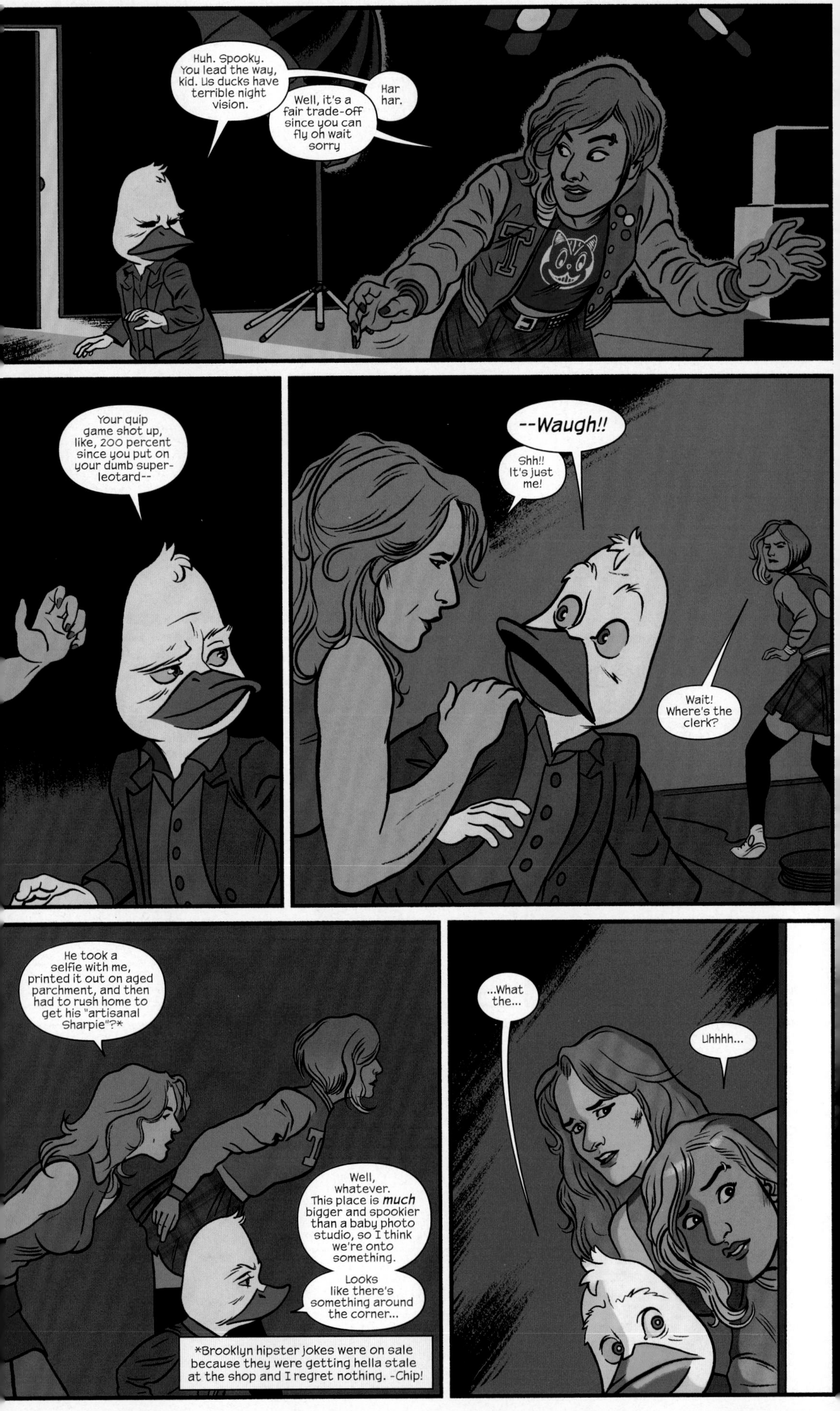
Huh. Spooky. You lead the way, kid. Us ducks have terrible night vision.
Well, it's a fair trade-off since you can fly oh wait sorry
Har har.
Your quip game shot up, like, 200 percent since you put on your dumb super-leotard--
--Waugh!!
Shh!! It's just me!
Wait! Where's the clerk?
He took a selfie with me, printed it out on aged parchment, and then had to rush home to get his "artisanal Sharpie"?*
Well, whatever. This place is *much* bigger and spookier than a baby photo studio, so I think we're onto something.
Looks like there's something around the corner...
*Brooklyn hipster jokes were on sale because they were getting hella stale at the shop and I regret nothing. -Chip!
...What the...
Uhhhh...

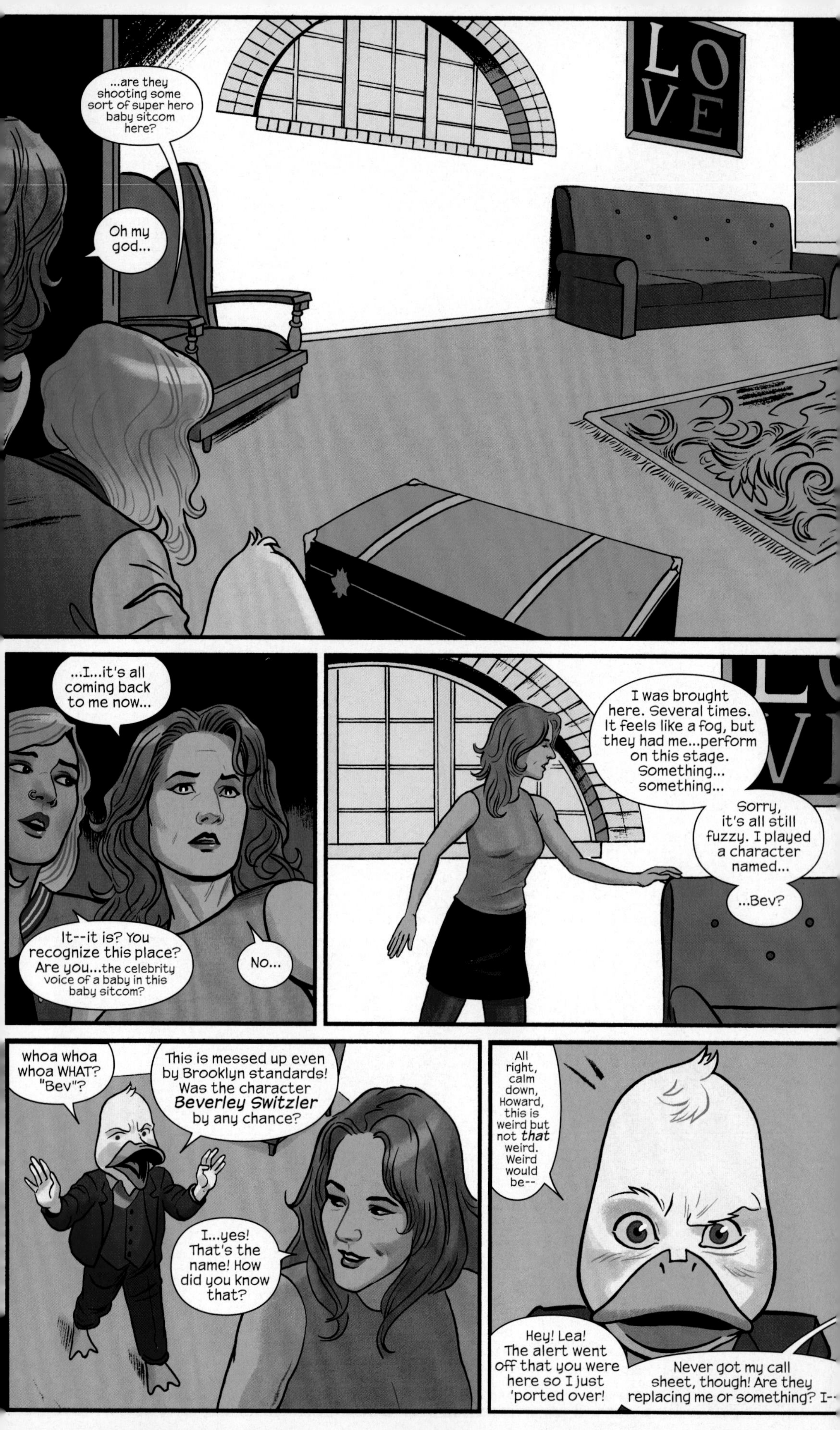
...are they shooting some sort of super hero baby sitcom here?
Oh my god...
...I...it's all coming back to me now...
It--it is? You recognize this place? Are you...the celebrity voice of a baby in this baby sitcom?
No...
I was brought here. Several times. It feels like a fog, but they had me...perform on this stage. Something... something...
Sorry, it's all still fuzzy. I played a character named...
...Bev?
whoa whoa whoa WHAT? "Bev"?
This is messed up even by Brooklyn standards! Was the character *Beverley Switzler* by any chance?
I...yes! That's the name! How did you know that?
All right, calm down, Howard, this is weird but not *that* weird. Weird would be--
Hey! Lea! The alert went off that you were here so I just 'ported over!
Never got my call sheet, though! Are they replacing me or something? I--

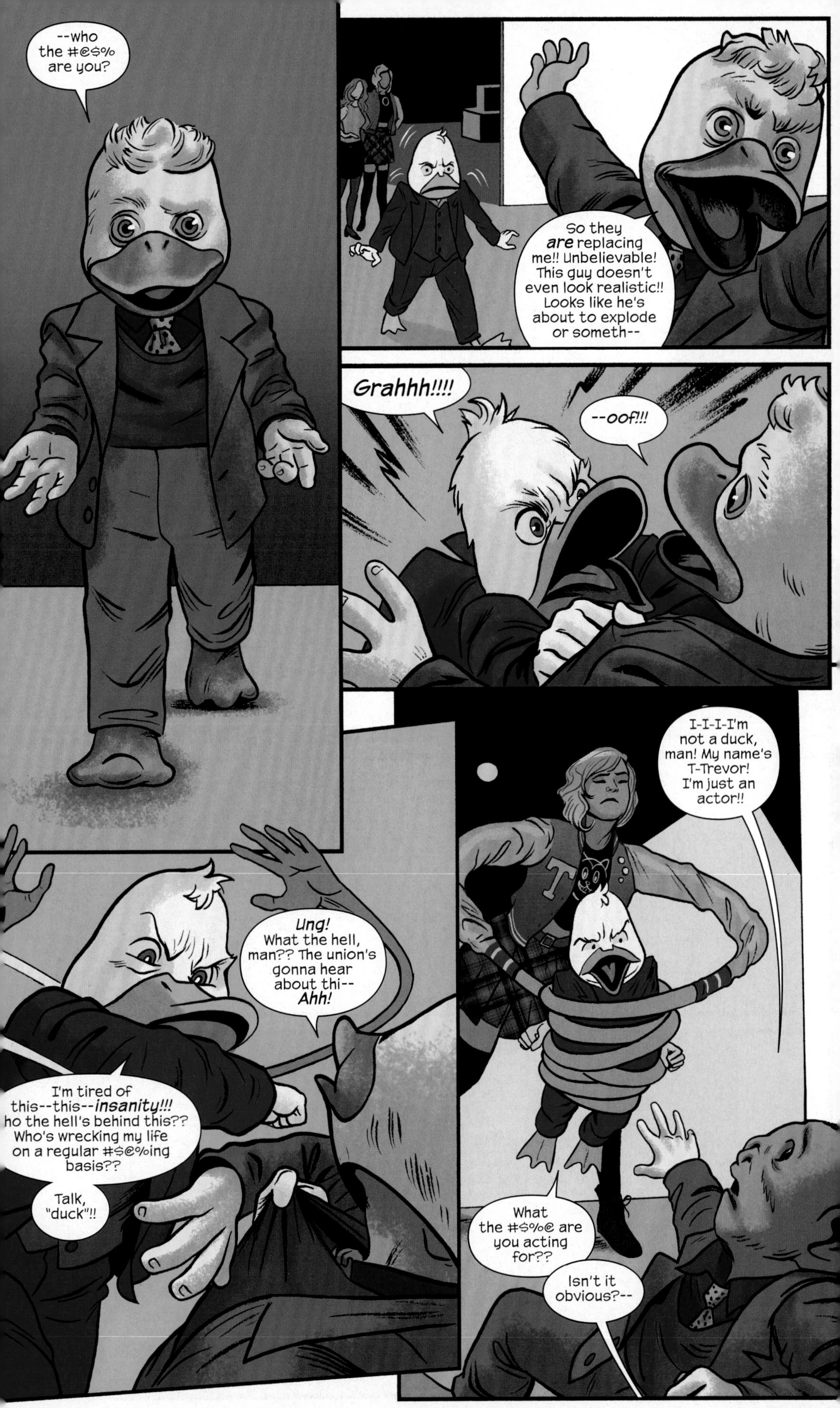
--who the #@$% are you?
So they *are* replacing me!! Unbelievable! This guy doesn't even look realistic!! Looks like he's about to explode or someth--
Grahhh!!!!
--oof!!!
I'm tired of this--this--*insanity!!!* ho the hell's behind this?? Who's wrecking my life on a regular #$@%ing basis??
Talk, "duck"!!
Ung! What the hell, man?? The union's gonna hear about thi-- *Ahh!*
I-I-I-I'm not a duck, man! My name's T-Trevor! I'm just an actor!!
What the #$%@ are you acting for??
Isn't it obvious?--

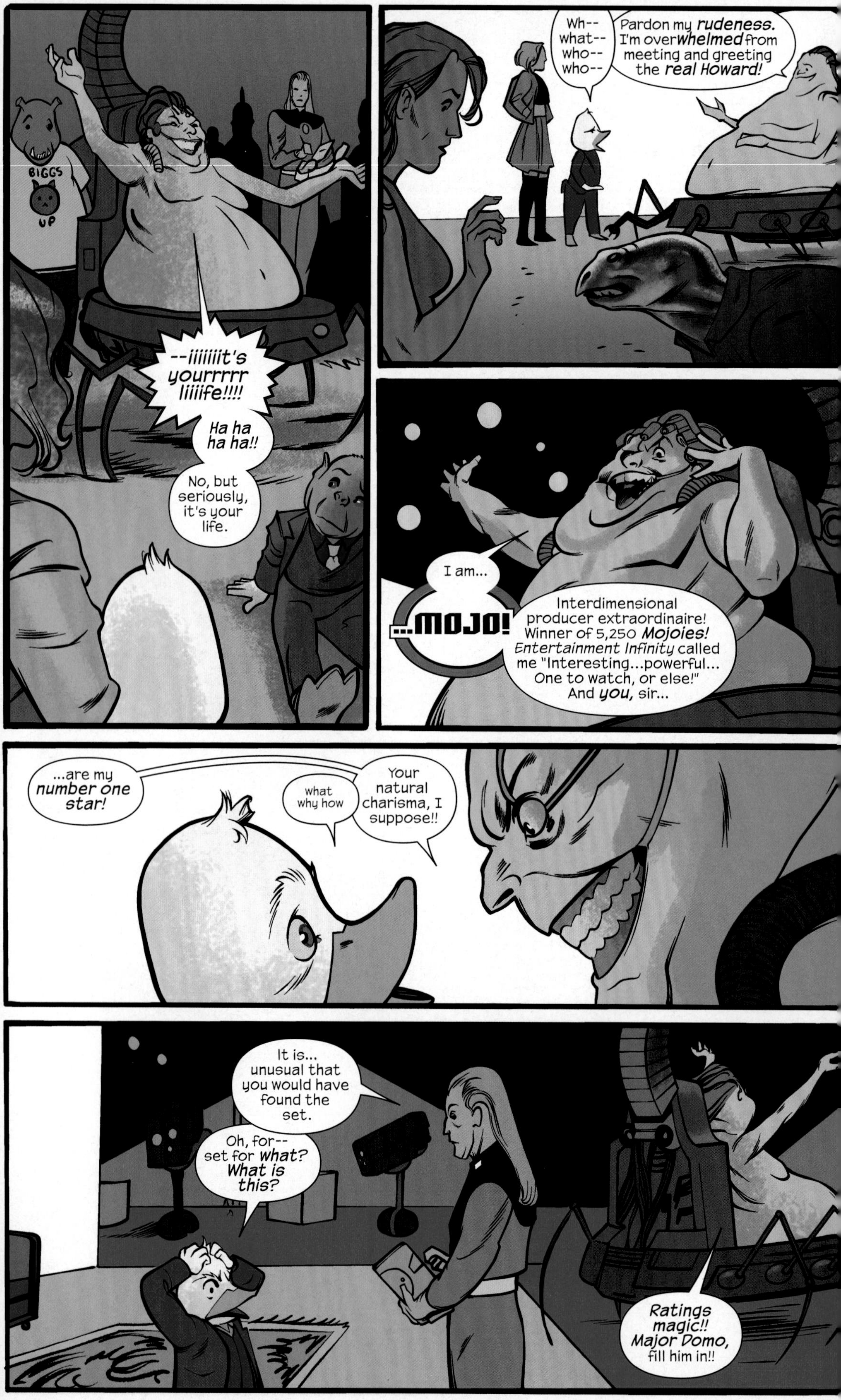

BIGGS UP
--iiiiiit's yourrrrr liiiife!!!!
Ha ha ha ha!!
No, but seriously, it's your life.
Wh-- what-- who-- who--
Pardon my rudeness. I'm overwhelmed from meeting and greeting the real Howard!
I am...
...MOJO!
Interdimensional producer extraordinaire! Winner of 5,250 Mojoies! Entertainment Infinity called me "Interesting...powerful... One to watch, or else!" And you, sir...
...are my number one star!
what why how
Your natural charisma, I suppose!!
It is... unusual that you would have found the set.
Oh, for-- set for what? What is this?
Ratings magic!! Major Domo, fill him in!!

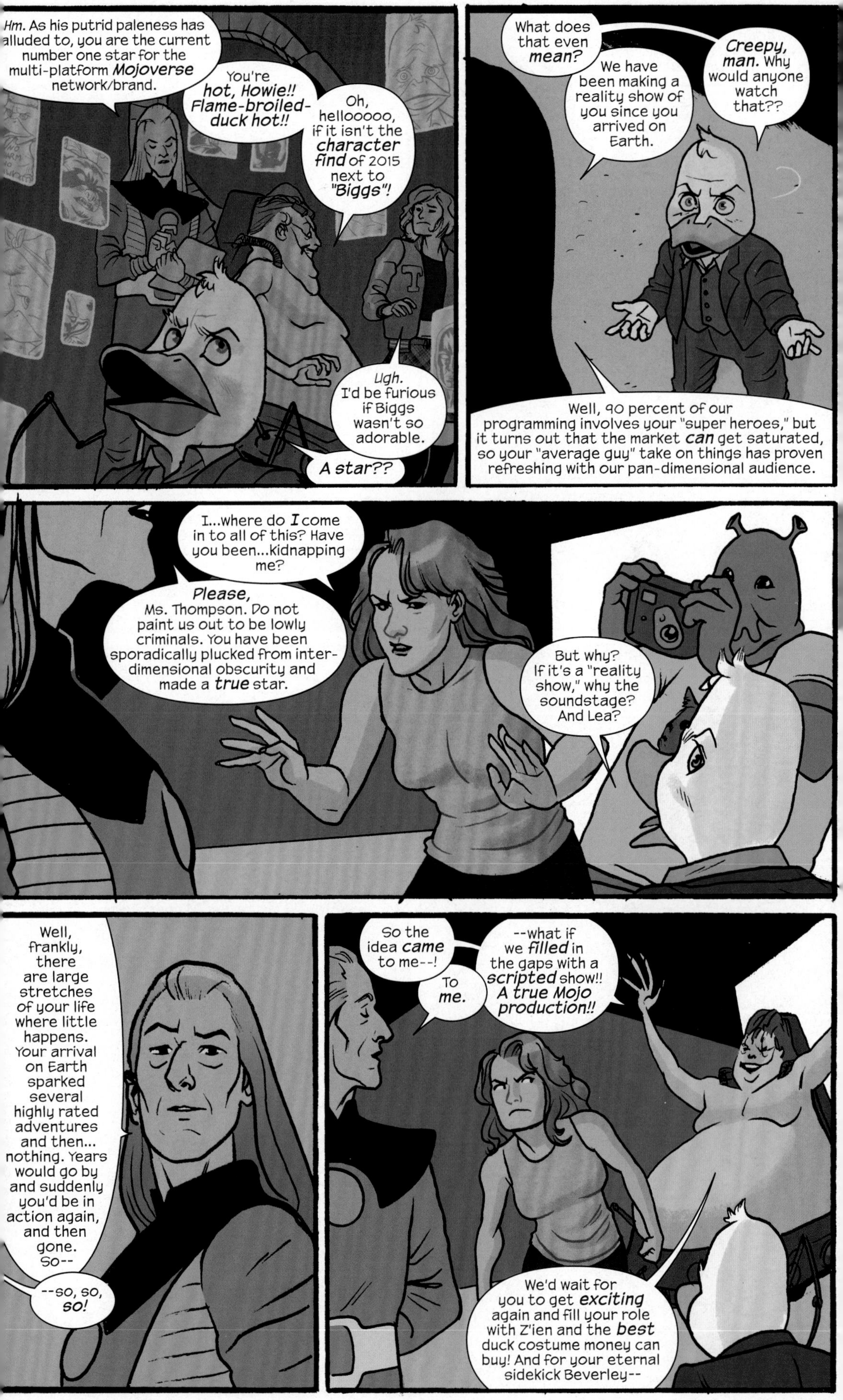
Hm. As his putrid paleness has alluded to, you are the current number one star for the multi-platform Mojoverse network/brand.
You're hot, Howie!! Flame-broiled-duck hot!!
Oh, hellooooo, if it isn't the character find of 2015 next to "Biggs"!
Ugh. I'd be furious if Biggs wasn't so adorable.
A star??
What does that even mean?
Creepy, man. Why would anyone watch that??
We have been making a reality show of you since you arrived on Earth.
Well, 90 percent of our programming involves your "super heroes," but it turns out that the market can get saturated, so your "average guy" take on things has proven refreshing with our pan-dimensional audience.
I...where do I come in to all of this? Have you been...kidnapping me?
Please, Ms. Thompson. Do not paint us out to be lowly criminals. You have been sporadically plucked from inter-dimensional obscurity and made a true star.
But why? If it's a "reality show," why the soundstage? And Lea?
Well, frankly, there are large stretches of your life where little happens. Your arrival on Earth sparked several highly rated adventures and then... nothing. Years would go by and suddenly you'd be in action again, and then gone. So--
--so, so, so!
So the idea came to me--!
To me.
--what if we filled in the gaps with a scripted show!! A true Mojo production!!
We'd wait for you to get exciting again and fill your role with Z'ien and the best duck costume money can buy! And for your eternal sidekick Beverley--

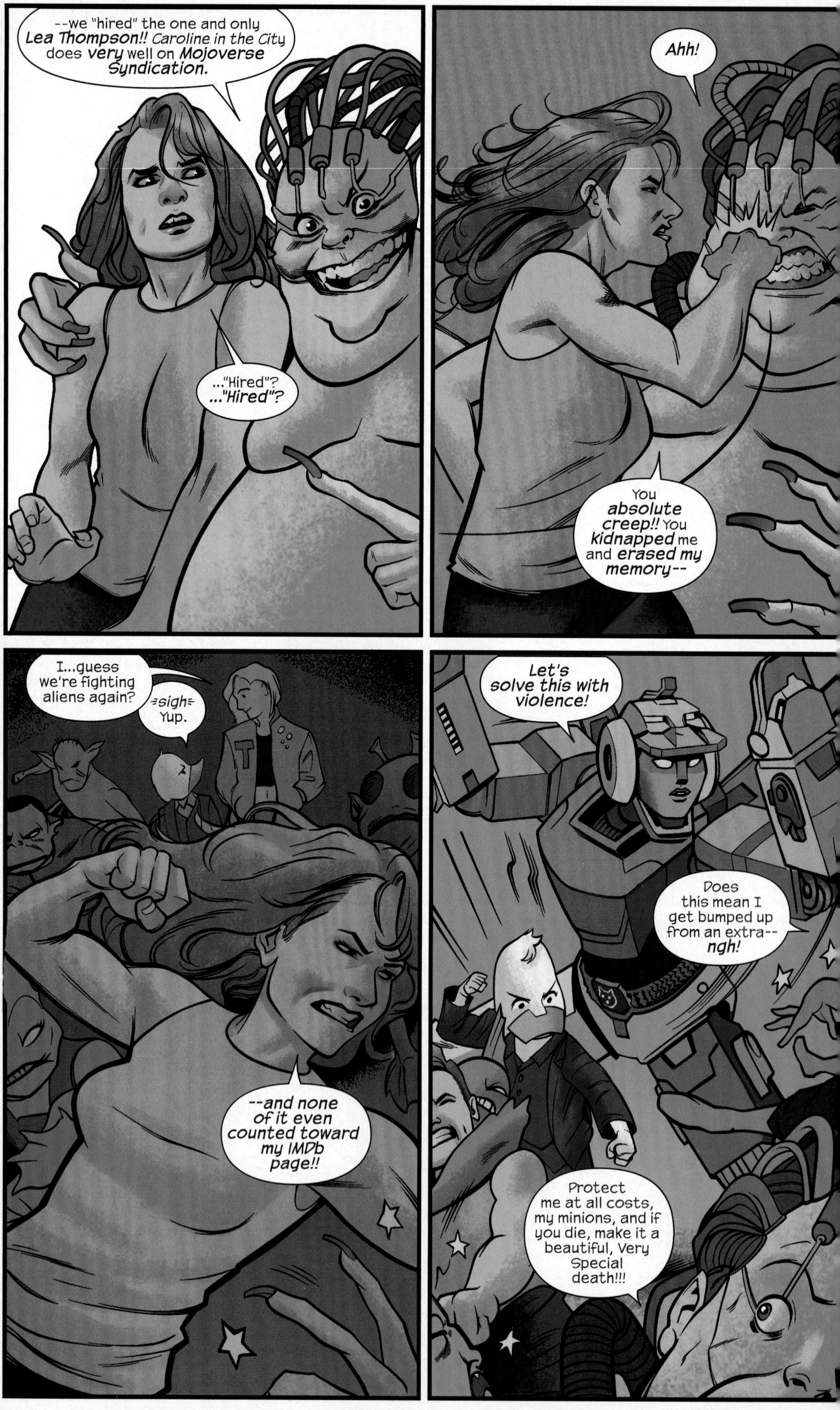
--we "hired" the one and only Lea Thompson!! Caroline in the City does very well on Mojoverse Syndication.
..."Hired"? ..."Hired"?
Ahh!
You absolute creep!! You kidnapped me and erased my memory--
I...guess we're fighting aliens again?
=sigh= Yup.
--and none of it even counted toward my IMDb page!!
Let's solve this with violence!
Does this mean I get bumped up from an extra-- ngh!
Protect me at all costs, my minions, and if you die, make it a beautiful, Very Special death!!!

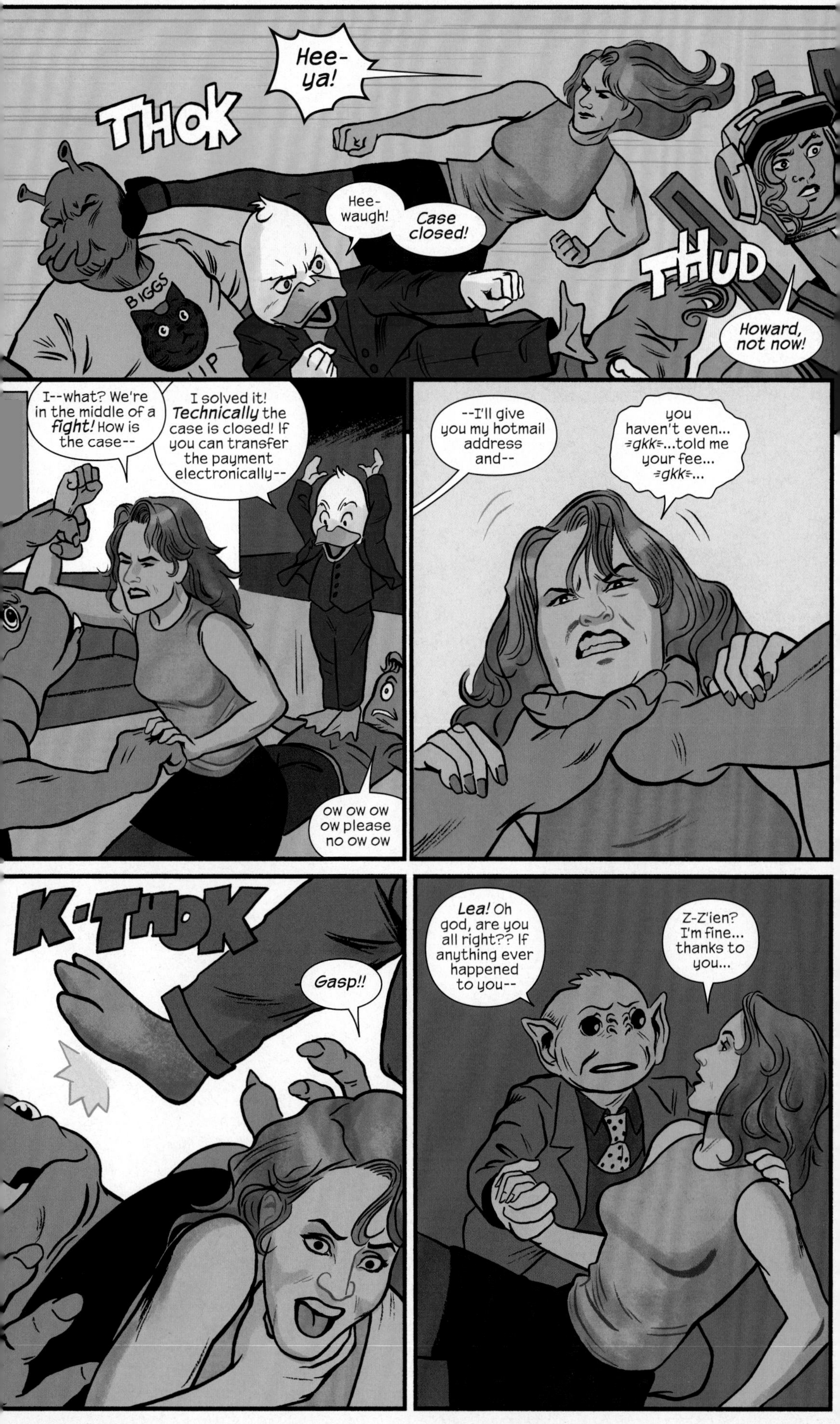
THOK
Hee-ya!
Hee-waugh!
Case closed!
THUD
Howard, not now!
BIGGS
I--what? We're in the middle of a *fight!* How is the case--
I solved it! *Technically* the case is closed! If you can transfer the payment electronically--
ow ow ow ow please no ow ow
--I'll give you my hotmail address and--
you haven't even... *gkk*...told me your fee... *gkk*...
K-THOK
Gasp!!
Lea! Oh god, are you all right?? If anything ever happened to you--
Z-Z'ien? I'm fine... thanks to you...

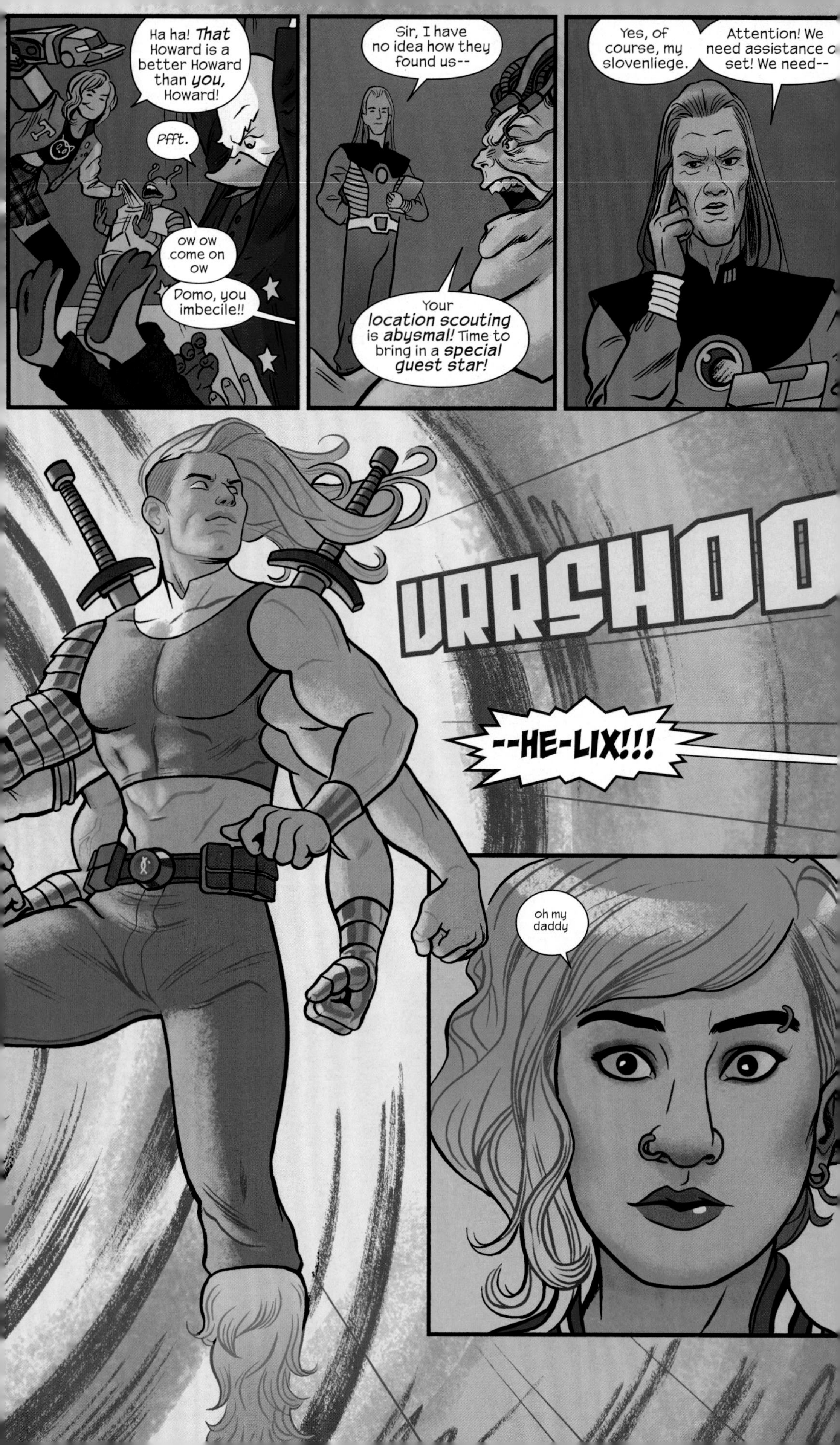

Ha ha! *That* Howard is a better Howard than *you,* Howard!
Pfft.
ow ow come on ow
Domo, you imbecile!!
Sir, I have no idea how they found us--
Your *location scouting* is *abysmal!* Time to bring in a *special guest star!*
Yes, of course, my slovenliege.
Attention! We need assistance o set! We need--
VRRSHOO
--HE-LIX!!!
oh my daddy

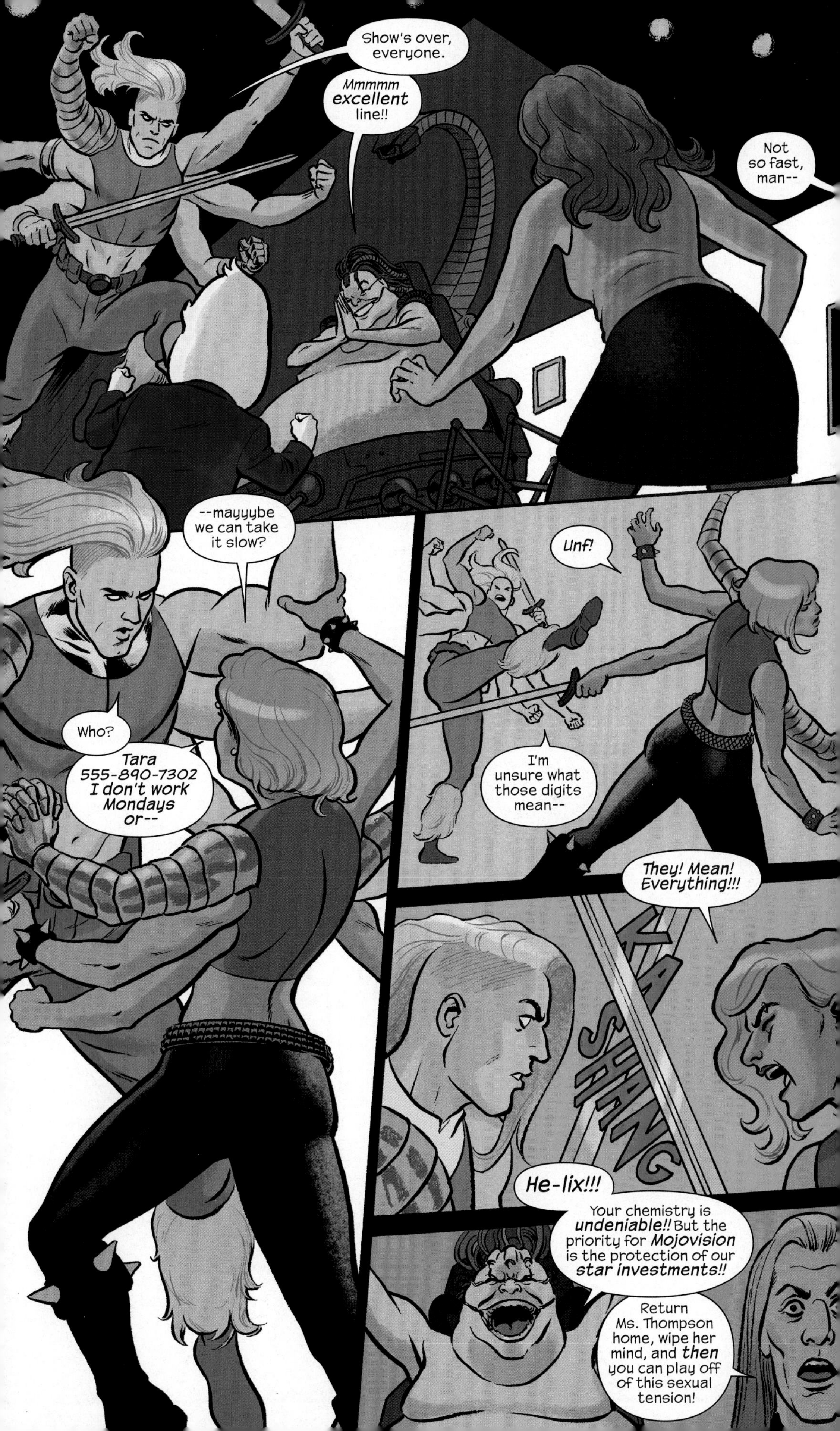

Show's over, everyone.
Mmmmm excellent line!!
Not so fast, man--
--mayyybe we can take it slow?
Who?
Tara 555-890-7302 I don't work Mondays or--
Unf!
I'm unsure what those digits mean--
They! Mean! Everything!!!
KA SHANG
He-lix!!!
Your chemistry is undeniable!! But the priority for Mojovision is the protection of our star investments!!
Return Ms. Thompson home, wipe her mind, and then you can play off of this sexual tension!

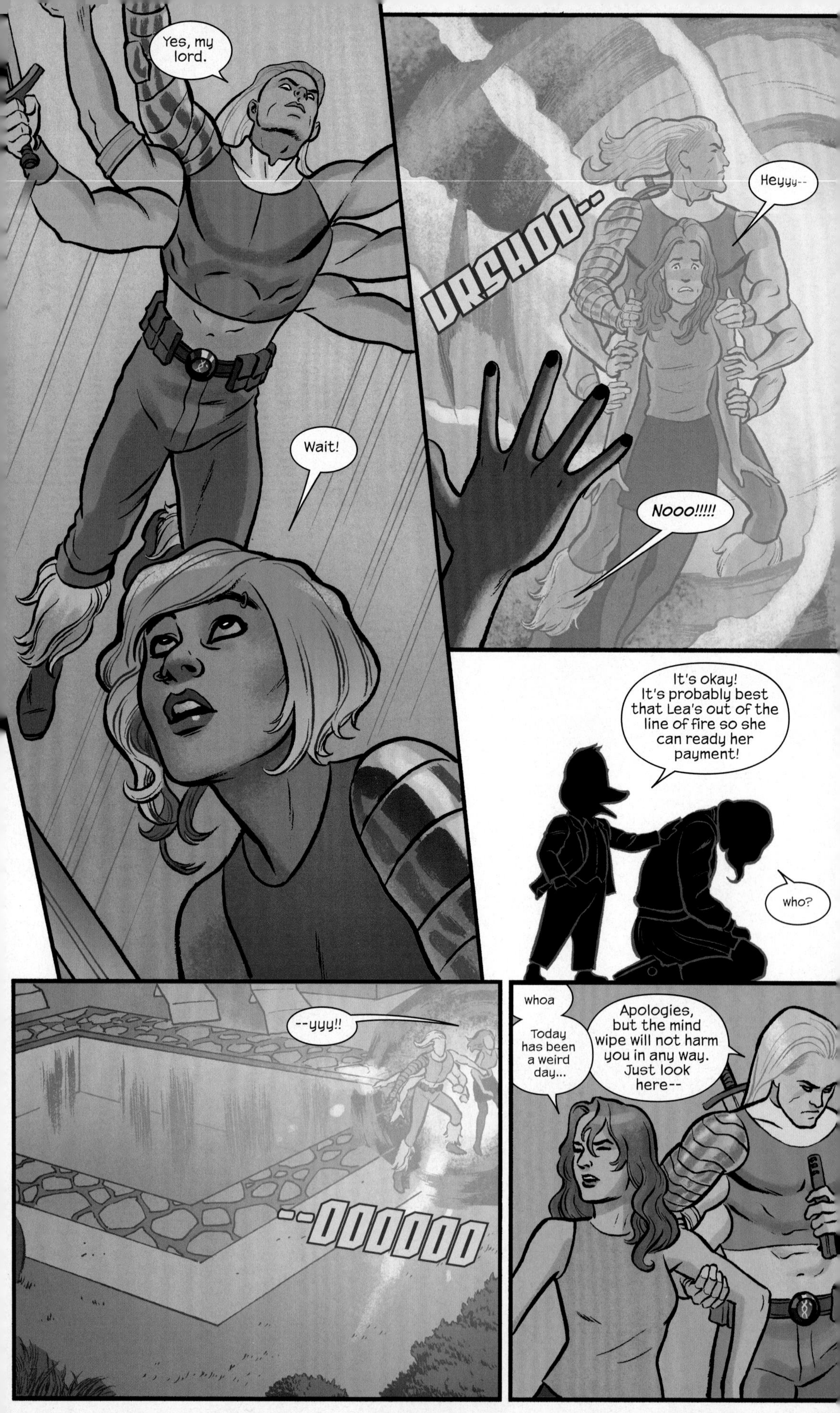
Yes, my lord.
Wait!
VRSHOO--
Heyyy--
Nooo!!!!!
It's okay! It's probably best that Lea's out of the line of fire so she can ready her payment!
who?
--yyy!!
--OOOOOO
whoa
Today has been a weird day...
Apologies, but the mind wipe will not harm you in any way. Just look here--

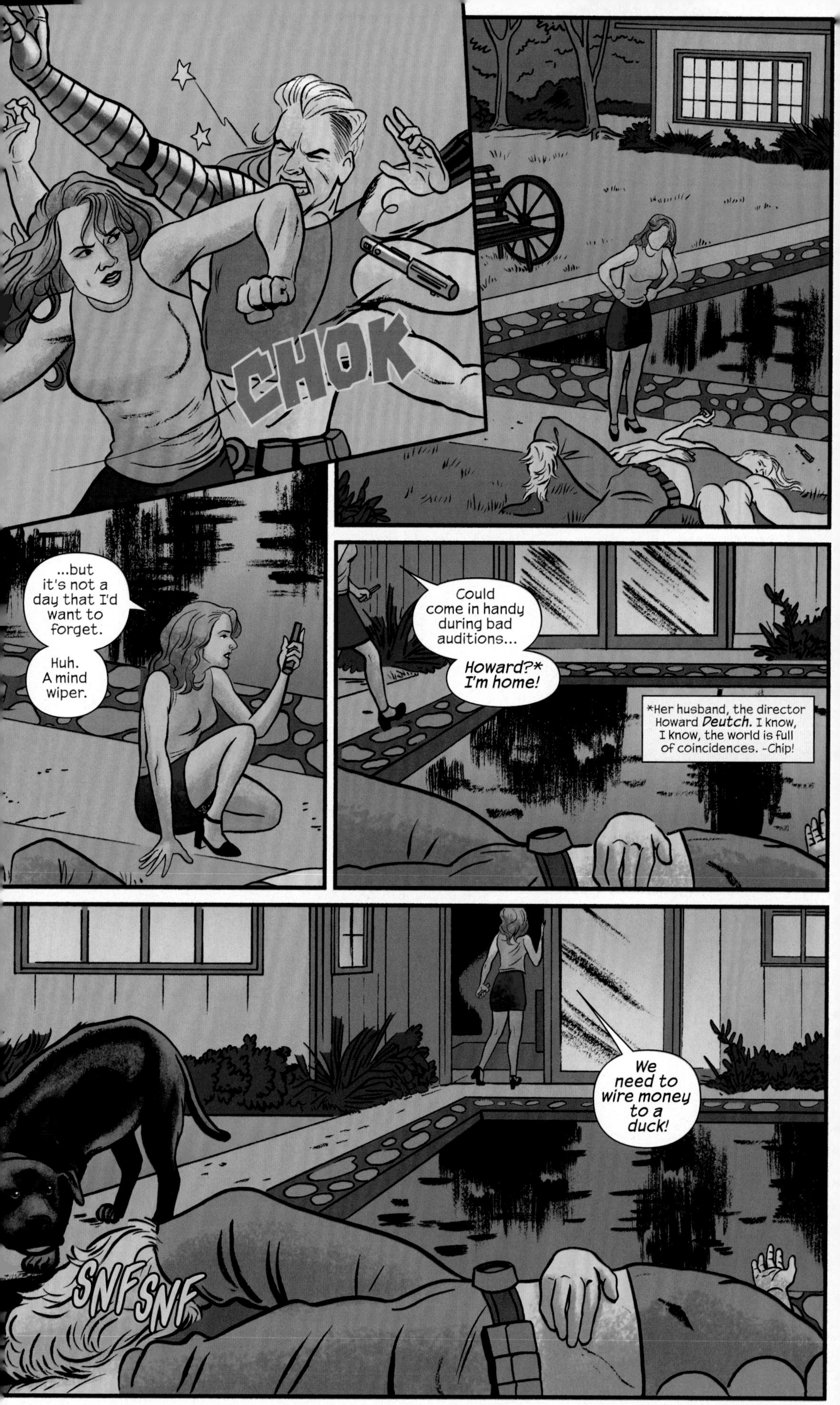
CHOK
...but it's not a day that I'd want to forget.
Huh. A mind wiper.
Could come in handy during bad auditions...
Howard?* I'm home!
*Her husband, the director Howard Deutch. I know, I know, the world is full of coincidences. -Chip!
SNF SNF
We need to wire money to a duck!

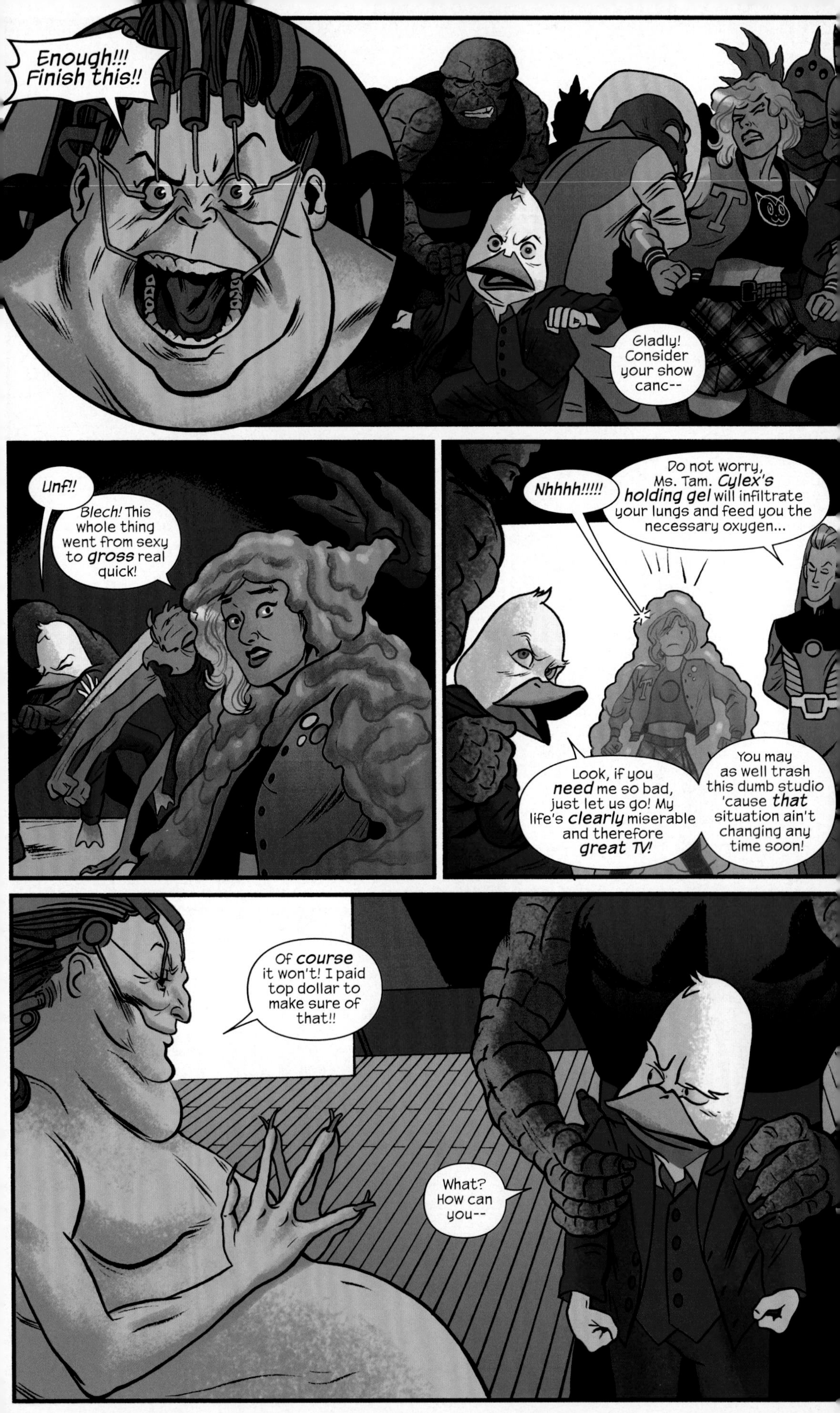

Enough!!! Finish this!!
Gladly! Consider your show canc--
Unf!!
Blech! This whole thing went from sexy to gross real quick!
Nhhhh!!!!!
Do not worry, Ms. Tam. Cylex's holding gel will infiltrate your lungs and feed you the necessary oxygen...
Look, if you need me so bad, just let us go! My life's clearly miserable and therefore great TV!
You may as well trash this dumb studio 'cause that situation ain't changing any time soon!
Of course it won't! I paid top dollar to make sure of that!!
What? How can you--

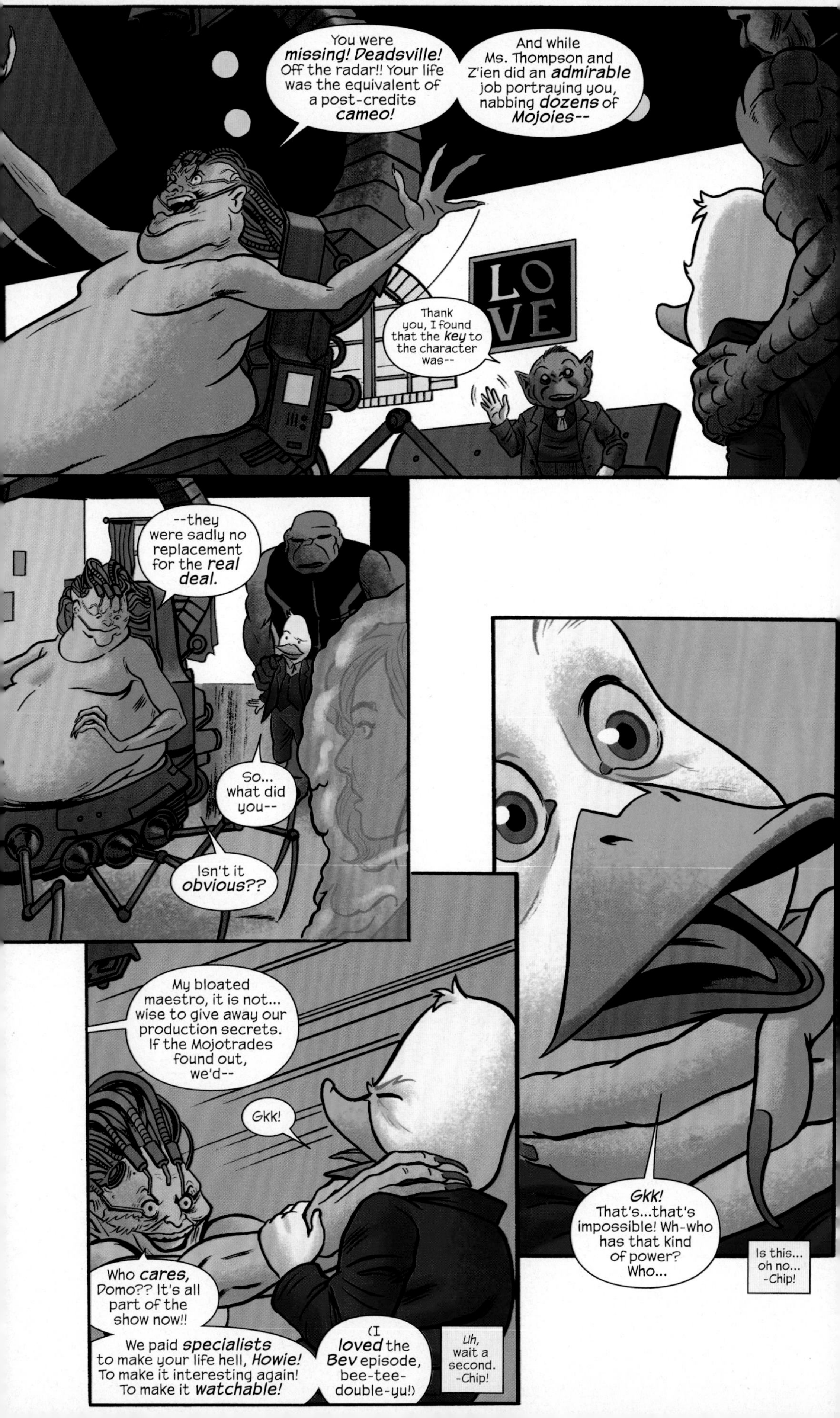
You were missing! Deadsville! Off the radar!! Your life was the equivalent of a post-credits cameo!
And while Ms. Thompson and Z'ien did an admirable job portraying you, nabbing dozens of Mojoies--
LO
VE
Thank you, I found that the key to the character was--
--they were sadly no replacement for the real deal.
So... what did you--
Isn't it obvious??
My bloated maestro, it is not... wise to give away our production secrets. If the Mojotrades found out, we'd--
Gkk!
Who cares, Domo?? It's all part of the show now!!
We paid specialists to make your life hell, Howie! To make it interesting again! To make it watchable!
(I loved the Bev episode, bee-tee-double-yu!)
Uh, wait a second. -Chip!
Gkk! That's...that's impossible! Wh-who has that kind of power? Who...
Is this... oh no... -Chip!

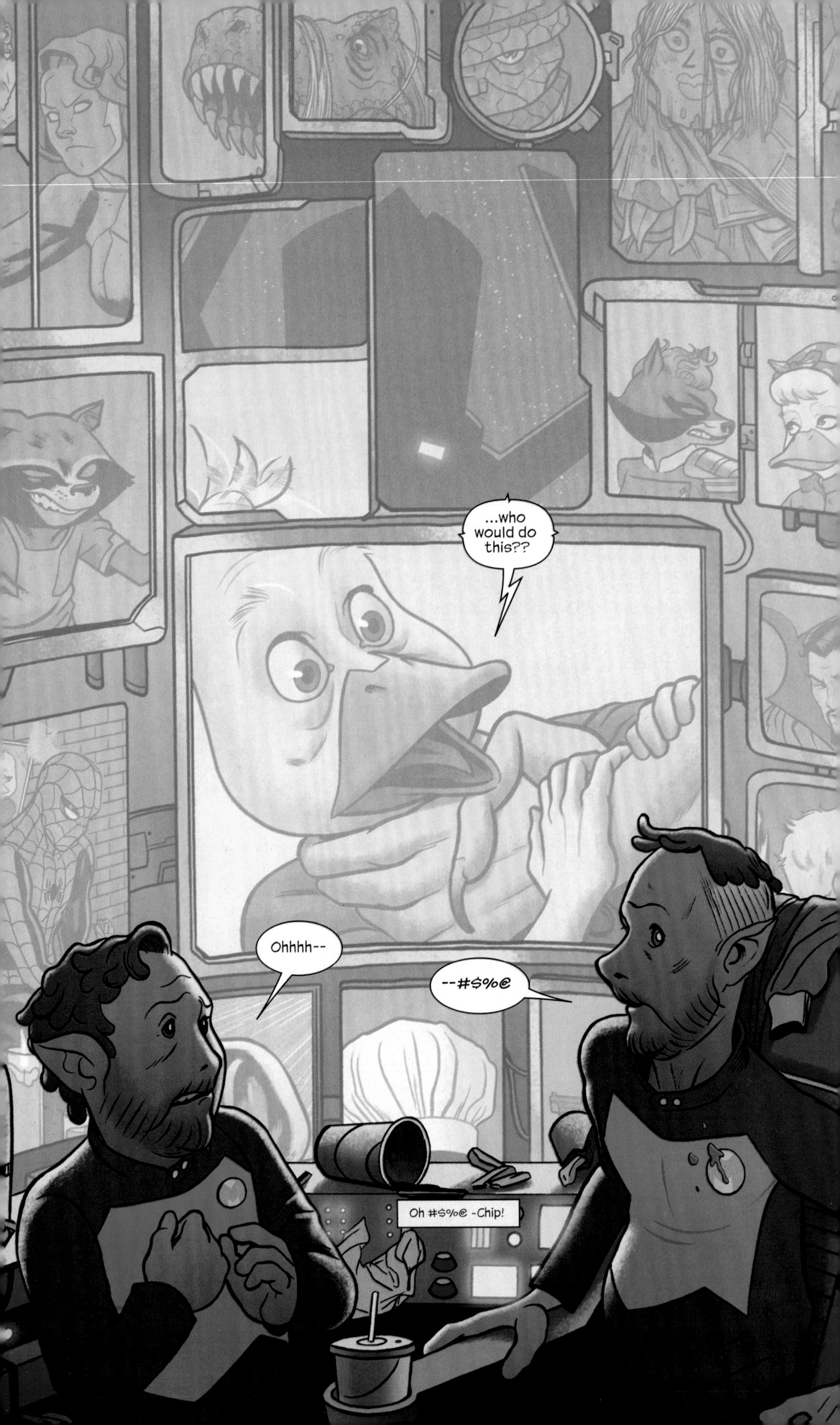
...who would do this??
Ohhhh--
--#$%@
Oh #$%@ -Chip!

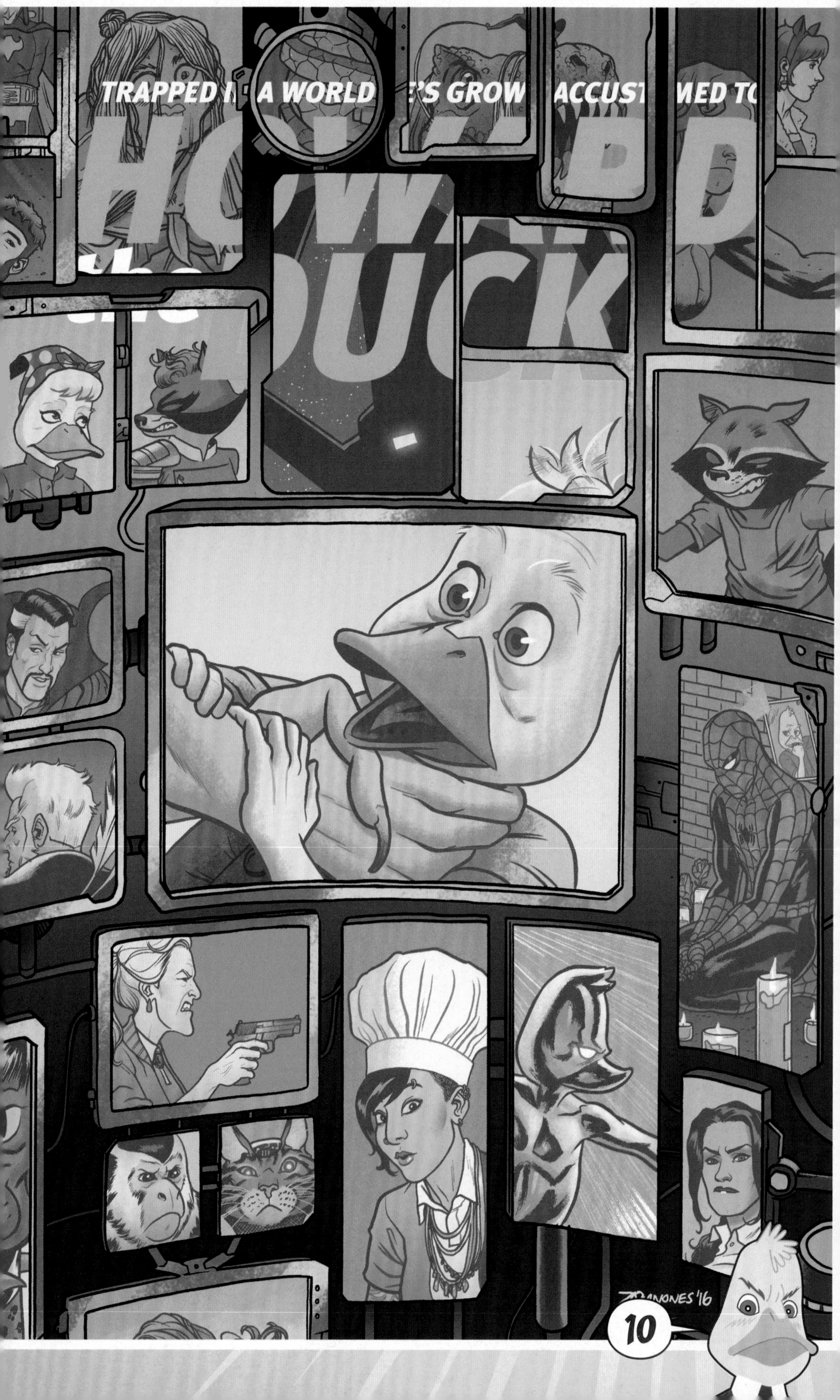

TRAPPED I A WORLD ’S GROW ACCUST MED T
10

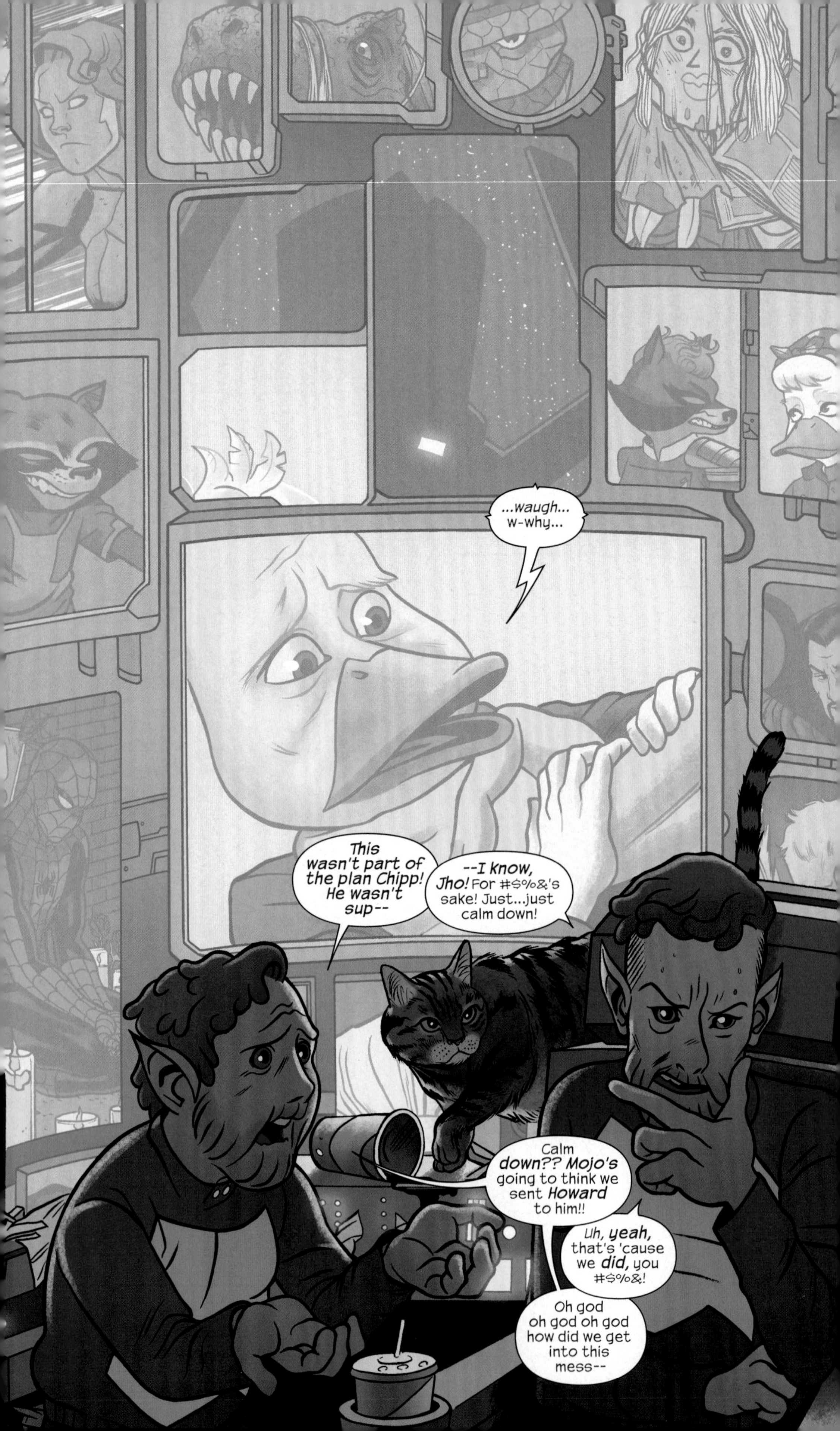
...waugh... w-why...
This wasn't part of the plan Chipp! He wasn't sup--
--I know, Jho! For #$%&'s sake! Just...just calm down!
Calm down?? Mojo's going to think we sent Howard to him!!
Uh, yeah, that's 'cause we did, you #$%&!
Oh god oh god oh god how did we get into this mess--

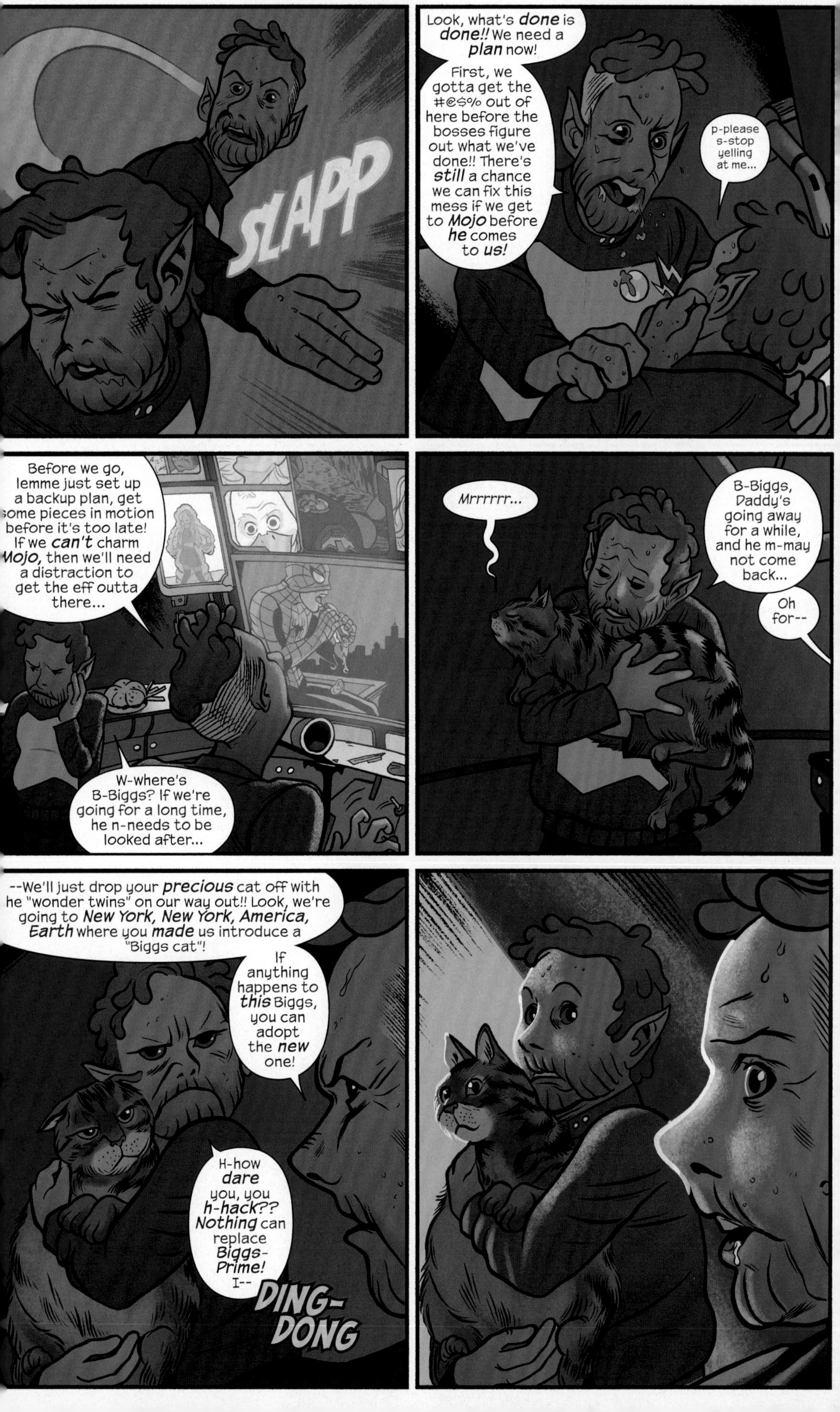
SLAPP
Look, what's done is done!! We need a plan now!
First, we gotta get the #@$% out of here before the bosses figure out what we've done!! There's still a chance we can fix this mess if we get to Mojo before he comes to us!
p-please s-stop yelling at me...
Before we go, lemme just set up a backup plan, get some pieces in motion before it's too late! If we can't charm Mojo, then we'll need a distraction to get the eff outta there...
W-where's B-Biggs? If we're going for a long time, he n-needs to be looked after...
Mrrrrrr...
B-Biggs, Daddy's going away for a while, and he m-may not come back...
Oh for--
--We'll just drop your precious cat off with the "wonder twins" on our way out!! Look, we're going to New York, New York, America, Earth where you made us introduce a "Biggs cat"!
If anything happens to this Biggs, you can adopt the new one!
H-how dare you, you h-hack?? Nothing can replace Biggs-Prime! I--
DING-DONG

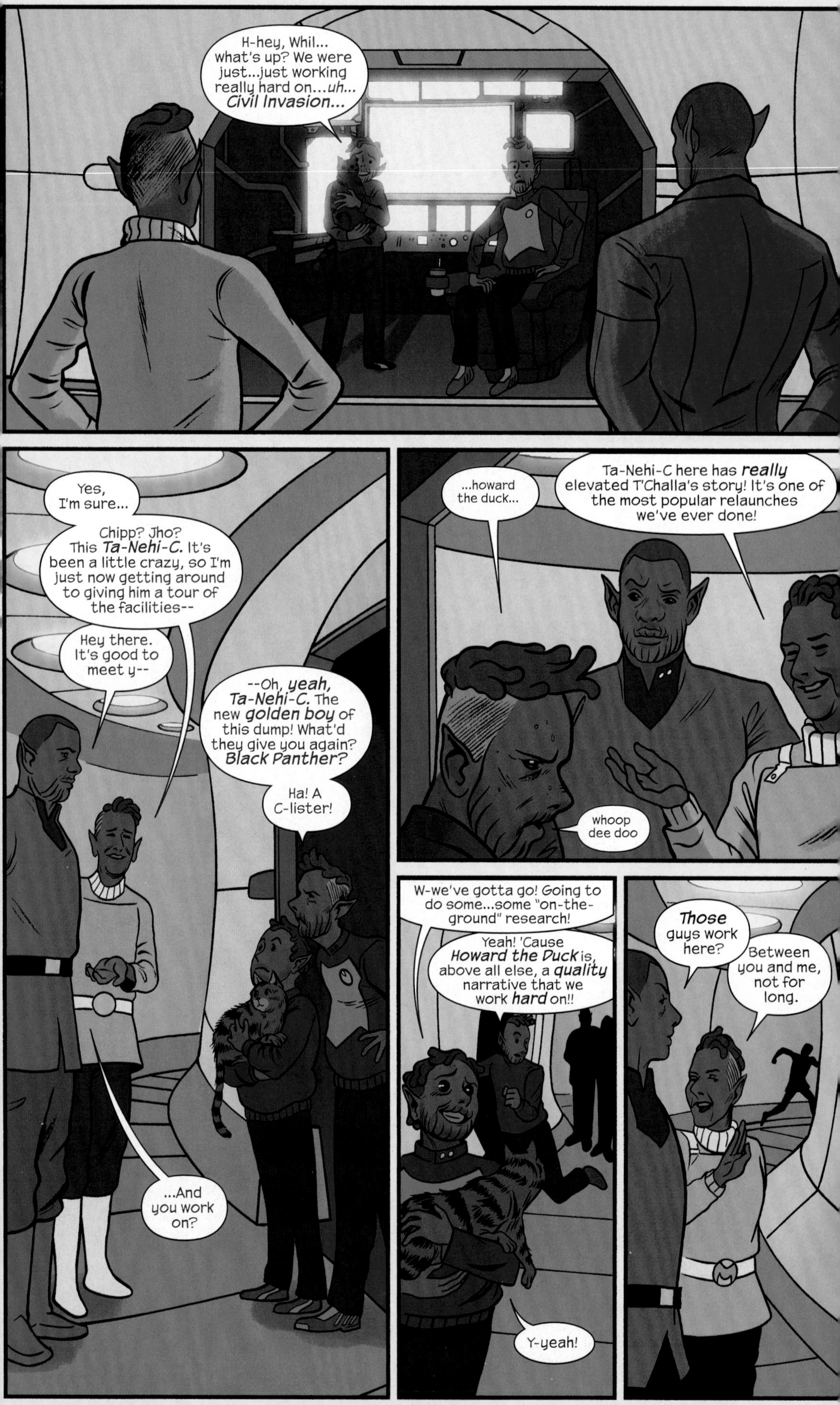
H-hey, Whil... what's up? We were just...just working really hard on...*uh...* ***Civil Invasion...***
Yes, I'm sure...
Chipp? Jho? This ***Ta-Nehi-C.*** It's been a little crazy, so I'm just now getting around to giving him a tour of the facilities--
Hey there. It's good to meet y--
--Oh, ***yeah, Ta-Nehi-C.*** The new ***golden boy*** of this dump! What'd they give you again? ***Black Panther?***
Ha! A C-lister!
...And you work on?
...howard the duck...
Ta-Nehi-C here has ***really*** elevated T'Challa's story! It's one of the most popular relaunches we've ever done!
whoop dee doo
W-we've gotta go! Going to do some...some "on-the-ground" research!
Yeah! 'Cause ***Howard the Duck*** is, above all else, a ***quality*** narrative that we work ***hard*** on!!
Y-yeah!
Those guys work here?
Between you and me, not for long.

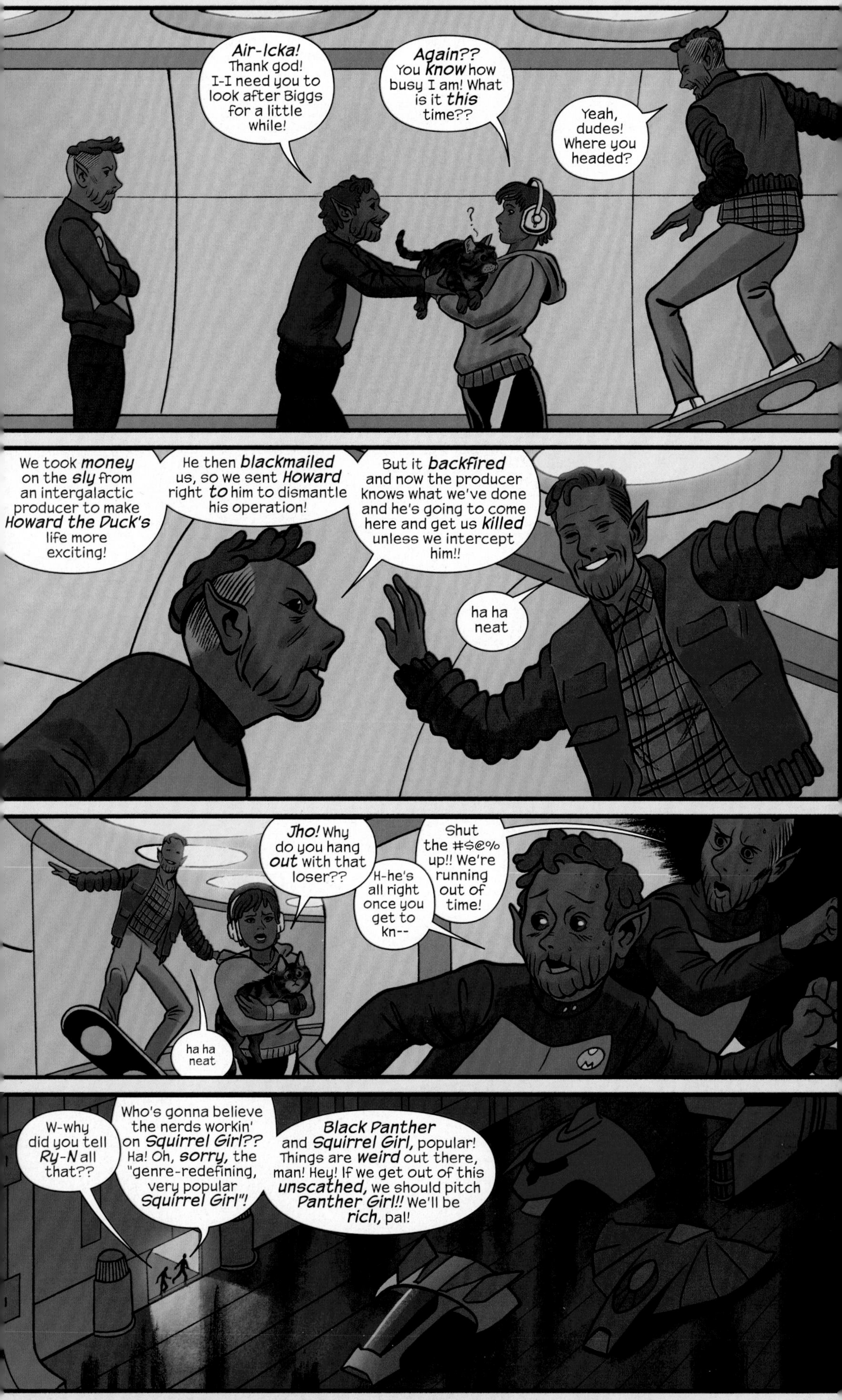

Air-Icka! Thank god! I-I need you to look after Biggs for a little while!
Again?? You know how busy I am! What is it this time??
?
Yeah, dudes! Where you headed?
We took money on the sly from an intergalactic producer to make Howard the Duck's life more exciting!
He then blackmailed us, so we sent Howard right to him to dismantle his operation!
But it backfired and now the producer knows what we've done and he's going to come here and get us killed unless we intercept him!!
ha ha neat
Jho! Why do you hang out with that loser??
H-he's all right once you get to kn--
Shut the #$@% up!! We're running out of time!
ha ha neat
W-why did you tell Ry-N all that??
Who's gonna believe the nerds workin' on Squirrel Girl?? Ha! Oh, sorry, the "genre-redefining, very popular Squirrel Girl"!
Black Panther and Squirrel Girl, popular! Things are weird out there, man! Hey! If we get out of this unscathed, we should pitch Panther Girl!! We'll be rich, pal!

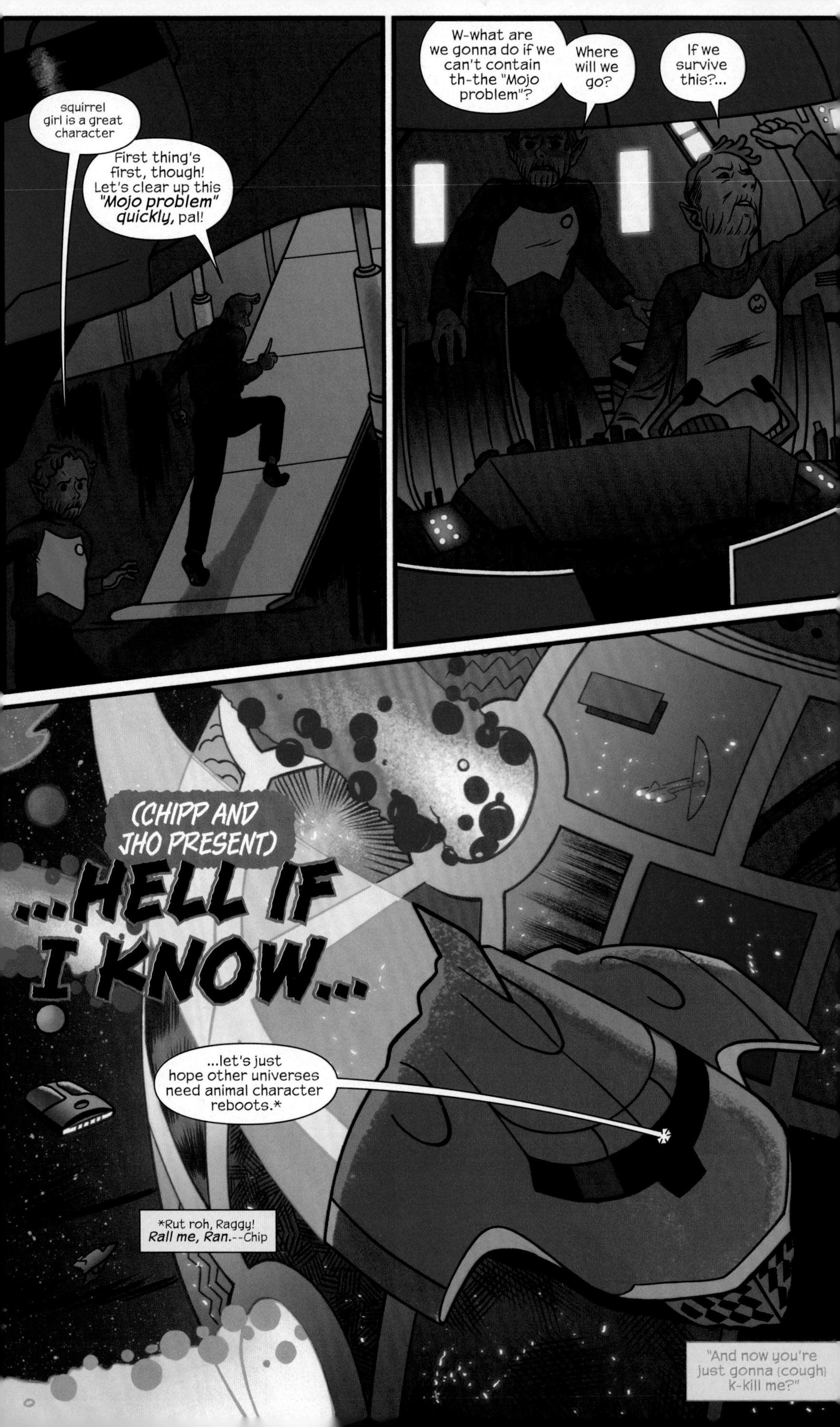
squirrel girl is a great character
First thing's first, though! Let's clear up this *"Mojo problem" quickly,* pal!
W-what are we gonna do if we can't contain th-the "Mojo problem"?
Where will we go?
If we survive this?...
(CHIPP AND JHO PRESENT)
...HELL IF I KNOW...
...let's just hope other universes need animal character reboots.*
*Rut roh, Raggy! *Rall me, Ran.*--Chip
"And now you're just gonna {cough} K-Kill me?"

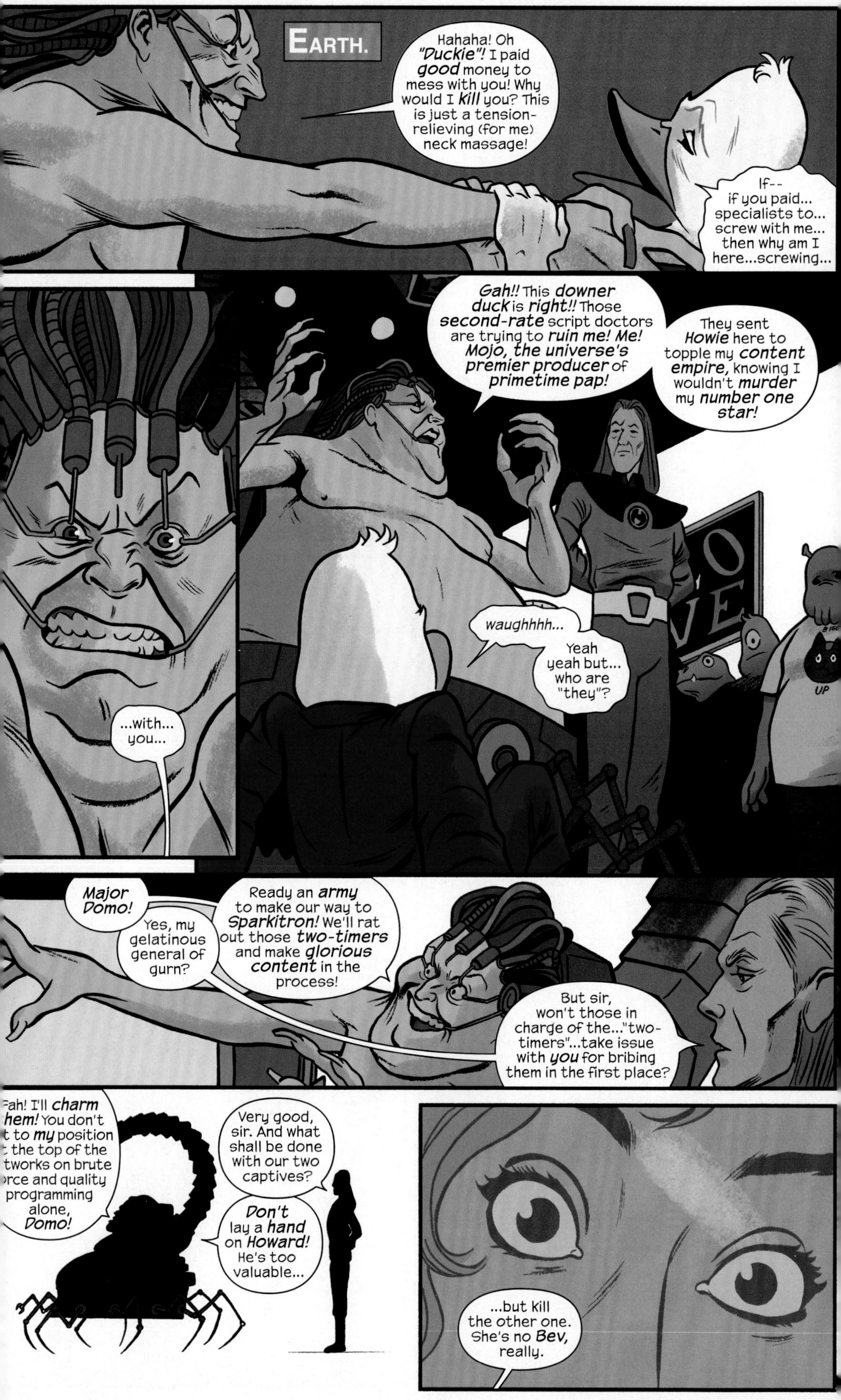
EARTH.
Hahaha! Oh "Duckie"! I paid good money to mess with you! Why would I kill you? This is just a tension-relieving (for me) neck massage!
If-- if you paid... specialists to... screw with me... then why am I here...screwing...
...with... you...
Gah!! This downer duck is right!! Those second-rate script doctors are trying to ruin me! Me! Mojo, the universe's premier producer of primetime pap!
They sent Howie here to topple my content empire, knowing I wouldn't murder my number one star!
waughhhh...
Yeah yeah but... who are "they"?
Major Domo!
Yes, my gelatinous general of gurn?
Ready an army to make our way to Sparkitron! We'll rat out those two-timers and make glorious content in the process!
But sir, won't those in charge of the..."two-timers"...take issue with you for bribing them in the first place?
Fah! I'll charm them! You don't get to my position at the top of the networks on brute force and quality programming alone, Domo!
Very good, sir. And what shall be done with our two captives?
Don't lay a hand on Howard! He's too valuable...
...but kill the other one. She's no Bev, really.

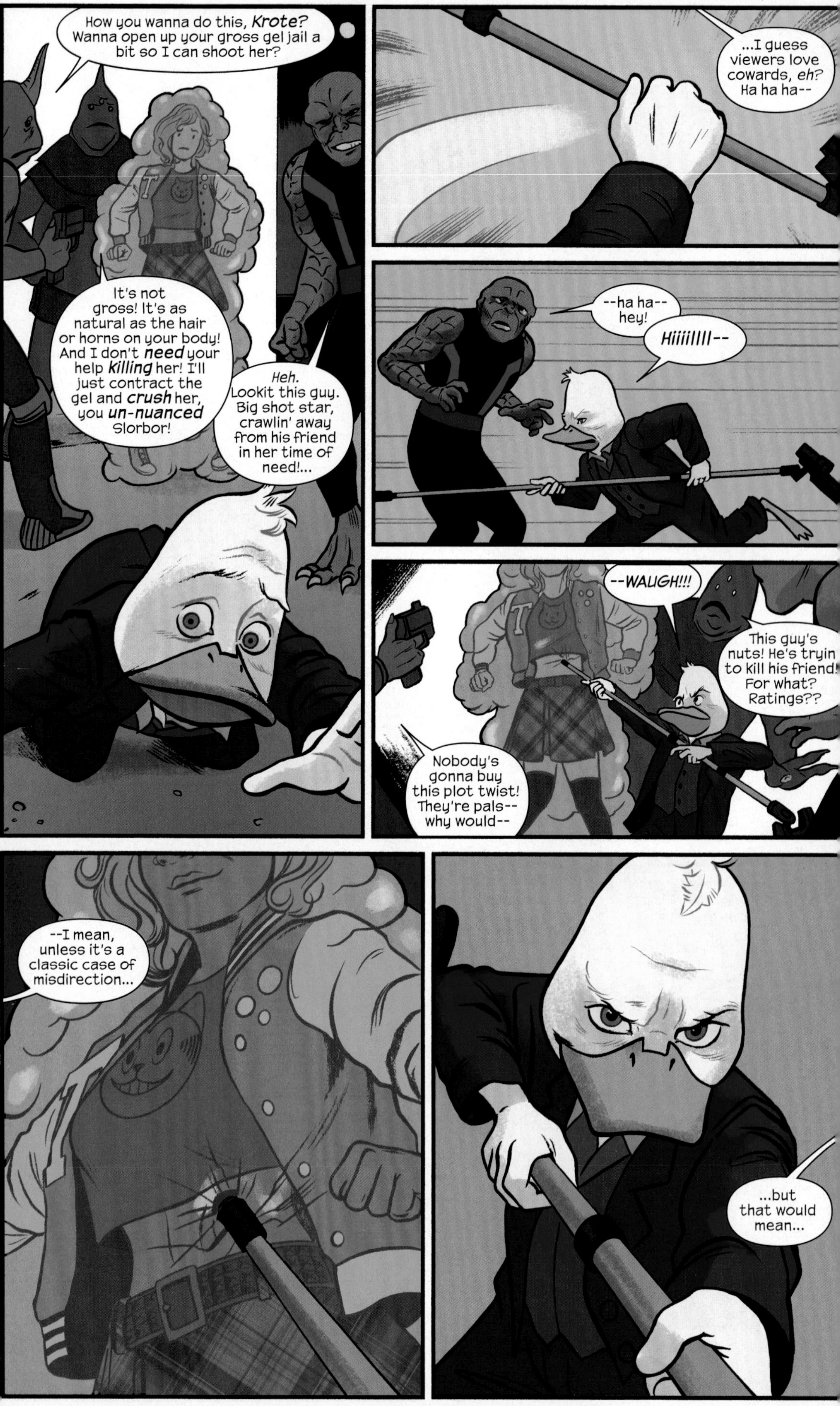
How you wanna do this, *Krote?* Wanna open up your gross gel jail a bit so I can shoot her?
It's not gross! It's as natural as the hair or horns on your body! And I don't ***need*** your help ***killing*** her! I'll just contract the gel and ***crush*** her, you ***un-nuanced*** Slorbor!
Heh. Lookit this guy. Big shot star, crawlin' away from his friend in her time of need!...
...I guess viewers love cowards, *eh?* Ha ha ha--
--ha ha-- hey!
Hiiiillll--
--WAUGH!!!
This guy's nuts! He's tryin to kill his friend! For what? Ratings??
Nobody's gonna buy this plot twist! They're pals-- why would--
--I mean, unless it's a classic case of misdirection...
...but that would mean...

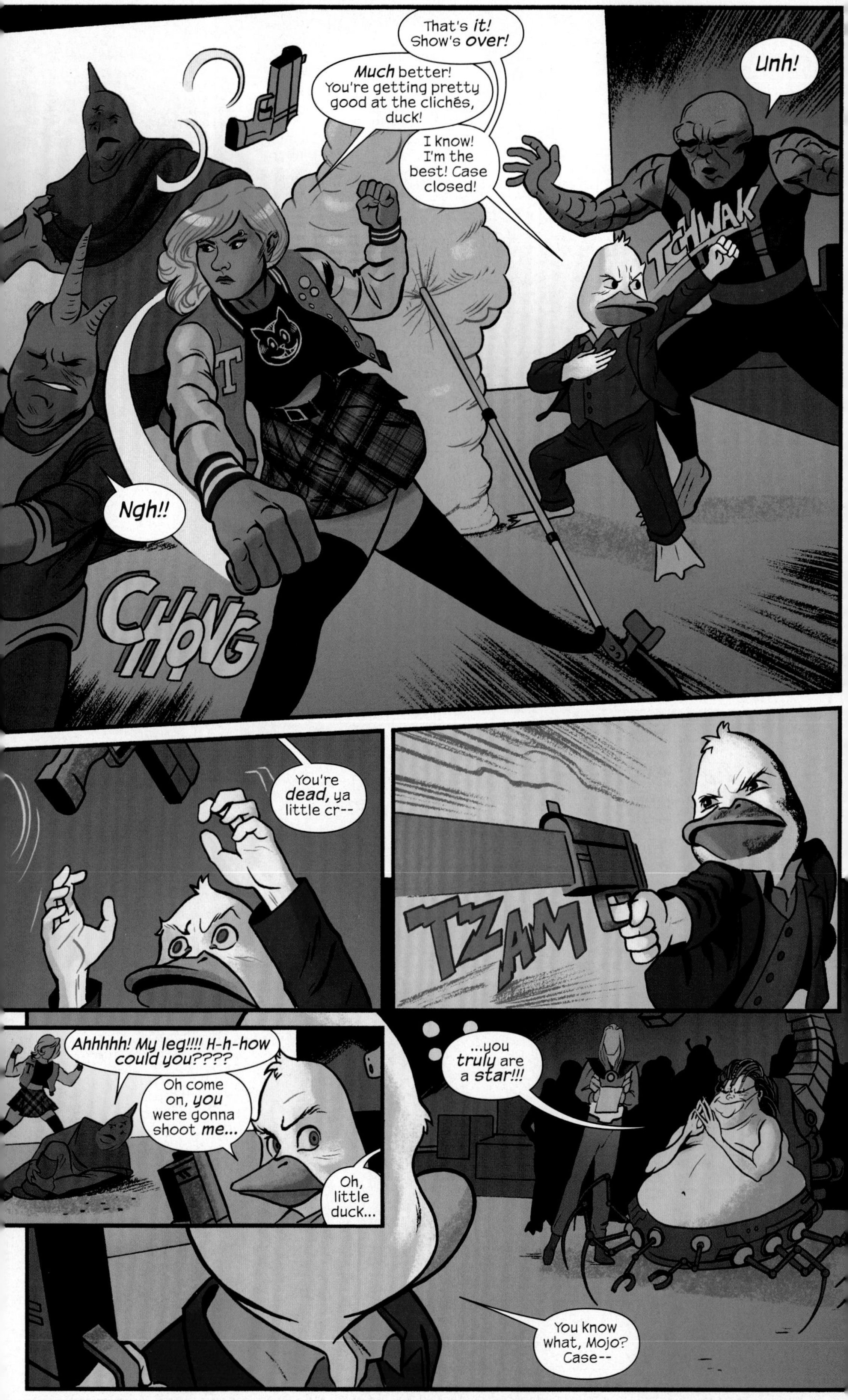

Much better! You're getting pretty good at the clichés, duck!
That's it! Show's over!
I know! I'm the best! Case closed!
Unh!
TCHWAK
Ngh!!
CHONG
You're dead, ya little cr--
TZAM
Ahhhhh! My leg!!!! H-h-how could you????
Oh come on, you were gonna shoot me...
Oh, little duck...
...you truly are a star!!!
You know what, Mojo? Case--

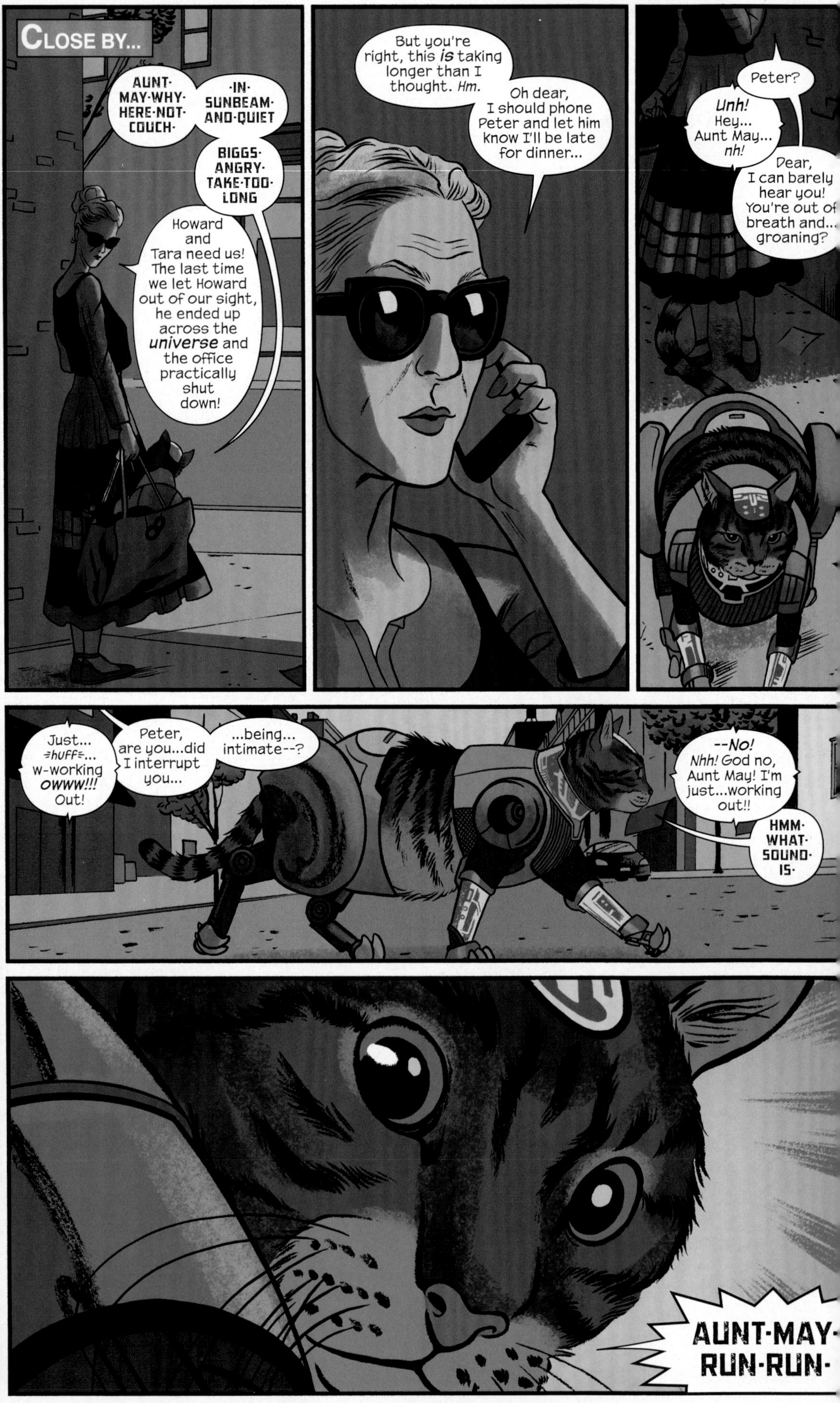
CLOSE BY...
AUNT·MAY·WHY·HERE·NOT·COUCH·
·IN·SUNBEAM·AND·QUIET
BIGGS·ANGRY·TAKE·TOO·LONG
Howard and Tara need us! The last time we let Howard out of our sight, he ended up across the *universe* and the office practically shut down!
But you're right, this *is* taking longer than I thought. *Hm.*
Oh dear, I should phone Peter and let him know I'll be late for dinner...
Peter?
Unh! Hey... Aunt May... *nh!*
Dear, I can barely hear you! You're out of breath and... groaning?
Just... *huff*... w-working *OWWW!!!* Out!
Peter, are you...did I interrupt you...
...being... intimate--?
--*NO!* *Nhh!* God no, Aunt May! I'm just...working out!!
HMM·WHAT·SOUND·IS·
AUNT·MAY·RUN·RUN·

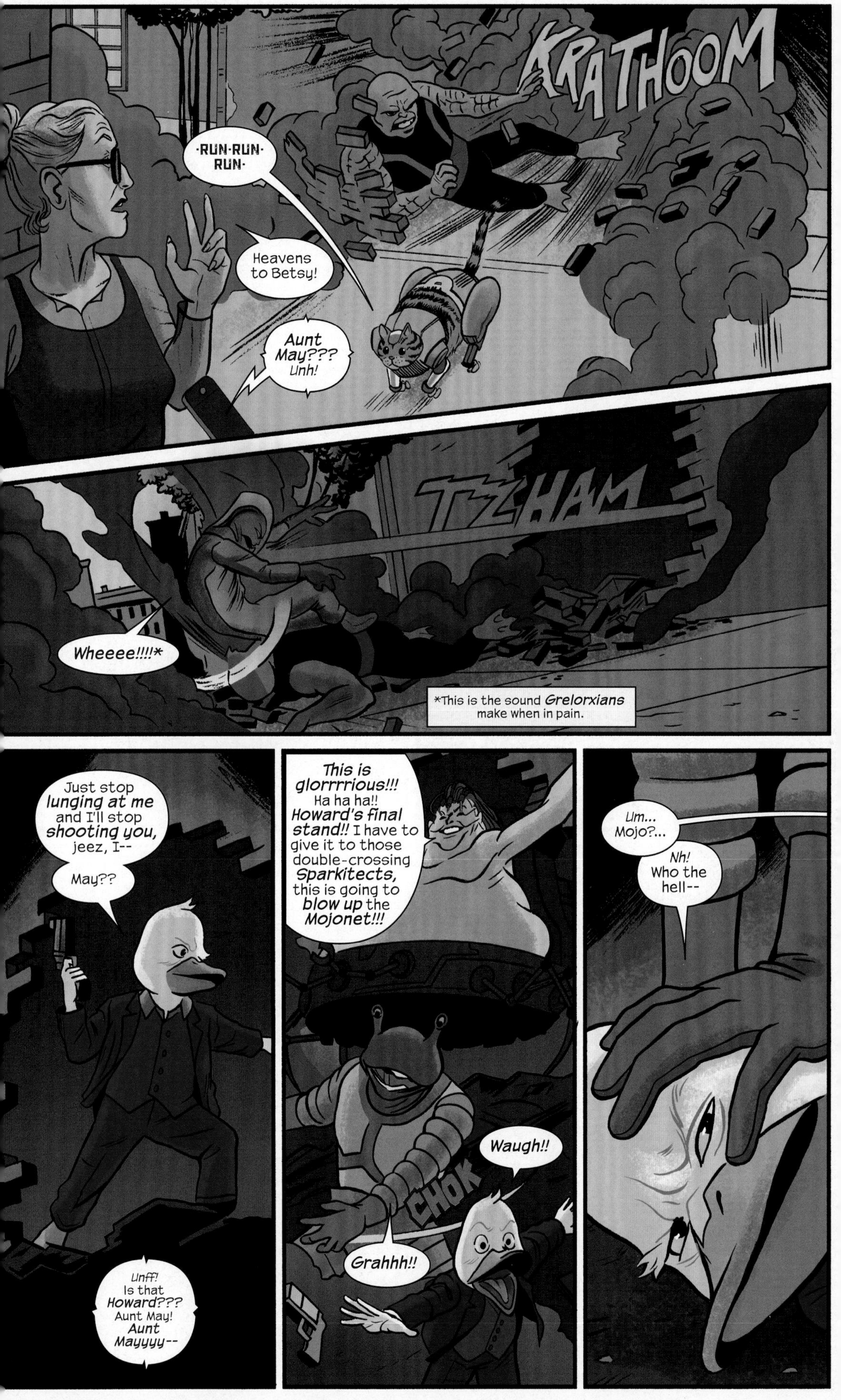
KRATHOOM
·RUN·RUN· RUN·
Heavens to Betsy!
Aunt May??? Unh!
TZHAM
Wheeee!!!!*
*This is the sound Grelorxians make when in pain.
Just stop lunging at me and I'll stop shooting you, jeez, I--
May??
Unff! Is that Howard??? Aunt May! Aunt Mayyyy--
This is glorrrrious!!! Ha ha ha!! Howard's final stand!! I have to give it to those double-crossing Sparkitects, this is going to blow up the Mojonet!!!
Waugh!!
CHOK
Grahhh!!
Um... Mojo?...
Nh! Who the hell--

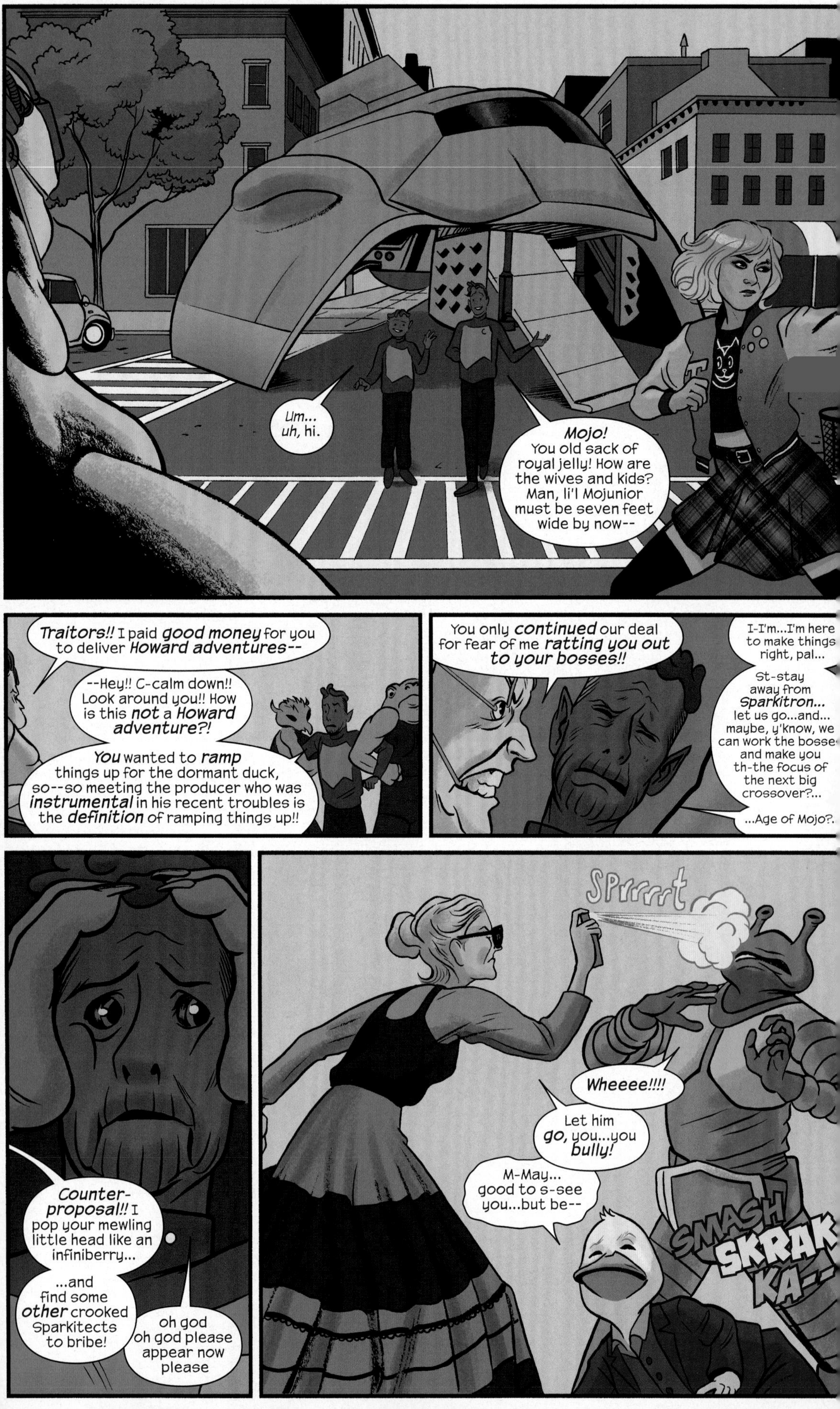

Um... uh, hi.
Mojo! You old sack of royal jelly! How are the wives and kids? Man, li'l Mojunior must be seven feet wide by now--
Traitors!! I paid good money for you to deliver Howard adventures--
--Hey!! C-calm down!! Look around you!! How is this not a Howard adventure?!
You wanted to ramp things up for the dormant duck, so--so meeting the producer who was instrumental in his recent troubles is the definition of ramping things up!!
You only continued our deal for fear of me ratting you out to your bosses!!
I-I'm...I'm here to make things right, pal...
St-stay away from Sparkitron... let us go...and... maybe, y'know, we can work the bosse and make you th-the focus of the next big crossover?...
...Age of Mojo?.
Counter-proposal!! I pop your mewling little head like an infiniberry...
...and find some other crooked Sparkitects to bribe!
oh god oh god please appear now please
SPrrrrrt
Wheeee!!!!
Let him go, you...you bully!
M-May... good to s-see you...but be--
SMASH
SKRAK
KA--

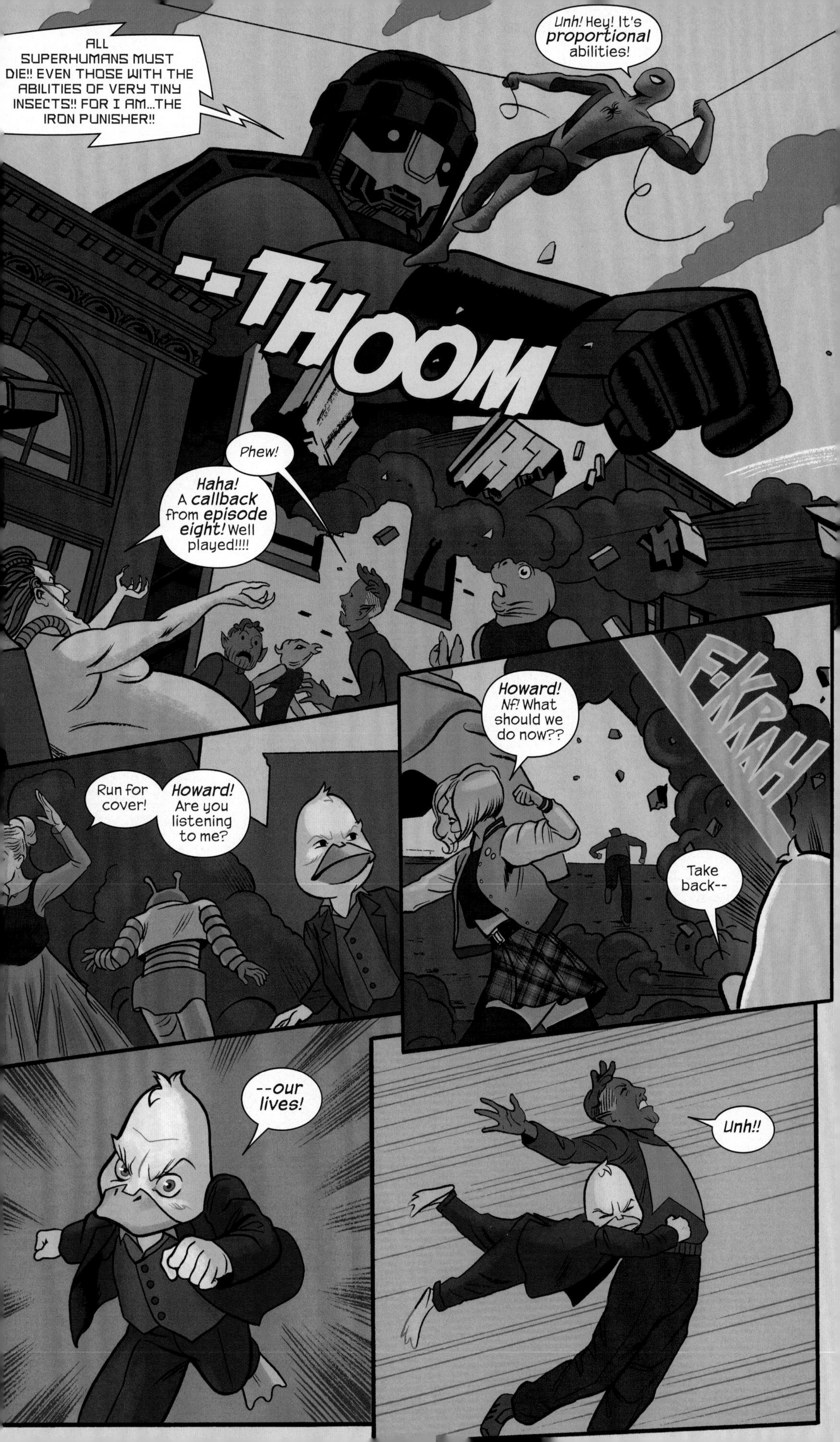

ALL SUPERHUMANS MUST DIE!! EVEN THOSE WITH THE ABILITIES OF VERY TINY INSECTS!! FOR I AM...THE IRON PUNISHER!!
Unh! Hey! It's proportional abilities!
--THOOM
Phew!
Haha! A callback from episode eight! Well played!!!!
KRAH
Run for cover!
Howard! Are you listening to me?
Howard! Nf! What should we do now??
Take back--
--our lives!
Unh!!

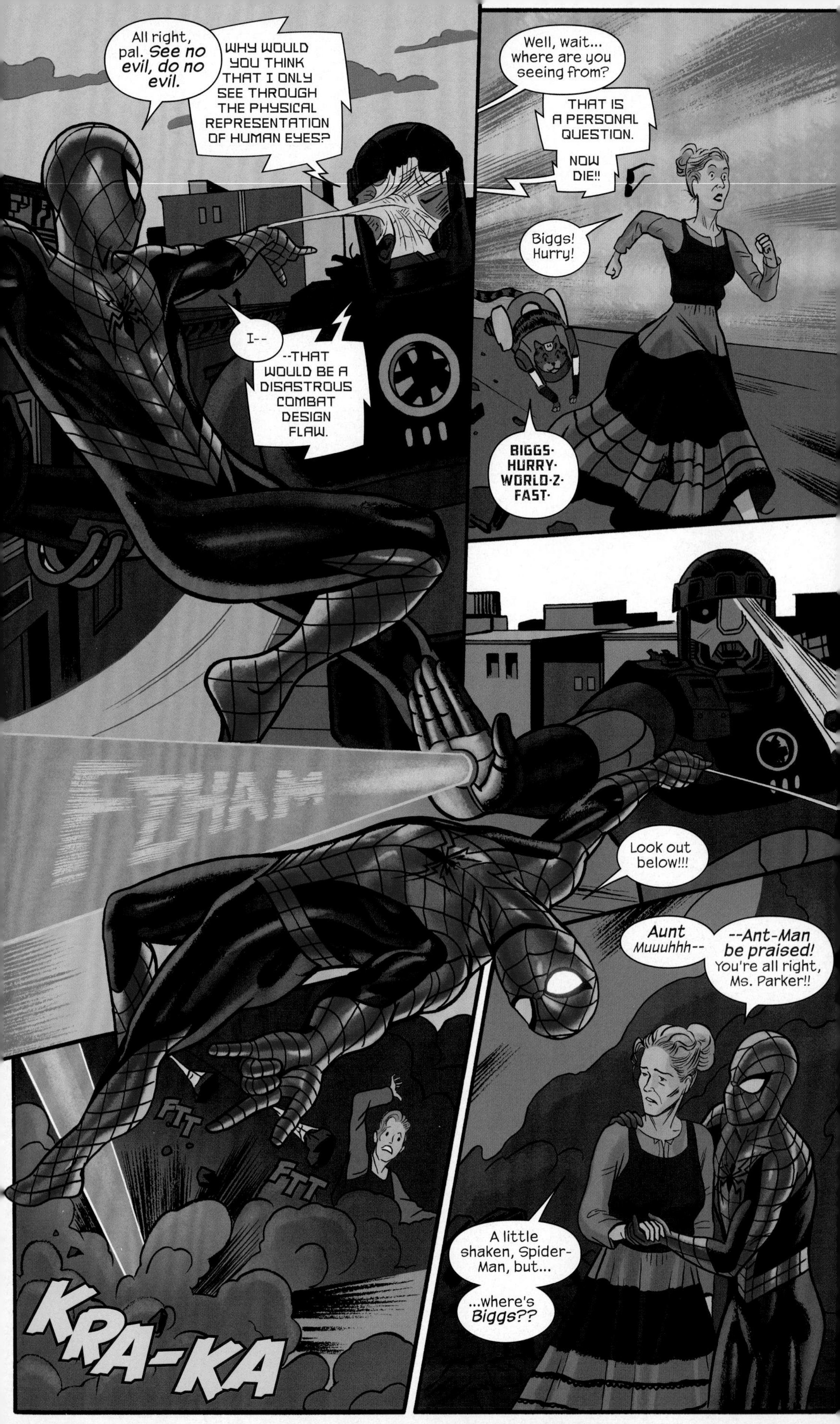
All right, pal. See no evil, do no evil.
WHY WOULD YOU THINK THAT I ONLY SEE THROUGH THE PHYSICAL REPRESENTATION OF HUMAN EYES?
I--
--THAT WOULD BE A DISASTROUS COMBAT DESIGN FLAW.
Well, wait... where are you seeing from?
THAT IS A PERSONAL QUESTION.
NOW DIE!!
Biggs! Hurry!
BIGGS· HURRY· WORLD·Z· FAST·
FZHAM
Look out below!!!
FTT
FTT
KRA-KA
Aunt Muuuhhh--
--Ant-Man be praised! You're all right, Ms. Parker!!
A little shaken, Spider-Man, but...
...where's Biggs??

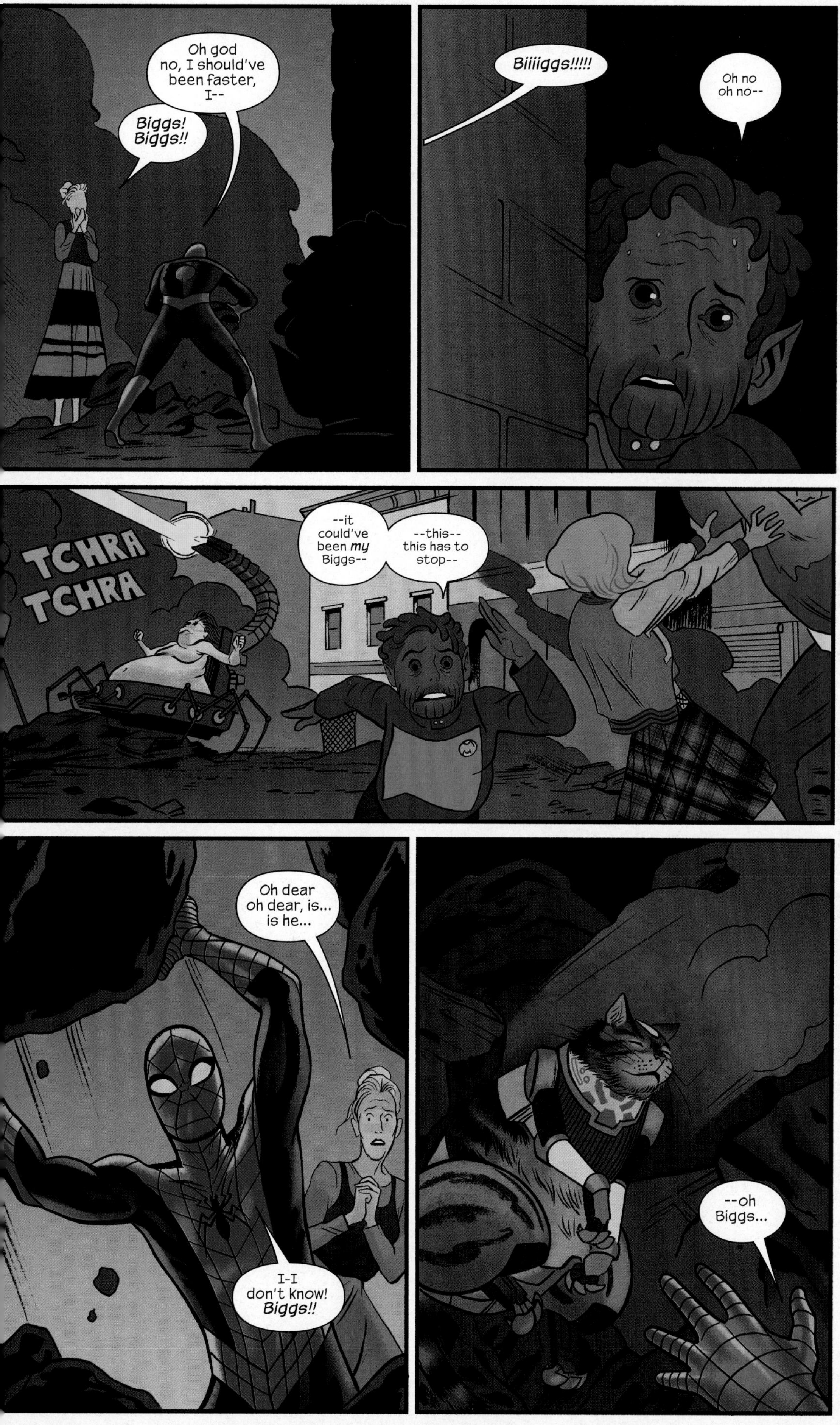

Oh god no, I should've been faster, I--
Biggs! Biggs!!
Biiiiggs!!!!!
Oh no oh no--
TCHRA TCHRA
--it could've been my Biggs--
--this-- this has to stop--
Oh dear oh dear, is... is he...
I-I don't know! Biggs!!
--oh Biggs...

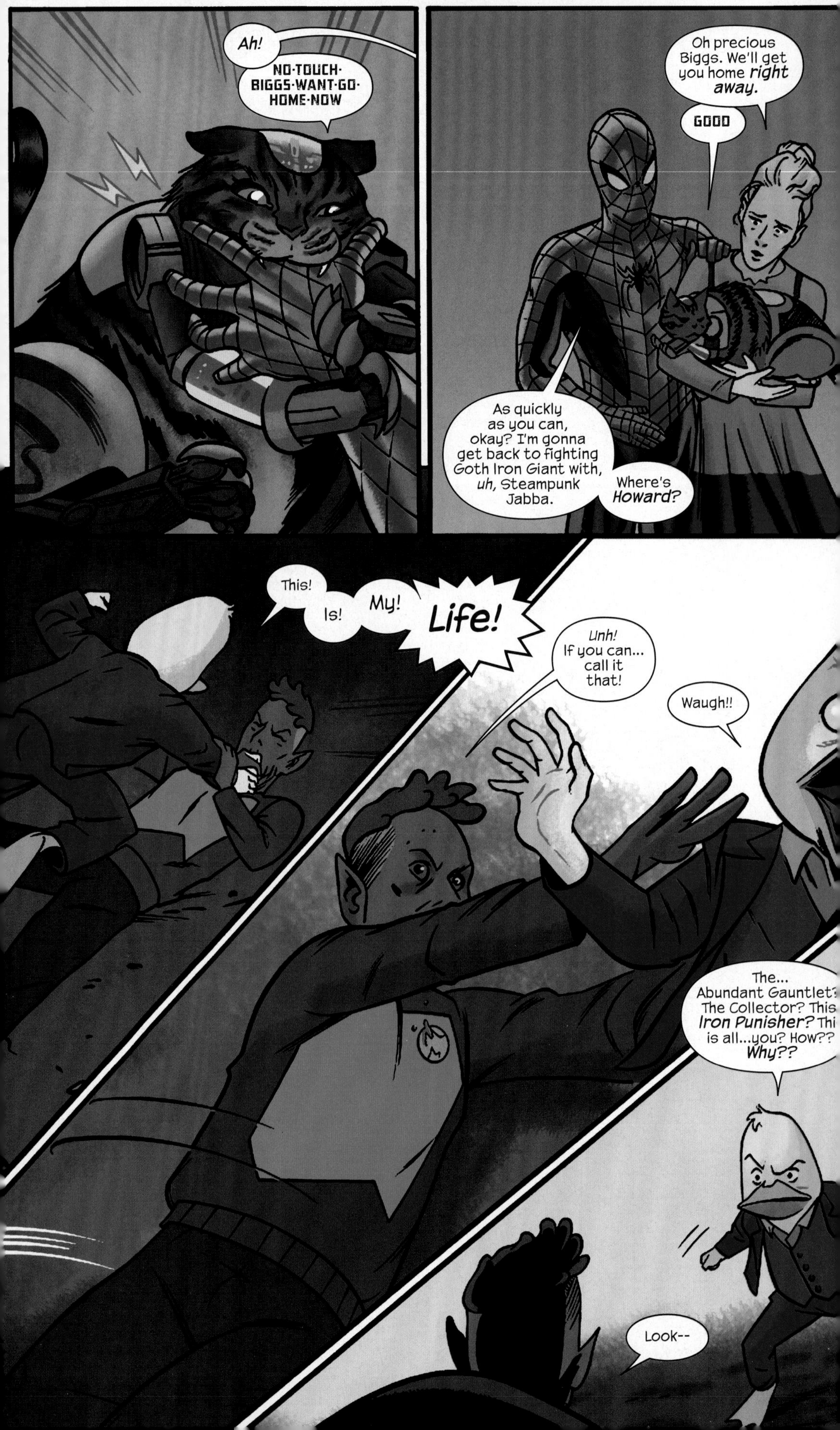

Ah!
NO·TOUCH·BIGGS·WANT·GO·HOME·NOW
Oh precious Biggs. We'll get you home *right away.*
GOOD
As quickly as you can, okay? I'm gonna get back to fighting Goth Iron Giant with, *uh,* Steampunk Jabba.
Where's *Howard?*
This!
Is!
My!
Life!
Unh! If you can... call it that!
Waugh!!
The... Abundant Gauntlet? The Collector? This *Iron Punisher?* Thi is all...you? How?? *Why??*
Look--

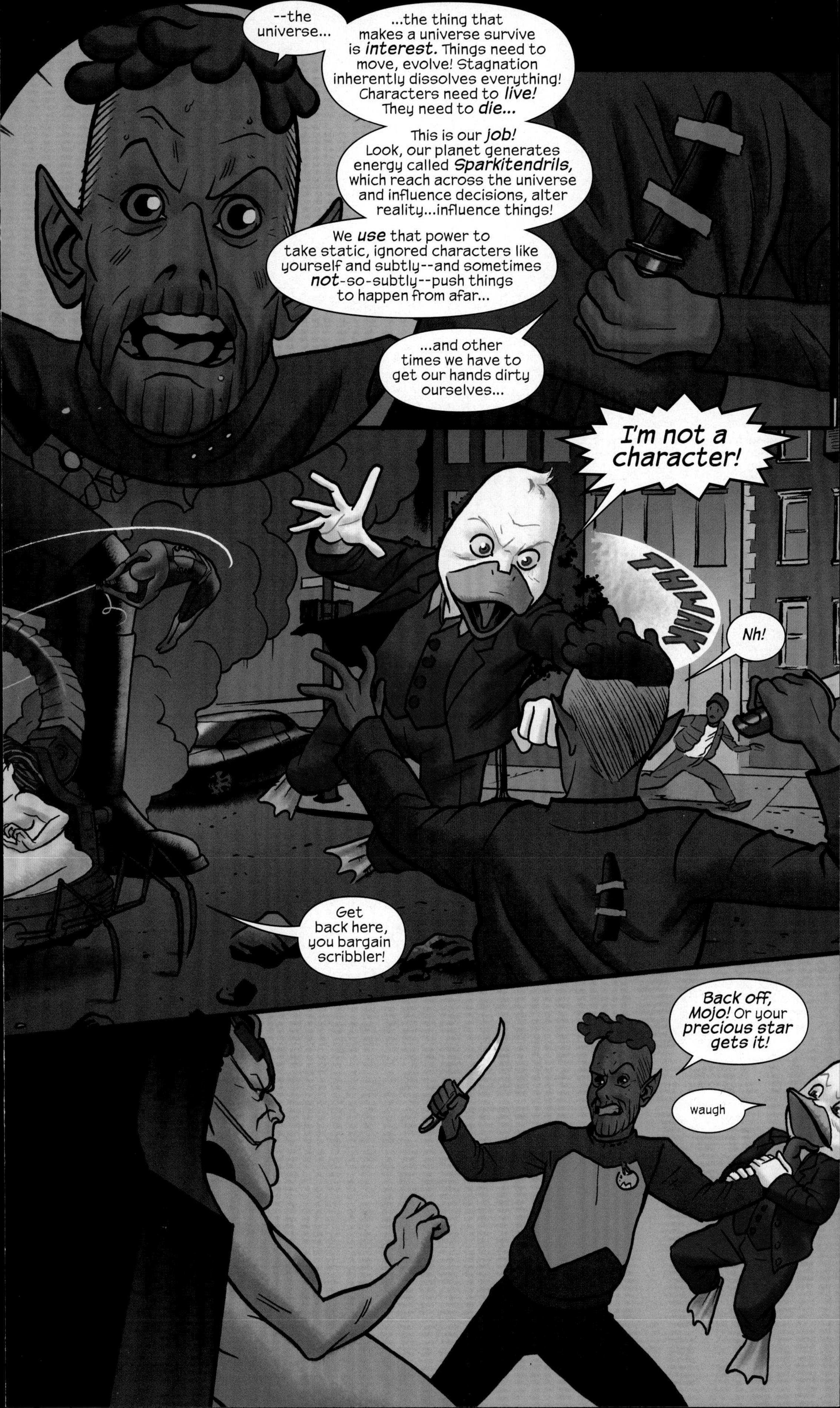
--the universe...
...the thing that makes a universe survive is *interest.* Things need to move, evolve! Stagnation inherently dissolves everything! Characters need to *live!* They need to *die...*
This is our *job!* Look, our planet generates energy called *Sparkitendrils,* which reach across the universe and influence decisions, alter reality...influence things!
We *use* that power to take static, ignored characters like yourself and subtly--and sometimes *not*-so-subtly--push things to happen from afar...
...and other times we have to get our hands dirty ourselves...
I'm not a character!
THWAK
Nh!
Get back here, you bargain scribbler!
Back off, Mojo! Or your precious star gets it!
waugh

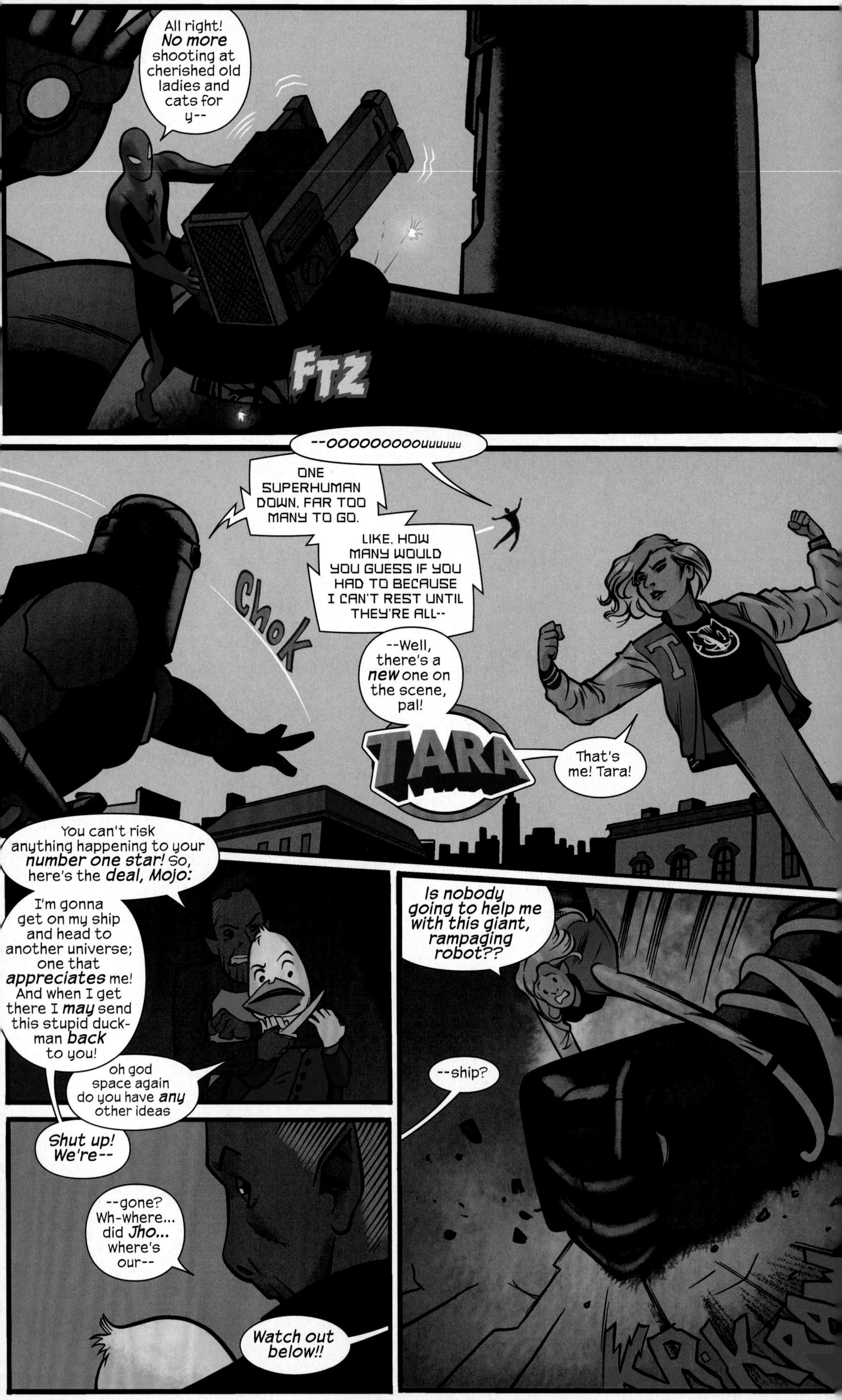

All right! No more shooting at cherished old ladies and cats for y--
FTZ
--OOOOOOOOOuuuuuu
ONE SUPERHUMAN DOWN, FAR TOO MANY TO GO.
LIKE, HOW MANY WOULD YOU GUESS IF YOU HAD TO BECAUSE I CAN'T REST UNTIL THEY'RE ALL--
Chok
--Well, there's a new one on the scene, pal!
TARA
That's me! Tara!
You can't risk anything happening to your number one star! So, here's the deal, Mojo:
I'm gonna get on my ship and head to another universe; one that appreciates me! And when I get there I may send this stupid duck-man back to you!
oh god space again do you have any other ideas
Shut up! We're--
--gone? Wh-where... did Jho... where's our--
Watch out below!!
Is nobody going to help me with this giant, rampaging robot??
--ship?

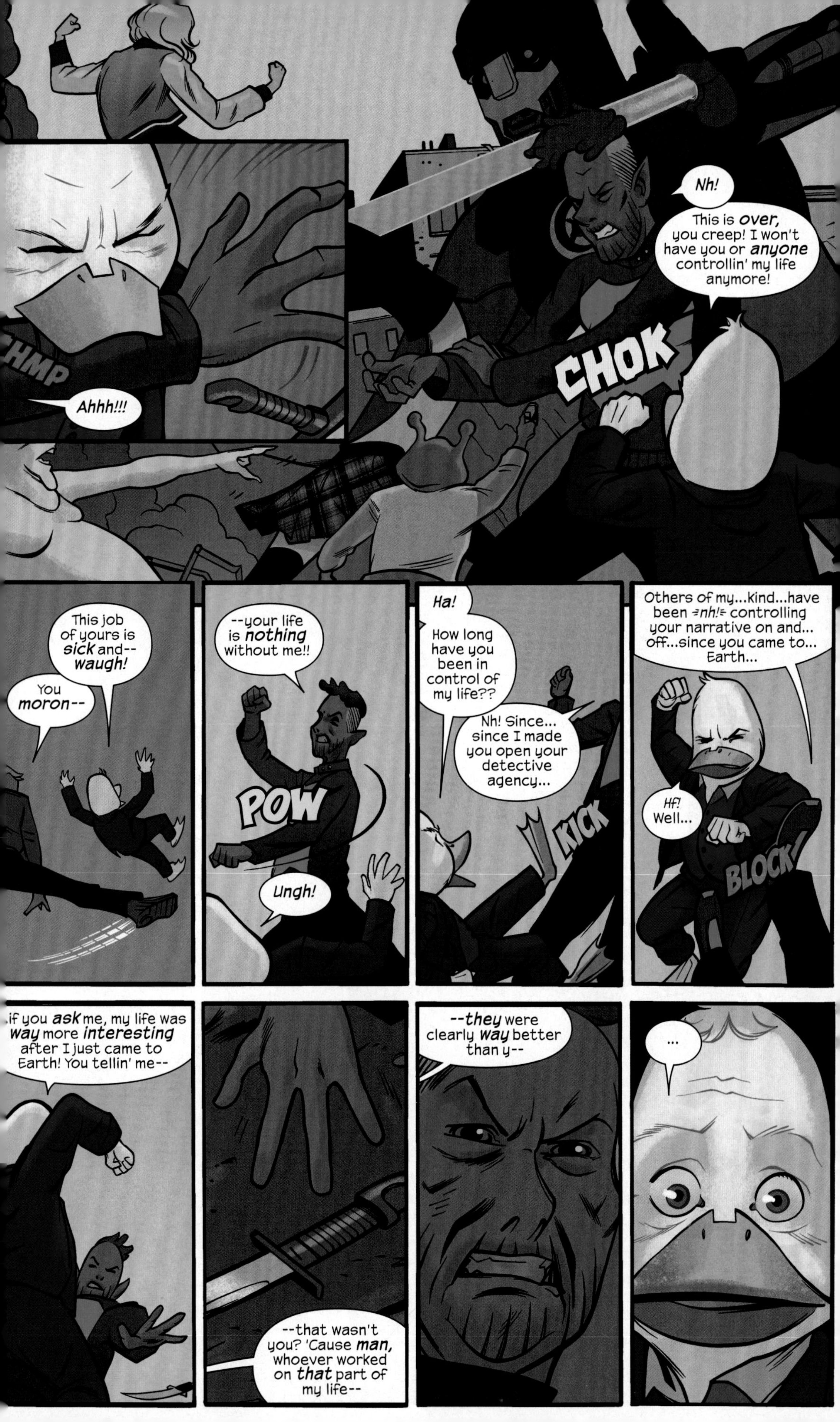
HMP
Ahhh!!!
Nh!
This is over, you creep! I won't have you or anyone controllin' my life anymore!
CHOK
This job of yours is sick and-- waugh!
You moron--
--your life is nothing without me!!
POW
Ungh!
Ha!
How long have you been in control of my life??
Nh! Since... since I made you open your detective agency...
KICK
Others of my...kind...have been =nh!= controlling your narrative on and... off...since you came to... Earth...
Hf! Well...
BLOCK
..if you ask me, my life was way more interesting after I just came to Earth! You tellin' me--
--that wasn't you? 'Cause man, whoever worked on that part of my life--
--they were clearly way better than y--
...

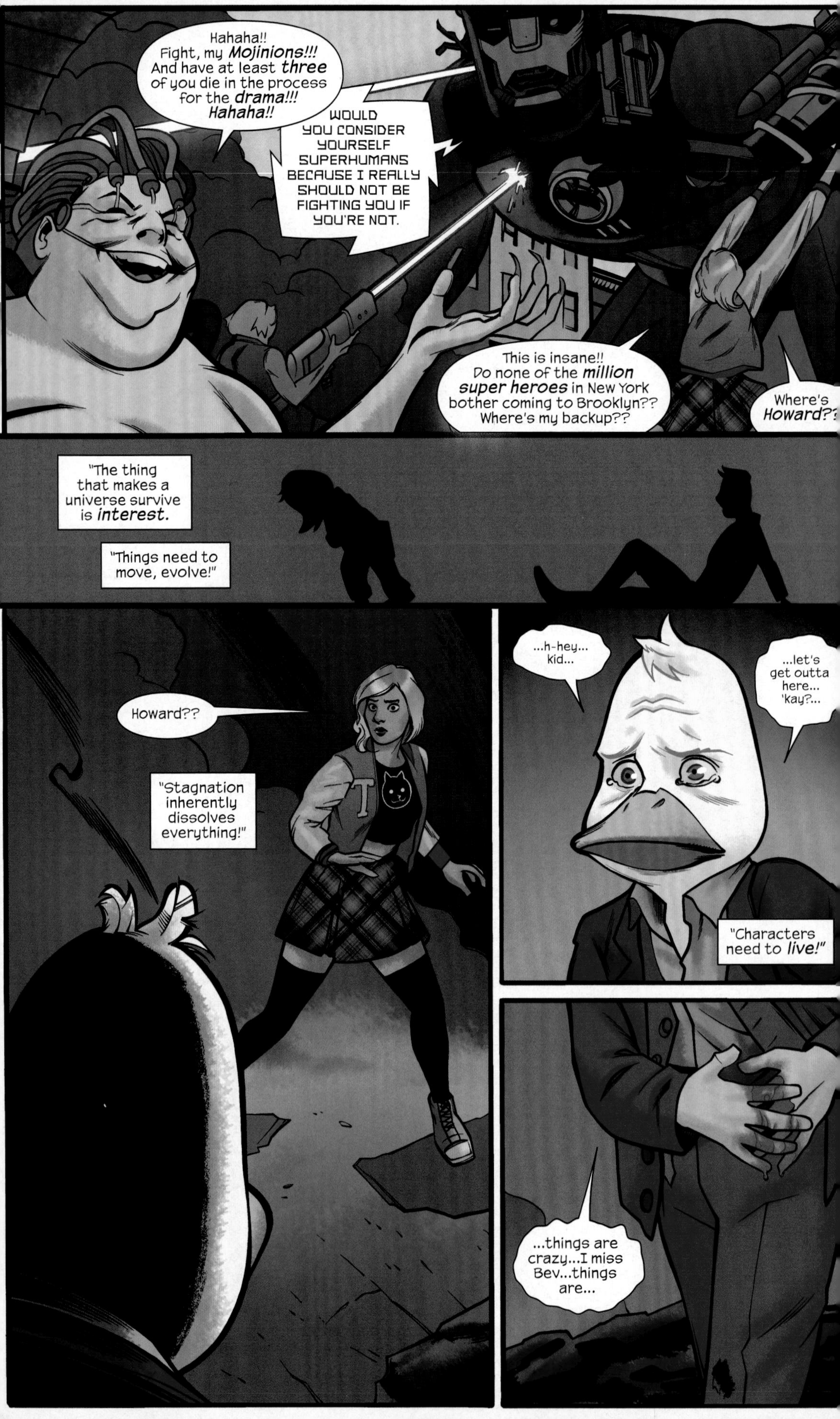
Hahaha!! Fight, my Mojinions!!! And have at least three of you die in the process for the drama!!! Hahaha!!
WOULD YOU CONSIDER YOURSELF SUPERHUMANS BECAUSE I REALLY SHOULD NOT BE FIGHTING YOU IF YOU'RE NOT.
This is insane!! Do none of the million super heroes in New York bother coming to Brooklyn?? Where's my backup??
Where's Howard??
"The thing that makes a universe survive is interest.
"Things need to move, evolve!"
Howard??
"Stagnation inherently dissolves everything!"
...h-hey... kid...
...let's get outta here... 'kay?...
"Characters need to live!"
...things are crazy...I miss Bev...things are...

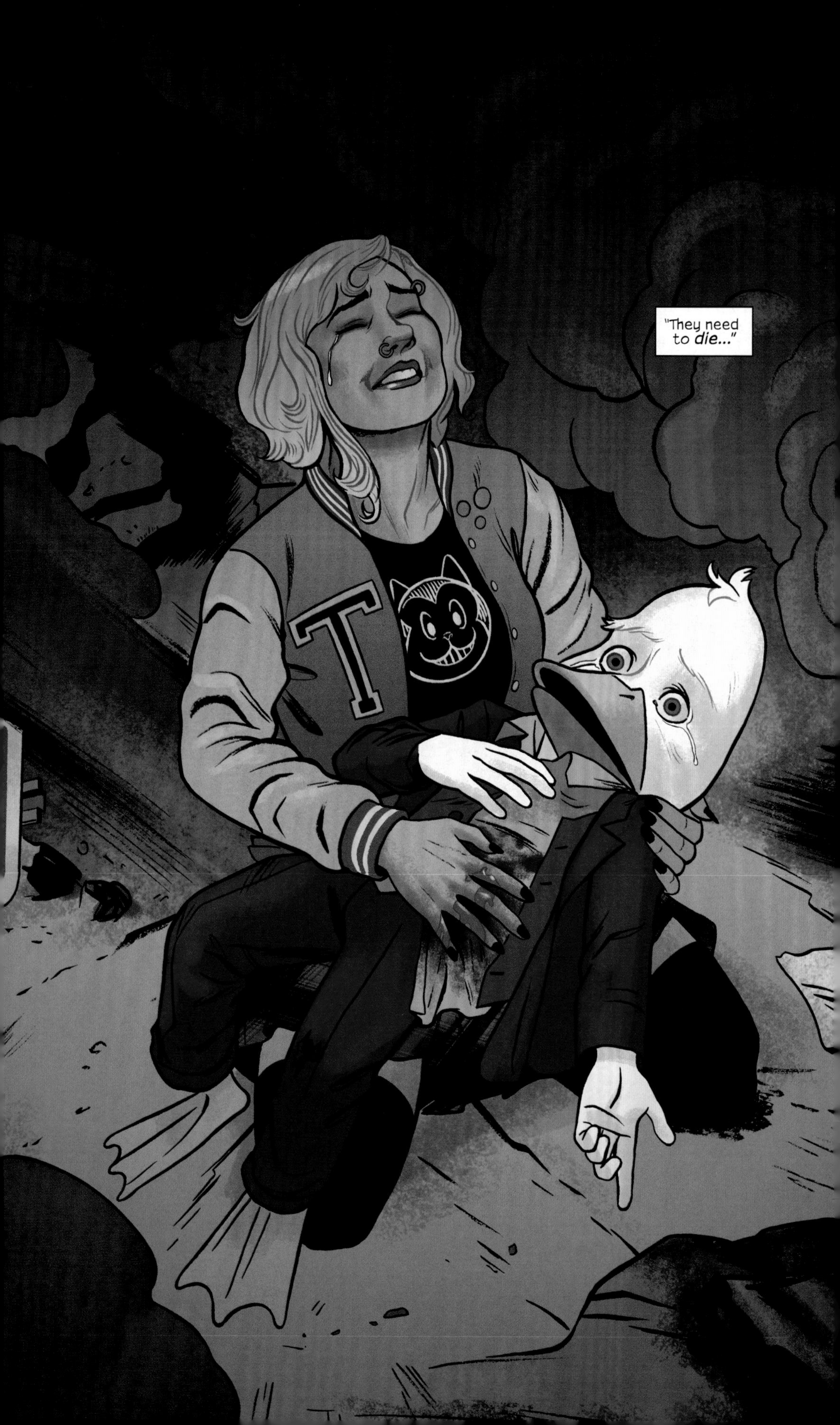
"They need to *die*..."

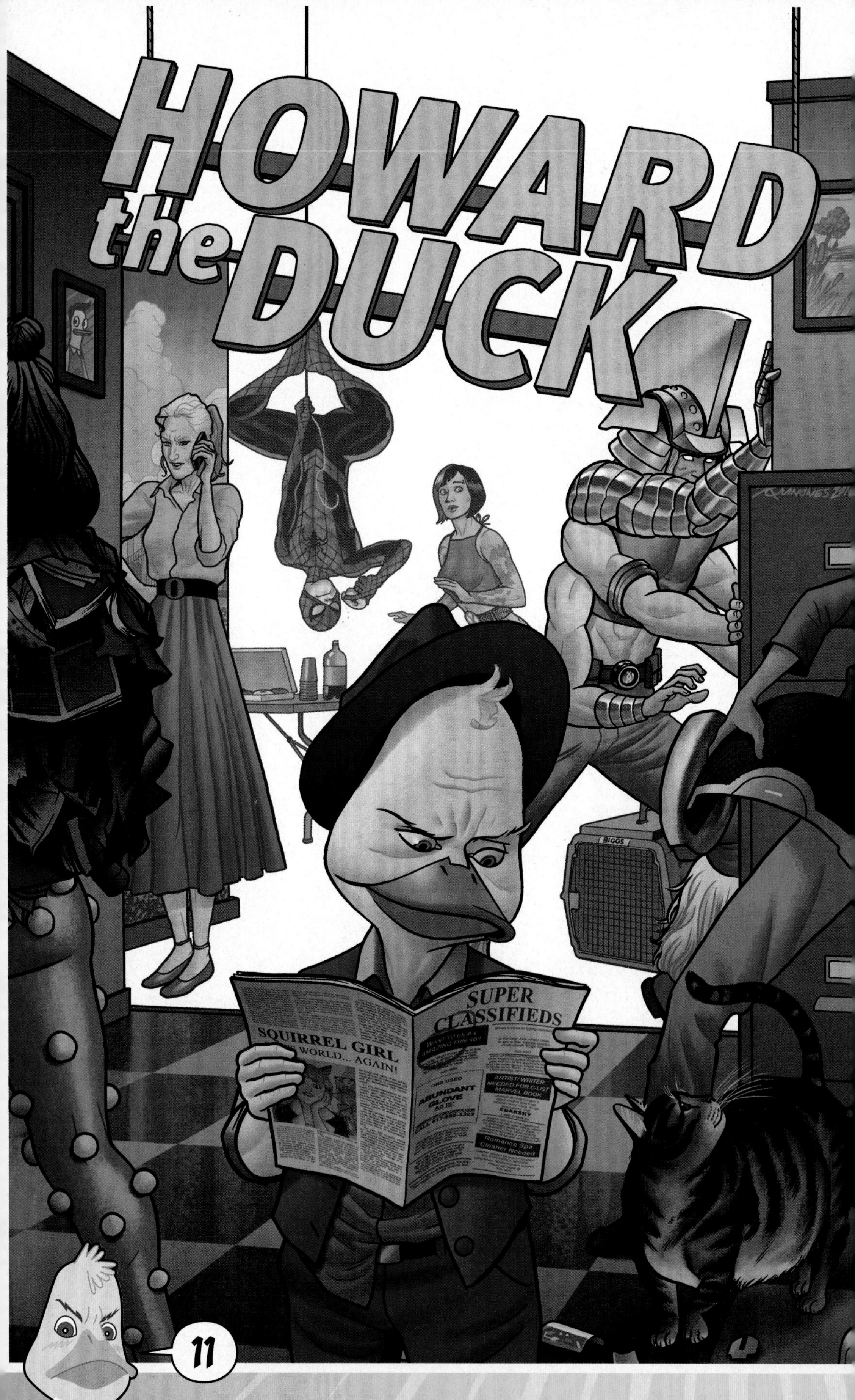

HOWARD the DUCK
SQUIRREL GIRL
WORLD... AGAIN!
SUPER CLASSIFIEDS
ONE USED
ABUNDANT GLOVE
ARTIST/WRITER NEEDED FOR C-LIST MARVEL BOOK
ZDARSKY
Romance Spa Cleaner Needed
BIGGS

HOWARD'S END

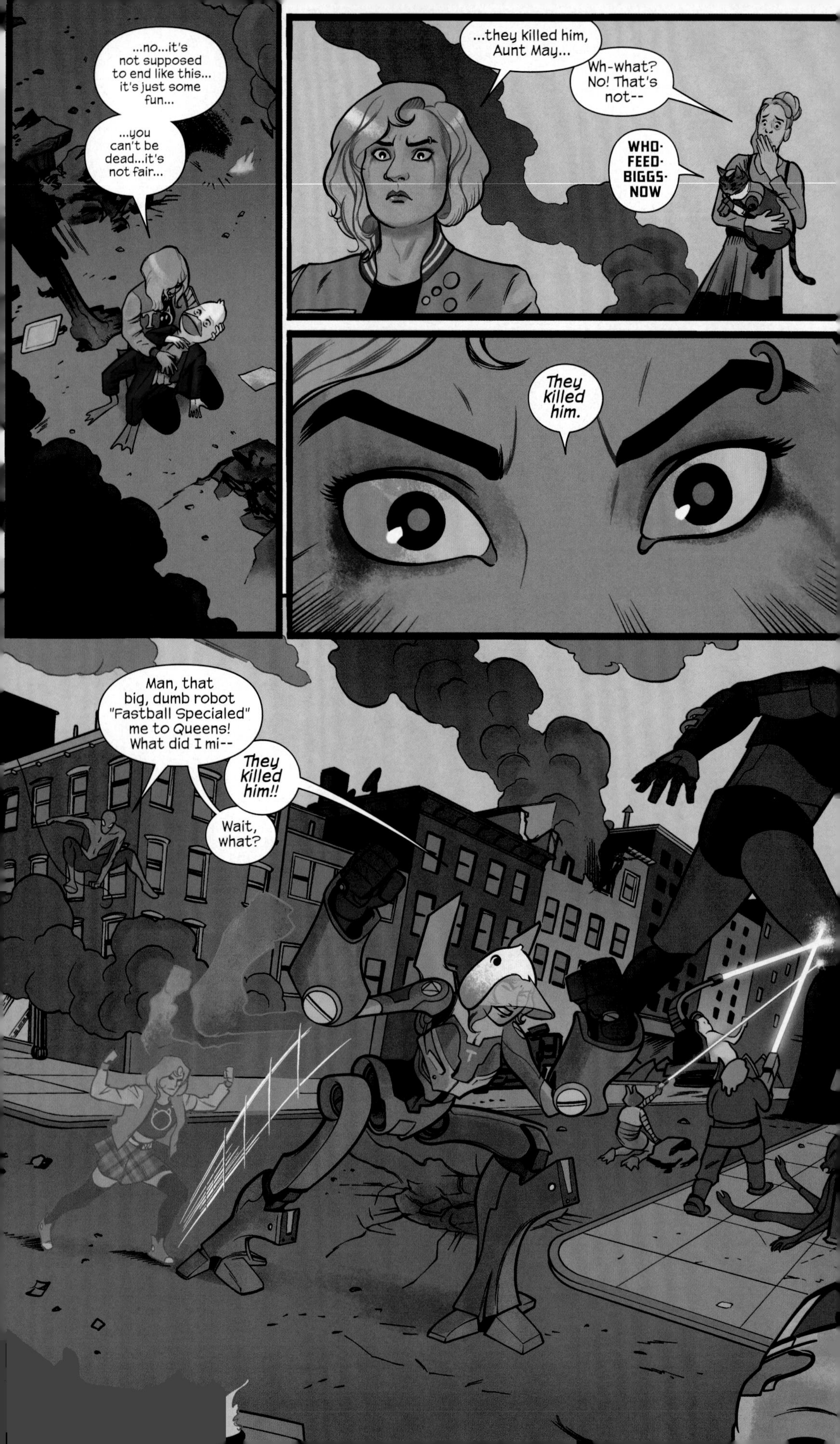
...no...it's not supposed to end like this... it's just some fun...
...you can't be dead...it's not fair...
...they killed him, Aunt May...
Wh-what? No! That's not--
WHO· FEED· BIGGS· NOW
They killed him.
Man, that big, dumb robot "Fastball Specialed" me to Queens! What did I mi--
They killed him!!
Wait, what?

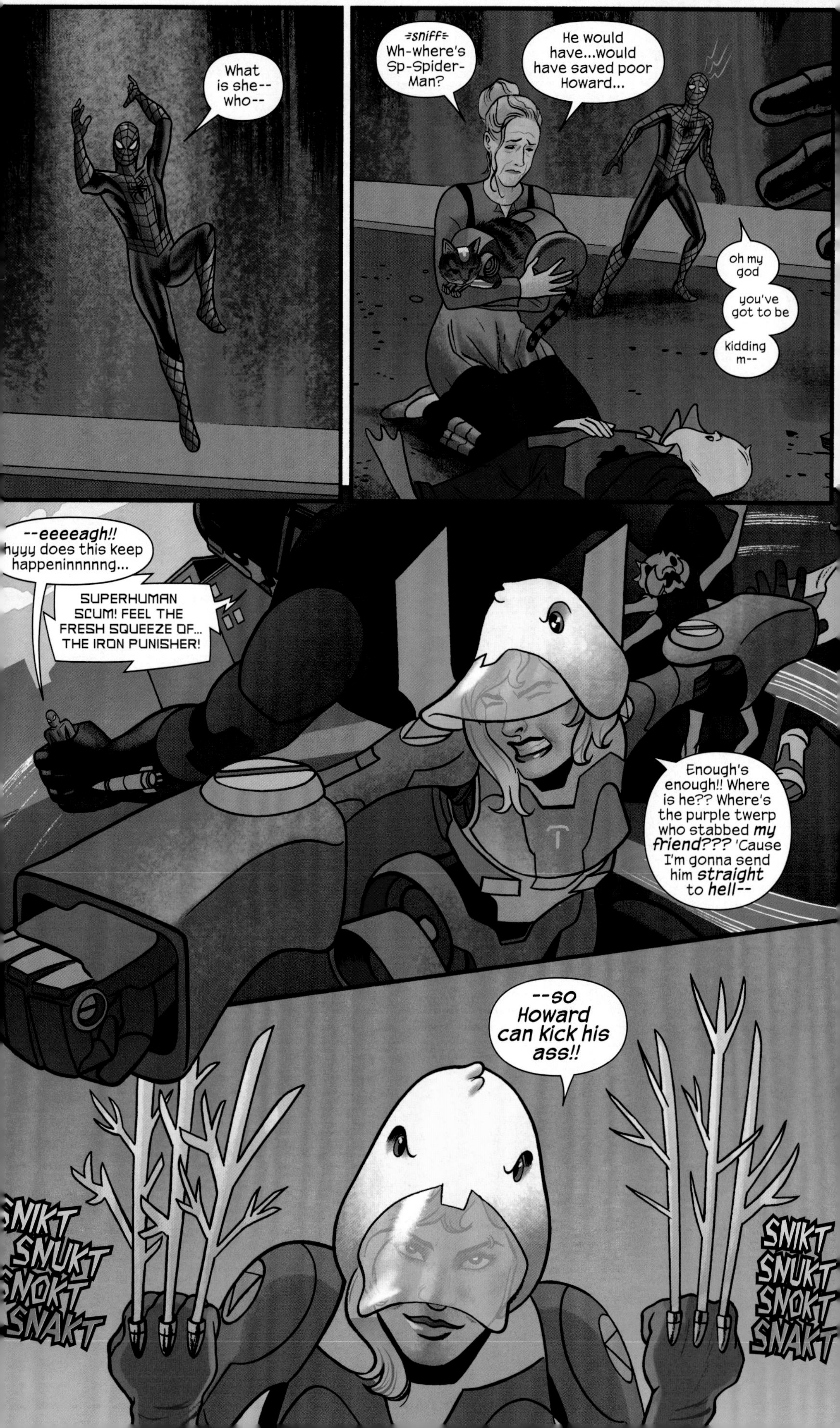
What is she-- who--
=sniff= Wh-where's Sp-Spider-Man?
He would have...would have saved poor Howard...
oh my god
you've got to be
kidding m--
--eeeeagh!! hyyy does this keep happeninnnnng...
SUPERHUMAN SCUM! FEEL THE FRESH SQUEEZE OF... THE IRON PUNISHER!
Enough's enough!! Where is he?? Where's the purple twerp who stabbed my friend??? 'Cause I'm gonna send him straight to hell--
--so Howard can kick his ass!!
SNIKT SNUKT SNOKT SNAKT
SNIKT SNUKT SNOKT SNAKT

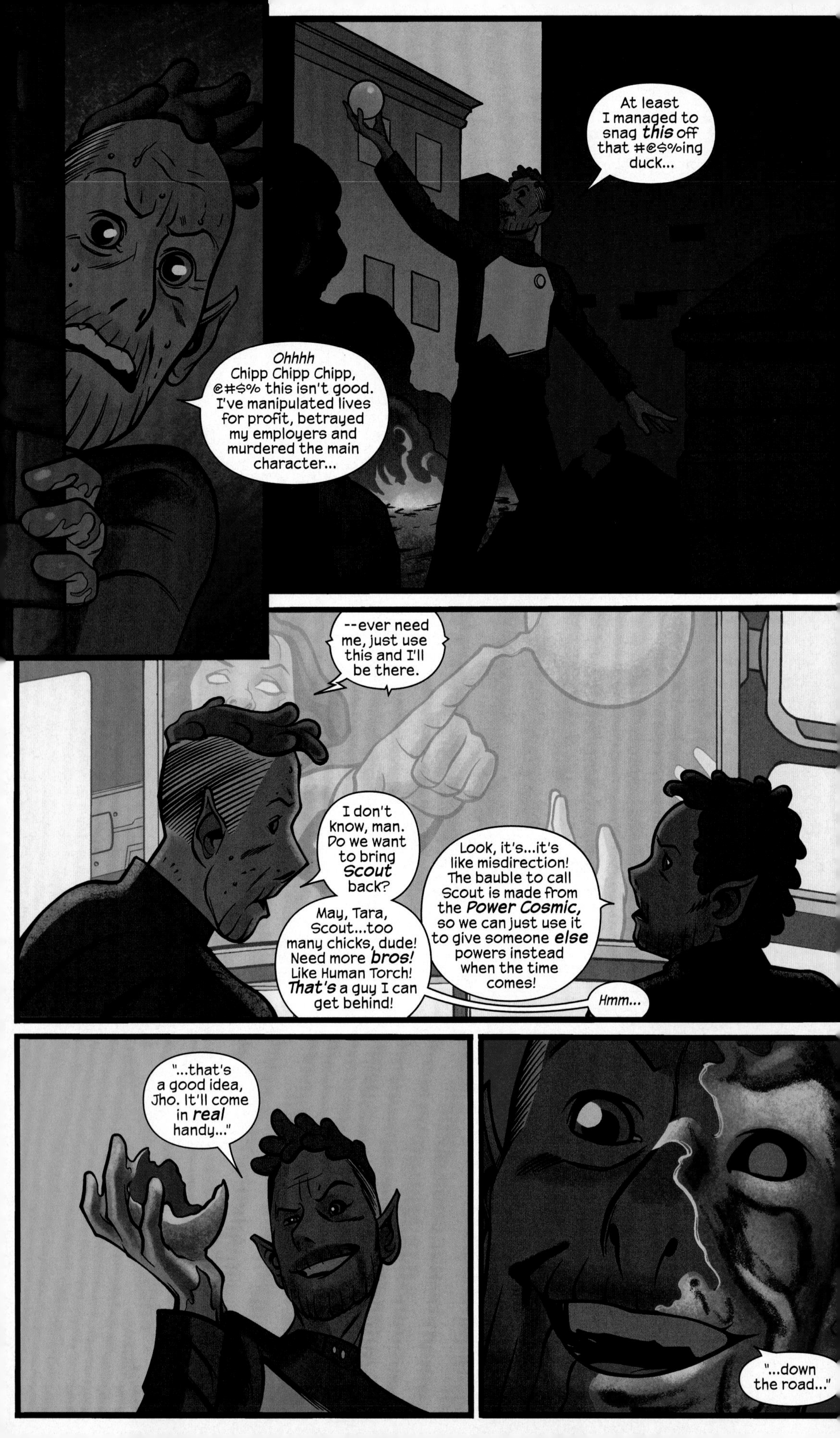
At least I managed to snag *this* off that #@$%ing duck...
Ohhhh Chipp Chipp Chipp, @#$% this isn't good. I've manipulated lives for profit, betrayed my employers and murdered the main character...
--ever need me, just use this and I'll be there.
I don't know, man. Do we want to bring *Scout* back?
May, Tara, Scout...too many chicks, dude! Need more *bros!* Like Human Torch! *That's* a guy I can get behind!
Look, it's...it's like misdirection! The bauble to call Scout is made from the *Power Cosmic,* so we can just use it to give someone *else* powers instead when the time comes!
Hmm...
"...that's a good idea, Jho. It'll come in *real* handy..."
"...down the road..."

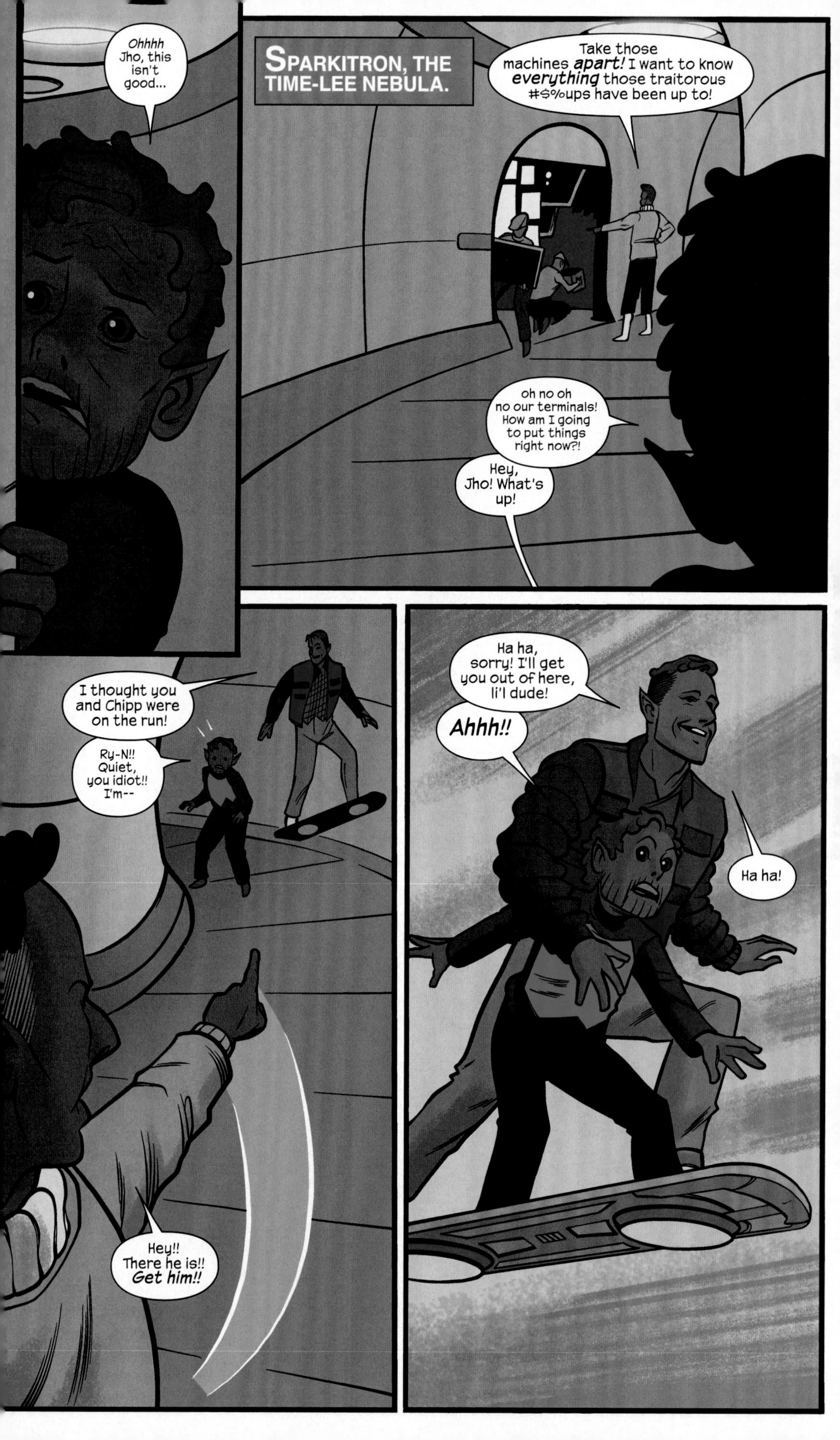
Ohhhh Jho, this isn't good...
SPARKITRON, THE TIME-LEE NEBULA.
Take those machines *apart!* I want to know *everything* those traitorous #$%ups have been up to!
oh no oh no our terminals! How am I going to put things right now?!
Hey, Jho! What's up!
I thought you and Chipp were on the run!
Ry-N!! Quiet, you idiot!! I'm--
Hey!! There he is!! *Get him!!*
Ha ha, sorry! I'll get you out of here, li'l dude!
Ahhh!!
Ha ha!

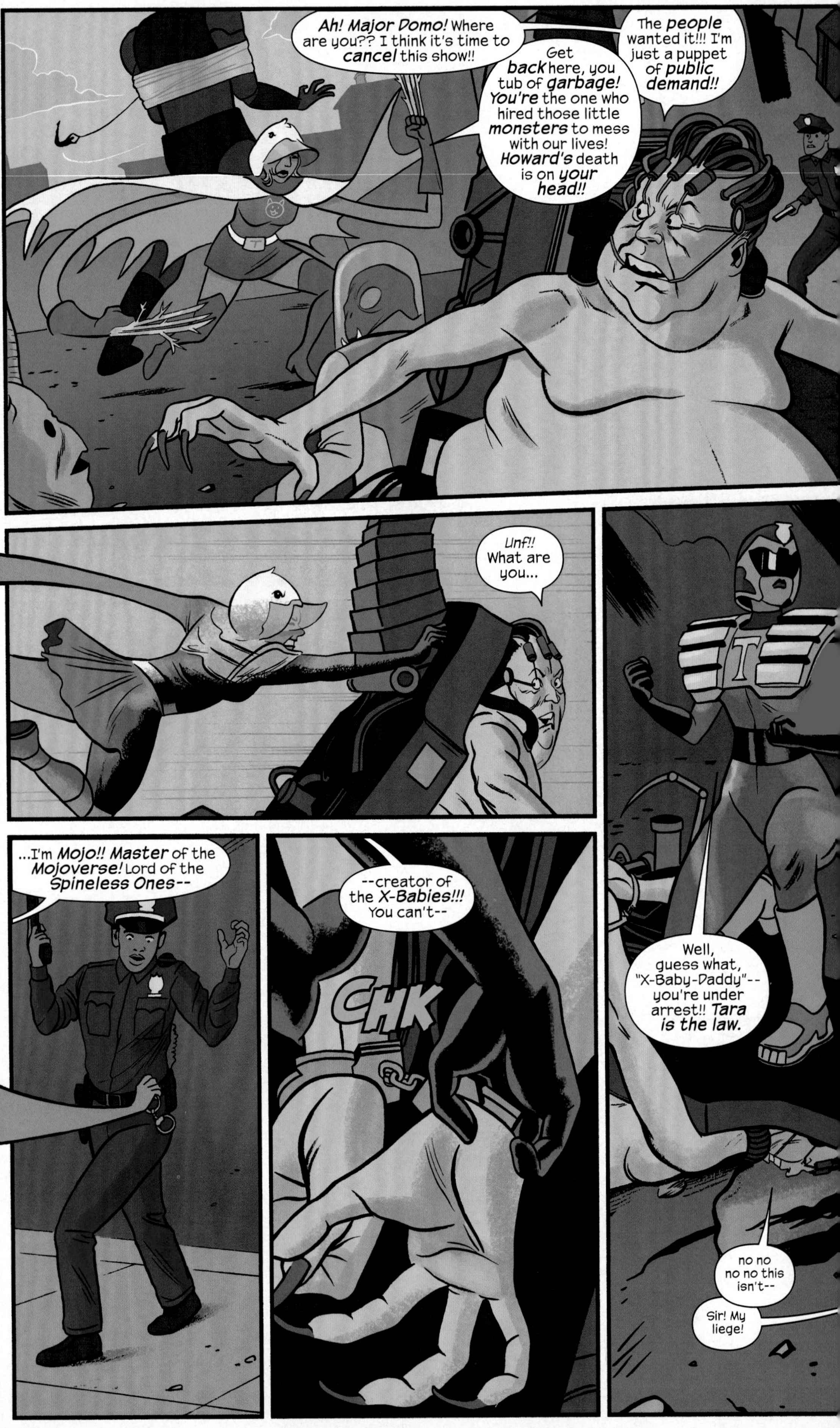
Ah! Major Domo! Where are you?? I think it's time to cancel this show!!
Get back here, you tub of garbage! You're the one who hired those little monsters to mess with our lives! Howard's death is on your head!!
The people wanted it!!! I'm just a puppet of public demand!!
Unf!! What are you...
...I'm Mojo!! Master of the Mojoverse! Lord of the Spineless Ones--
--creator of the X-Babies!!! You can't--
CHK
Well, guess what, "X-Baby-Daddy"-- you're under arrest!! Tara is the law.
no no no no this isn't--
Sir! My liege!

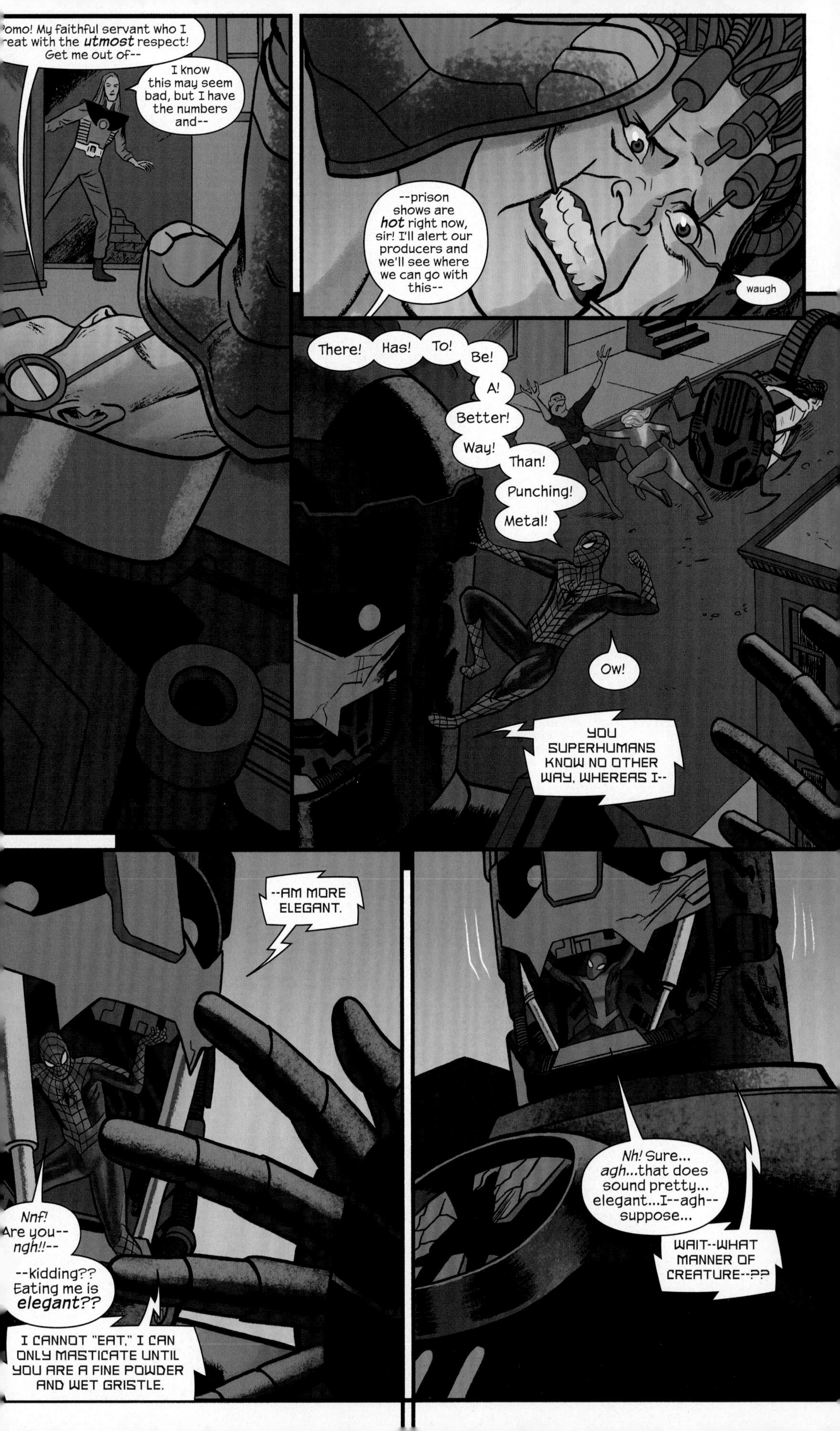

Pomo! My faithful servant who I treat with the utmost respect! Get me out of--
I know this may seem bad, but I have the numbers and--
--prison shows are hot right now, sir! I'll alert our producers and we'll see where we can go with this--
waugh
There!
Has!
To!
Be!
A!
Better!
Way!
Than!
Punching!
Metal!
Ow!
YOU SUPERHUMANS KNOW NO OTHER WAY, WHEREAS I--
--AM MORE ELEGANT.
Nnf! Are you-- ngh!!--
--kidding?? Eating me is elegant??
I CANNOT "EAT," I CAN ONLY MASTICATE UNTIL YOU ARE A FINE POWDER AND WET GRISTLE.
Nh! Sure... agh...that does sound pretty... elegant...I--agh-- suppose...
WAIT--WHAT MANNER OF CREATURE--??

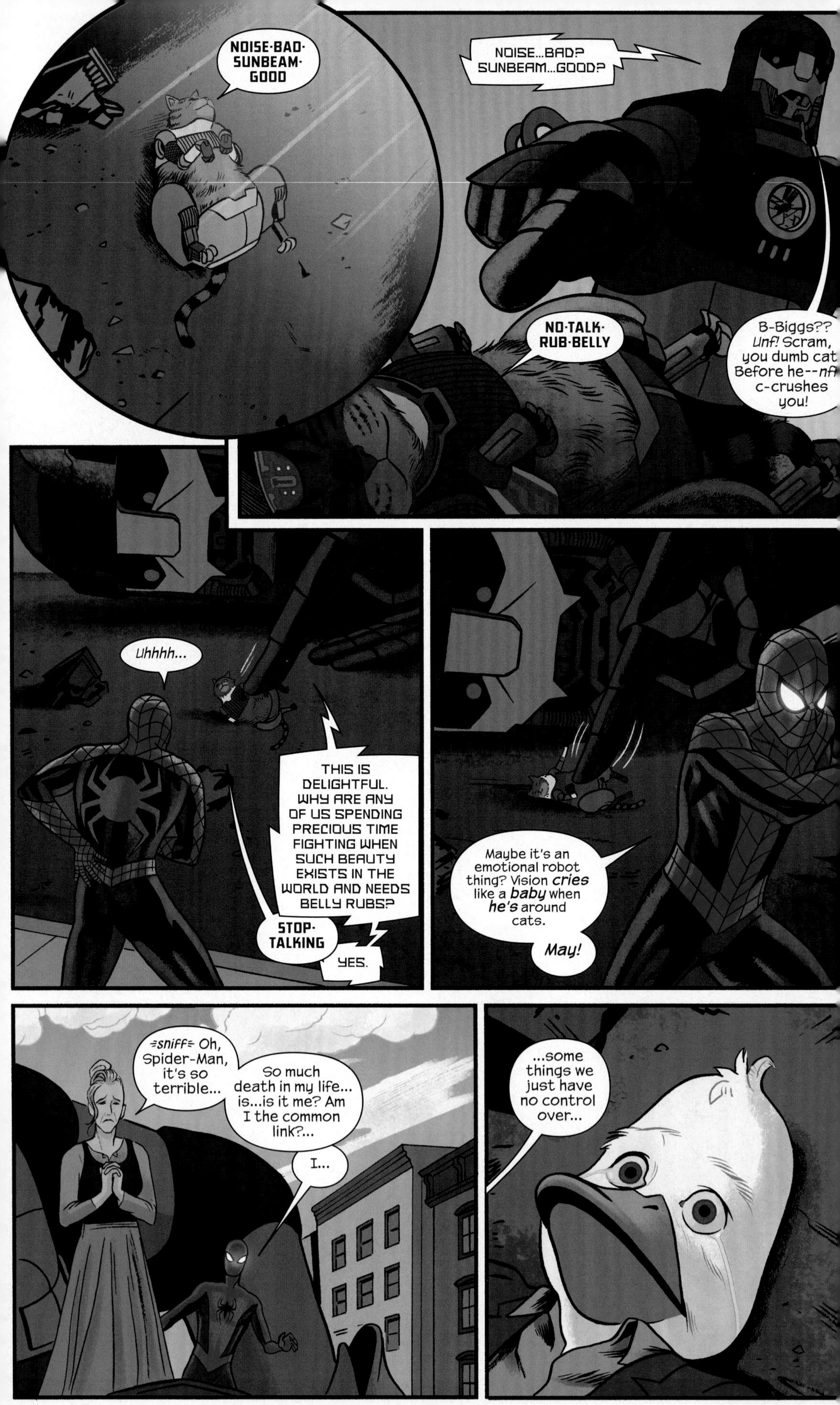
NOISE·BAD·
SUNBEAM·
GOOD
NOISE...BAD?
SUNBEAM...GOOD?
NO·TALK·
RUB·BELLY
B-Biggs??
Unf! Scram,
you dumb cat
Before he--*nf*
c-crushes
you!
Uhhhh...
THIS IS DELIGHTFUL. WHY ARE ANY OF US SPENDING PRECIOUS TIME FIGHTING WHEN SUCH BEAUTY EXISTS IN THE WORLD AND NEEDS BELLY RUBS?
STOP·
TALKING
YES.
Maybe it's an emotional robot thing? Vision *cries* like a *baby* when *he's* around cats.
May!
=*sniff*= Oh, Spider-Man, it's so terrible...
So much death in my life... is...is it me? Am I the common link?...
I...
...some things we just have no control over...

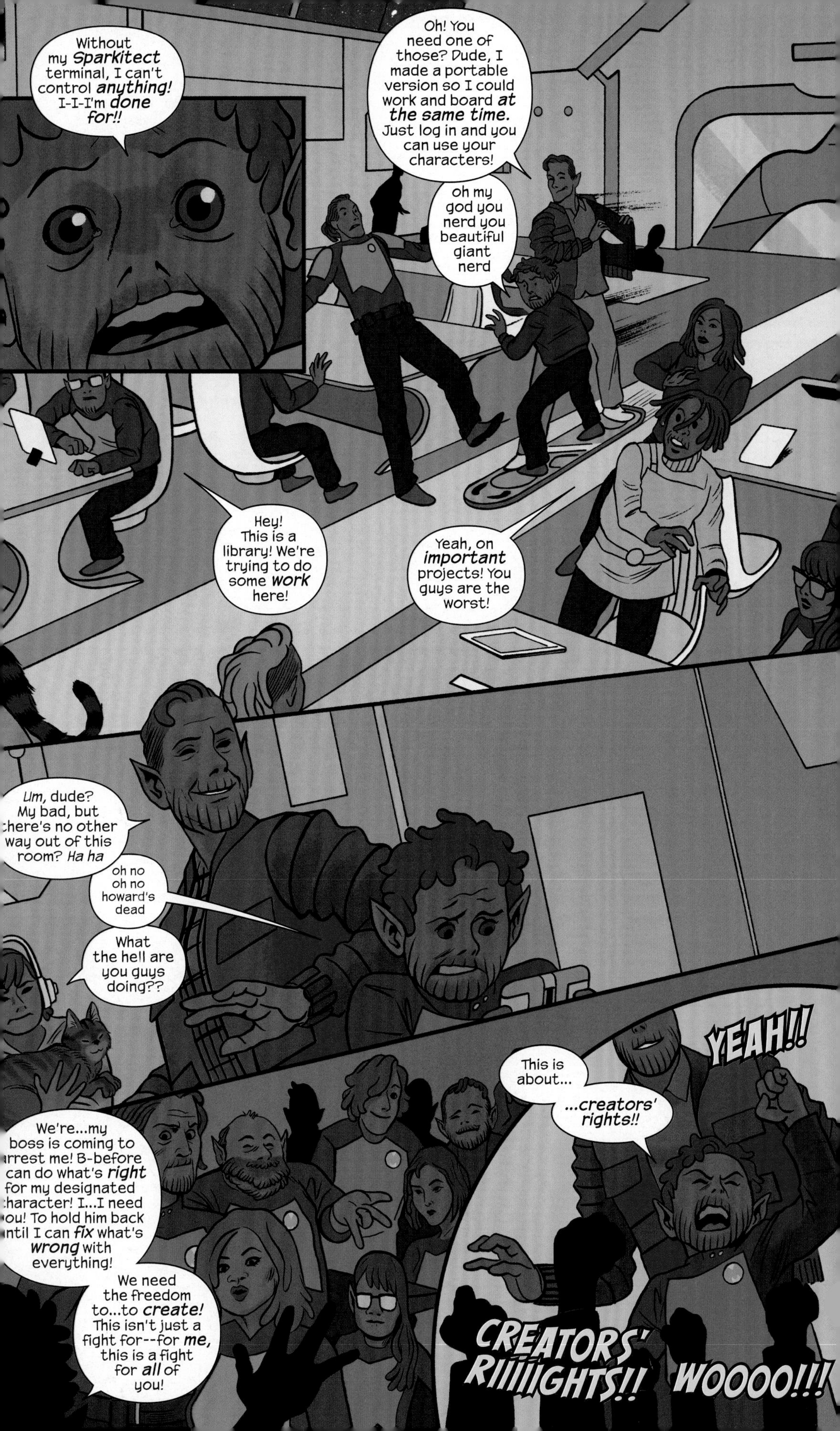
Without my *Sparkitect* terminal, I can't control *anything!* I-I-I'm *done for!!*
Oh! You need one of those? Dude, I made a portable version so I could work and board *at the same time.* Just log in and you can use your characters!
oh my god you nerd you beautiful giant nerd
Hey! This is a library! We're trying to do some *work* here!
Yeah, on *important* projects! You guys are the worst!
Um, dude? My bad, but here's no other way out of this room? *Ha ha*
oh no oh no howard's dead
What the hell are you guys doing??
We're...my boss is coming to arrest me! B-before can do what's *right* for my designated character! I...I need you! To hold him back until I can *fix* what's *wrong* with everything!
We need the freedom to...to *create!* This isn't just a fight for--for *me,* this is a fight for *all* of you!
This is about...
...creators' rights!!
YEAH!!
CREATORS' RIIIIIGHTS!!
WOOOO!!!

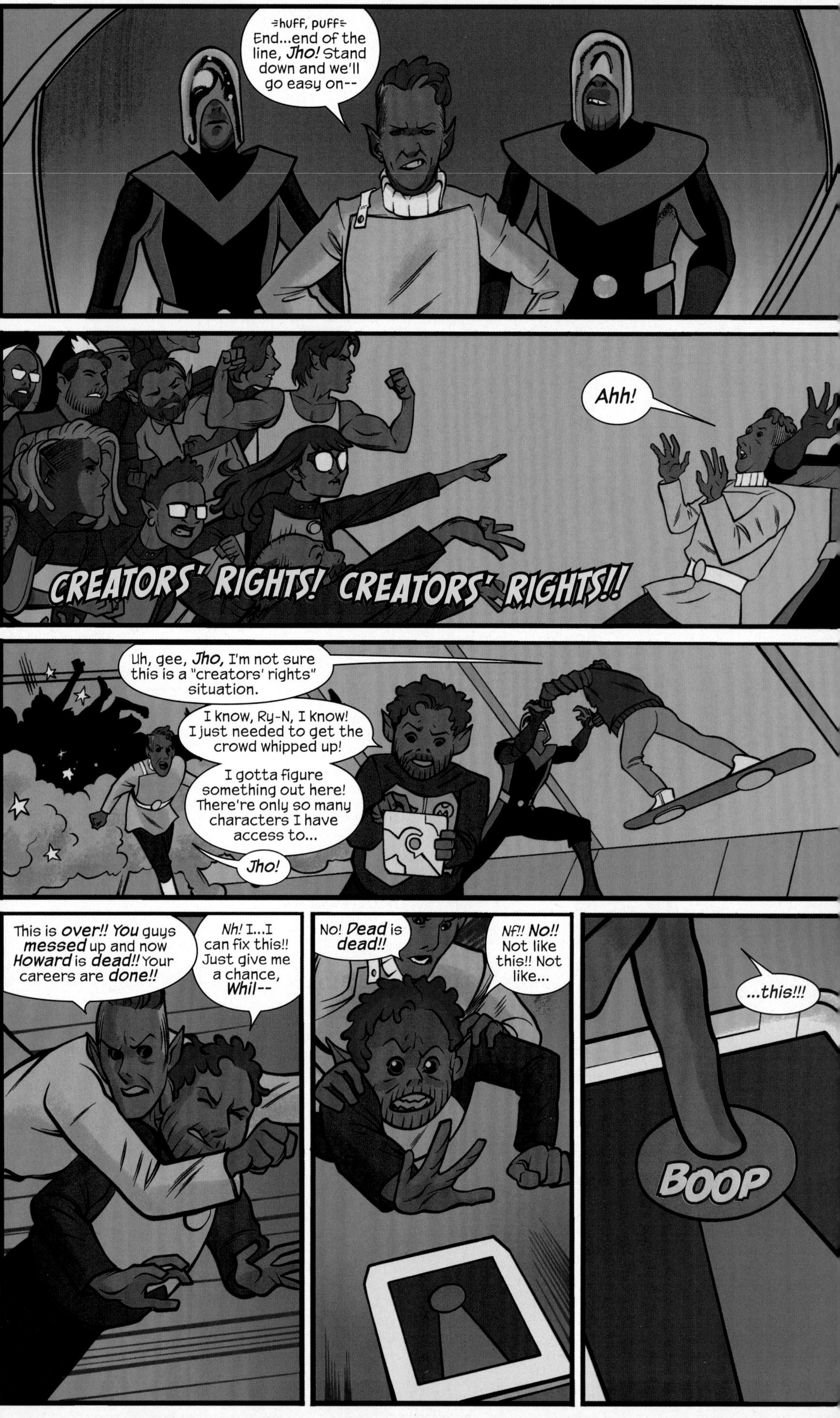

=huff, puff=
End...end of the line, Jho! Stand down and we'll go easy on--
CREATORS' RIGHTS! CREATORS' RIGHTS!!
Ahh!
Uh, gee, Jho, I'm not sure this is a "creators' rights" situation.
I know, Ry-N, I know! I just needed to get the crowd whipped up!
I gotta figure something out here! There're only so many characters I have access to...
Jho!
This is over!! You guys messed up and now Howard is dead!! Your careers are done!!
Nh! I...I can fix this!! Just give me a chance, Whil--
No! Dead is dead!!
Nf!! No!! Not like this!! Not like...
...this!!!
BOOP

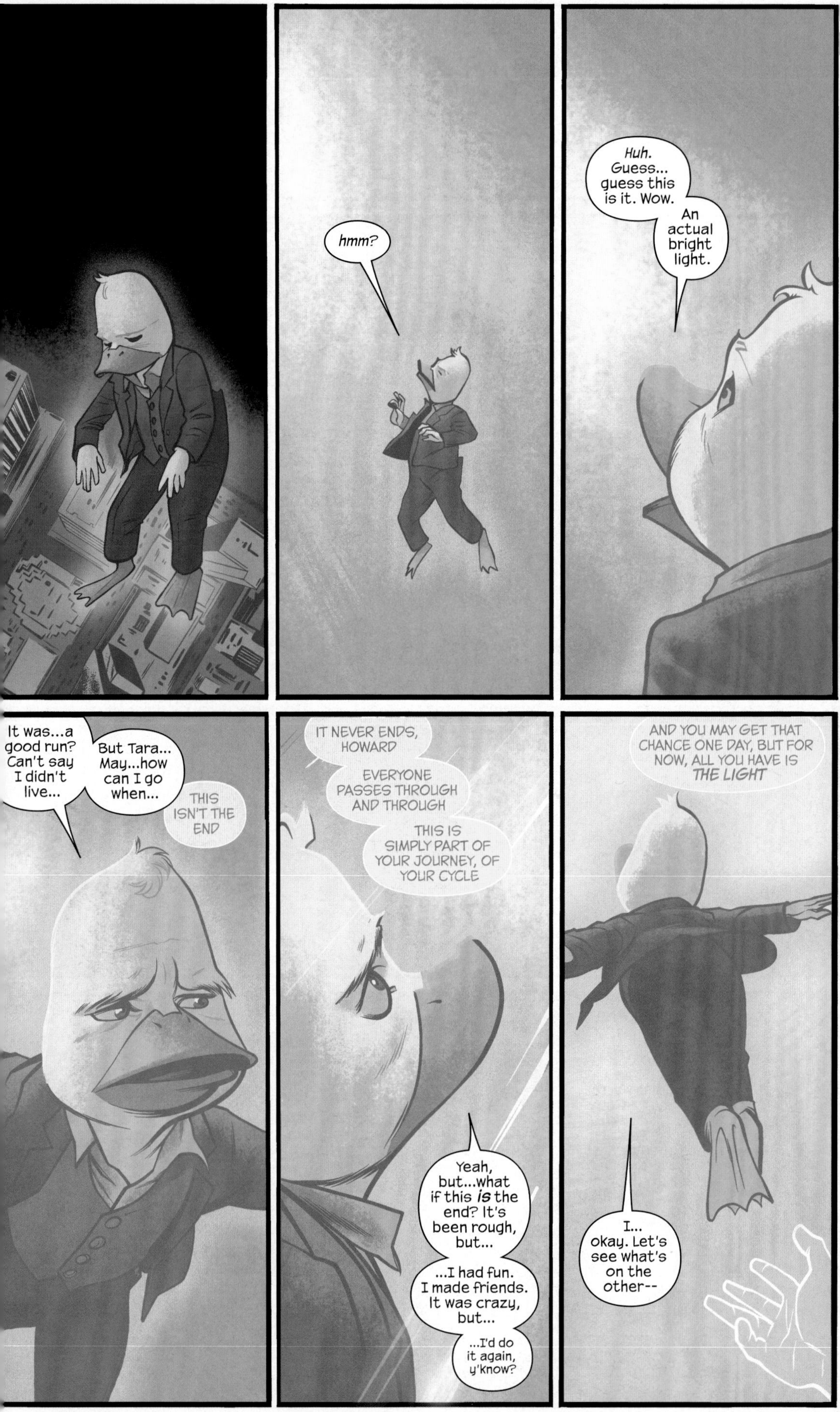
hmm?
Huh. Guess... guess this is it. Wow.
An actual bright light.
It was...a good run? Can't say I didn't live...
But Tara... May...how can I go when...
THIS ISN'T THE END
IT NEVER ENDS, HOWARD
EVERYONE PASSES THROUGH AND THROUGH
THIS IS SIMPLY PART OF YOUR JOURNEY, OF YOUR CYCLE
Yeah, but...what if this *is* the end? It's been rough, but...
...I had fun. I made friends. It was crazy, but...
...I'd do it again, y'know?
AND YOU MAY GET THAT CHANCE ONE DAY, BUT FOR NOW, ALL YOU HAVE IS *THE LIGHT*
I... okay. Let's see what's on the other--

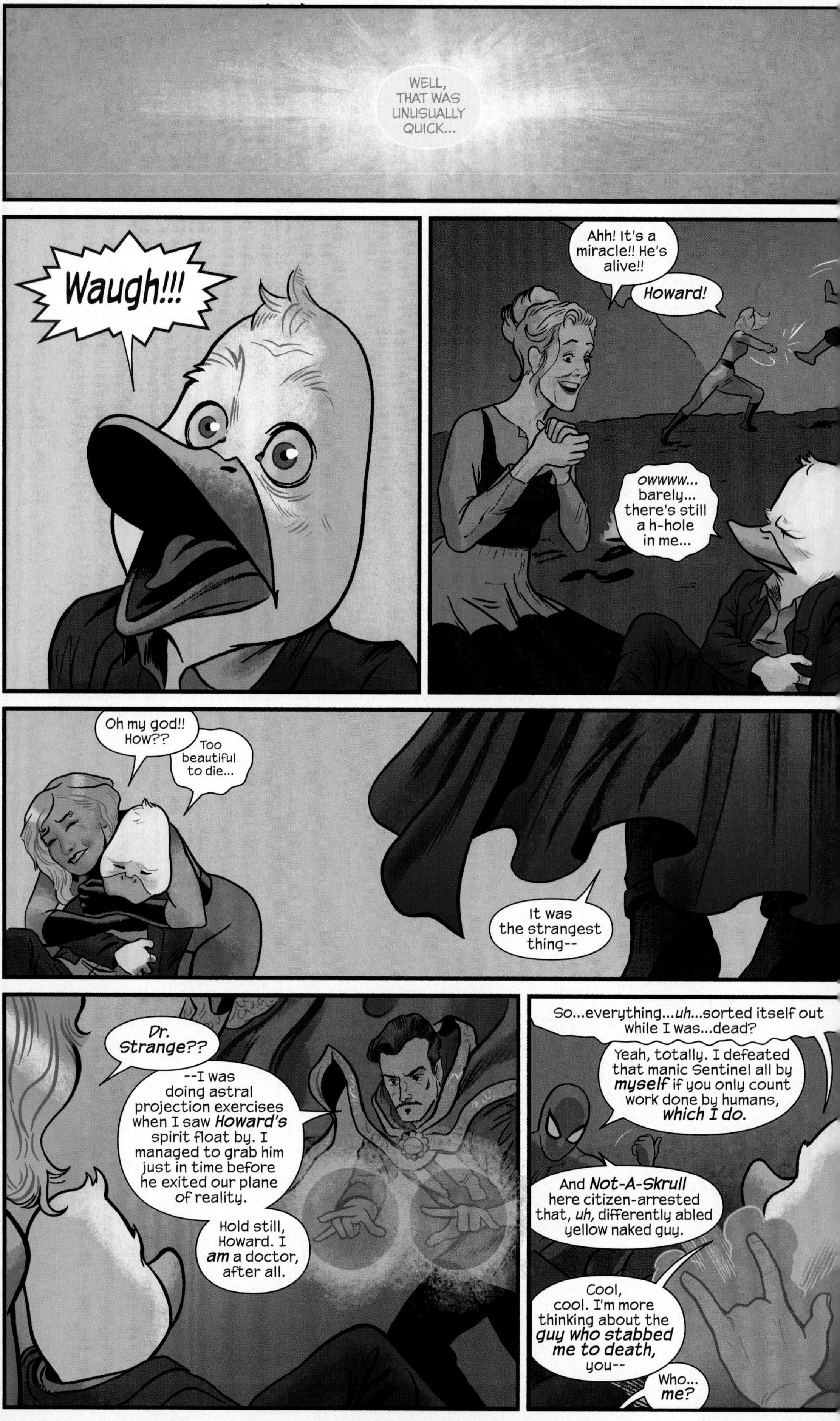
WELL, THAT WAS UNUSUALLY QUICK...
Waugh!!!
Ahh! It's a miracle!! He's alive!!
Howard!
owwww... barely... there's still a h-hole in me...
Oh my god!! How??
Too beautiful to die...
It was the strangest thing--
Dr. Strange??
--I was doing astral projection exercises when I saw Howard's spirit float by. I managed to grab him just in time before he exited our plane of reality.
Hold still, Howard. I am a doctor, after all.
So...everything...uh...sorted itself out while I was...dead?
Yeah, totally. I defeated that manic Sentinel all by myself if you only count work done by humans, which I do.
And Not-A-Skrull here citizen-arrested that, uh, differently abled yellow naked guy.
Cool, cool. I'm more thinking about the guy who stabbed me to death, you--
Who... me?

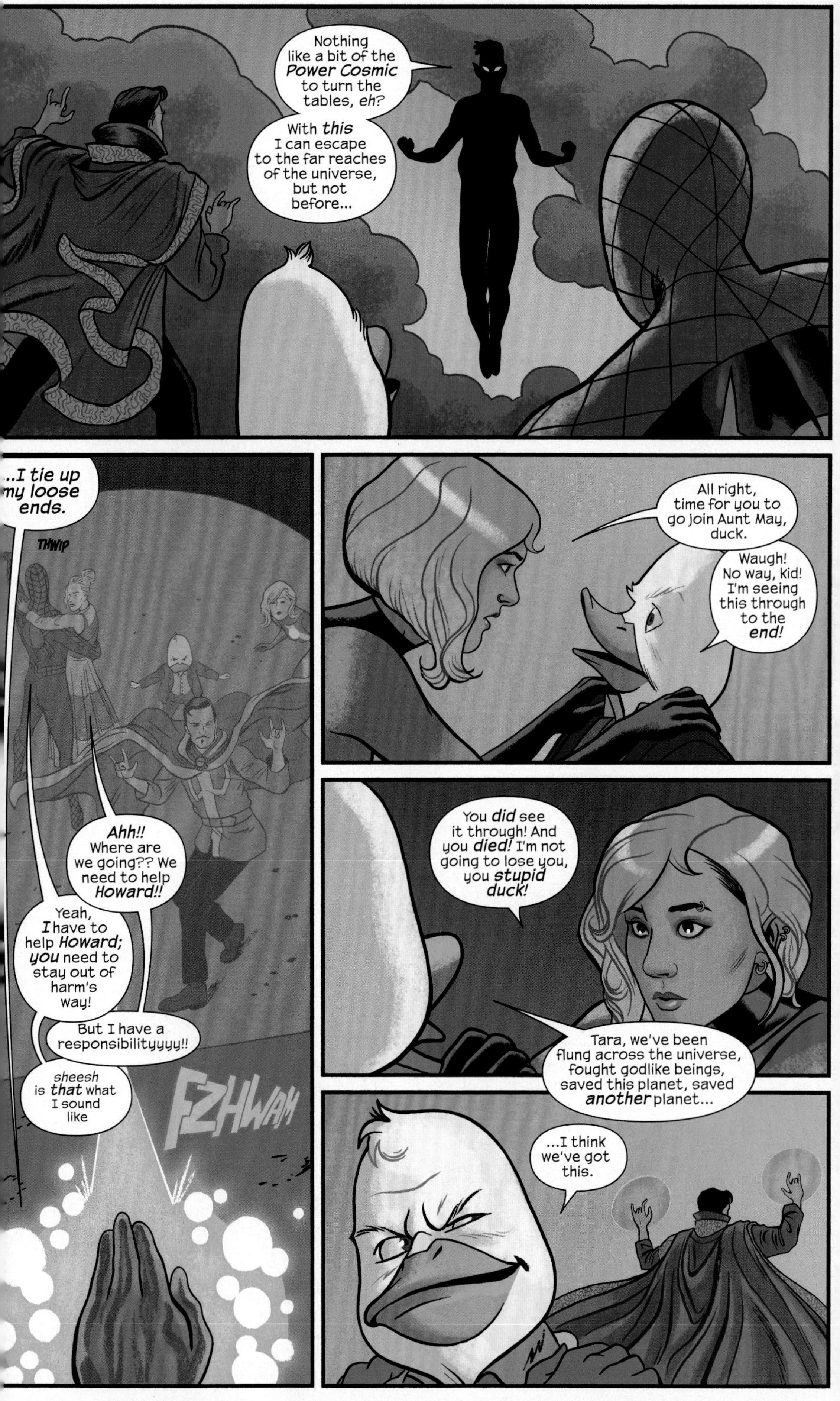
Nothing like a bit of the *Power Cosmic* to turn the tables, *eh?*
With *this* I can escape to the far reaches of the universe, but not before...
...I tie up my loose ends.
THWIP
Ahh!! Where are we going?? We need to help *Howard!!*
Yeah, *I* have to help *Howard; you* need to stay out of harm's way!
But I have a responsibilityyyy!!
sheesh is *that* what I sound like
FZHWAM
All right, time for you to go join Aunt May, duck.
Waugh! No way, kid! I'm seeing this through to the *end!*
You *did* see it through! And you *died!* I'm not going to lose you, you *stupid duck!*
Tara, we've been flung across the universe, fought godlike beings, saved this planet, saved *another* planet...
...I think we've got this.

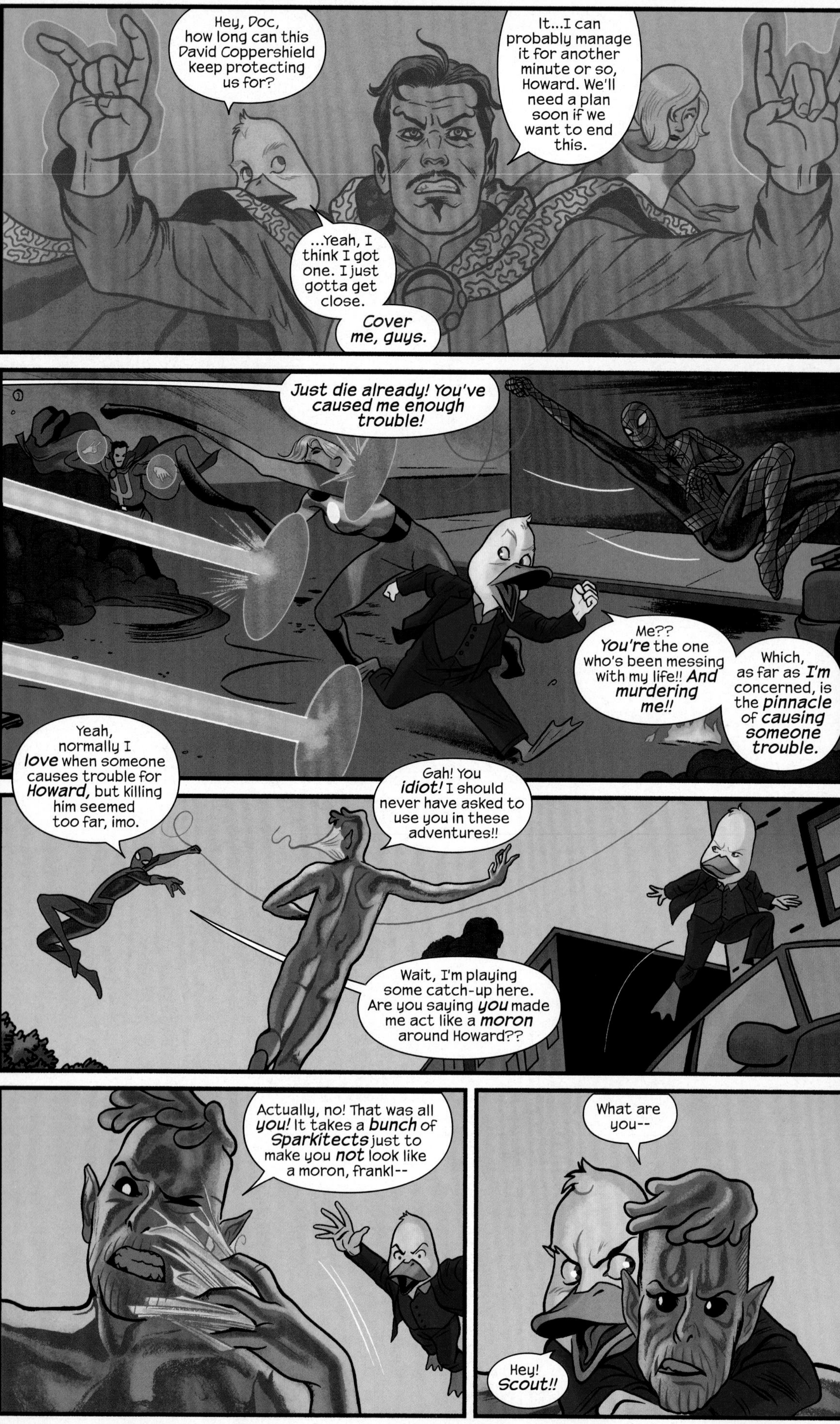

Hey, Doc, how long can this David Coppershield keep protecting us for?
It...I can probably manage it for another minute or so, Howard. We'll need a plan soon if we want to end this.
...Yeah, I think I got one. I just gotta get close.
Cover me, guys.
Just die already! You've caused me enough trouble!
Me?? You're the one who's been messing with my life!! And murdering me!!
Which, as far as I'm concerned, is the pinnacle of causing someone trouble.
Yeah, normally I love when someone causes trouble for Howard, but killing him seemed too far, imo.
Gah! You idiot! I should never have asked to use you in these adventures!!
Wait, I'm playing some catch-up here. Are you saying you made me act like a moron around Howard??
Actually, no! That was all you! It takes a bunch of Sparkitects just to make you not look like a moron, frankl--
What are you--
Hey! Scout!!

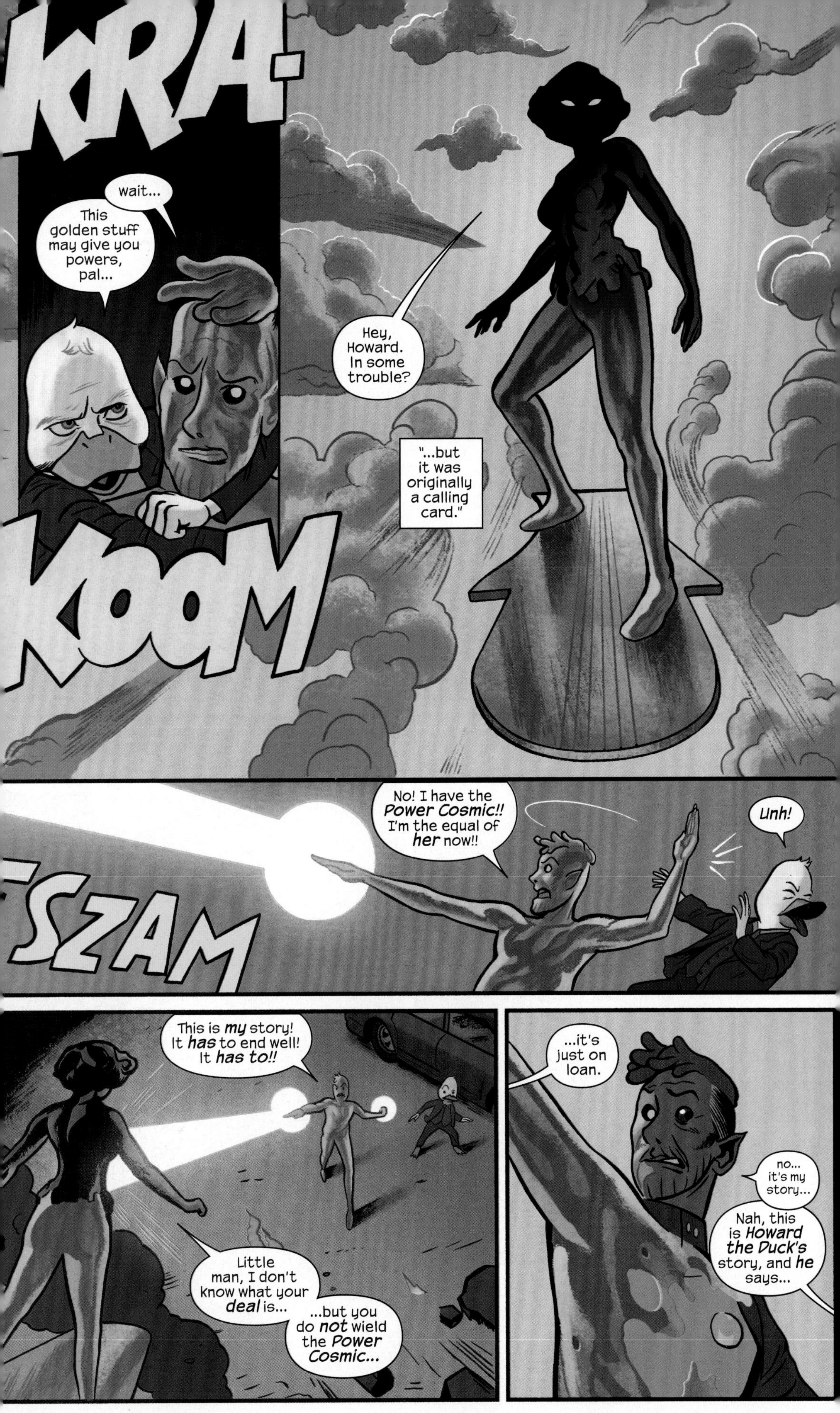
KRA-
wait...
This golden stuff may give you powers, pal...
Hey, Howard. In some trouble?
"...but it was originally a calling card."
KOOM
SZAM
No! I have the *Power Cosmic!!* I'm the equal of *her* now!!
Unh!
This is *my* story! It *has* to end well! It *has to!!*
Little man, I don't know what your *deal* is...
...but you do *not* wield the *Power Cosmic...*
...it's just on loan.
no... it's my story...
Nah, this is *Howard the Duck's* story, and *he* says...

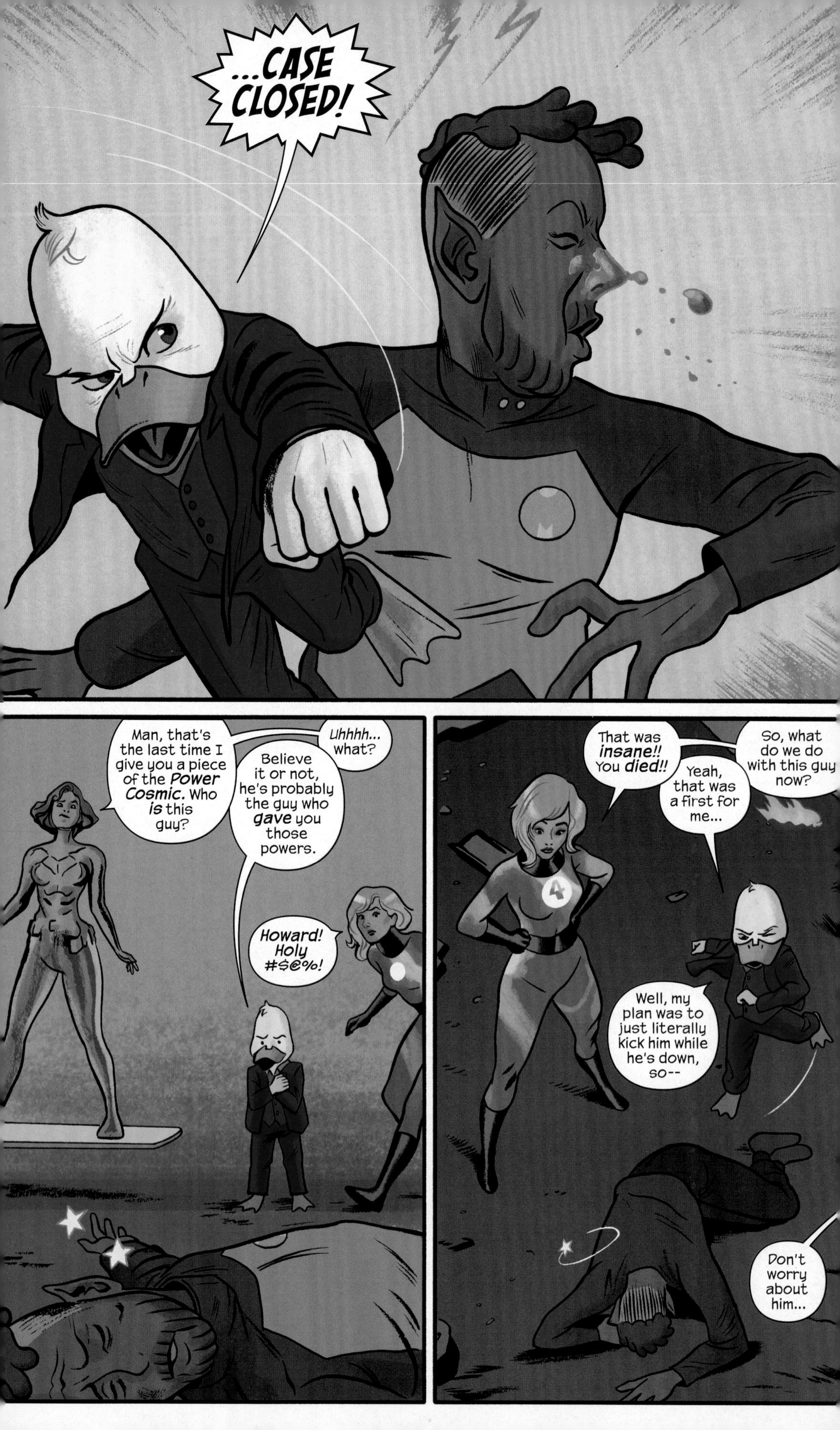
...CASE CLOSED!
Man, that's the last time I give you a piece of the *Power Cosmic.* Who *is* this guy?
Uhhhh... what?
Believe it or not, he's probably the guy who *gave* you those powers.
Howard! Holy #$@%!
That was *insane!!* You *died!!*
Yeah, that was a first for me...
So, what do we do with this guy now?
Well, my plan was to just literally kick him while he's down, so--
Don't worry about him...

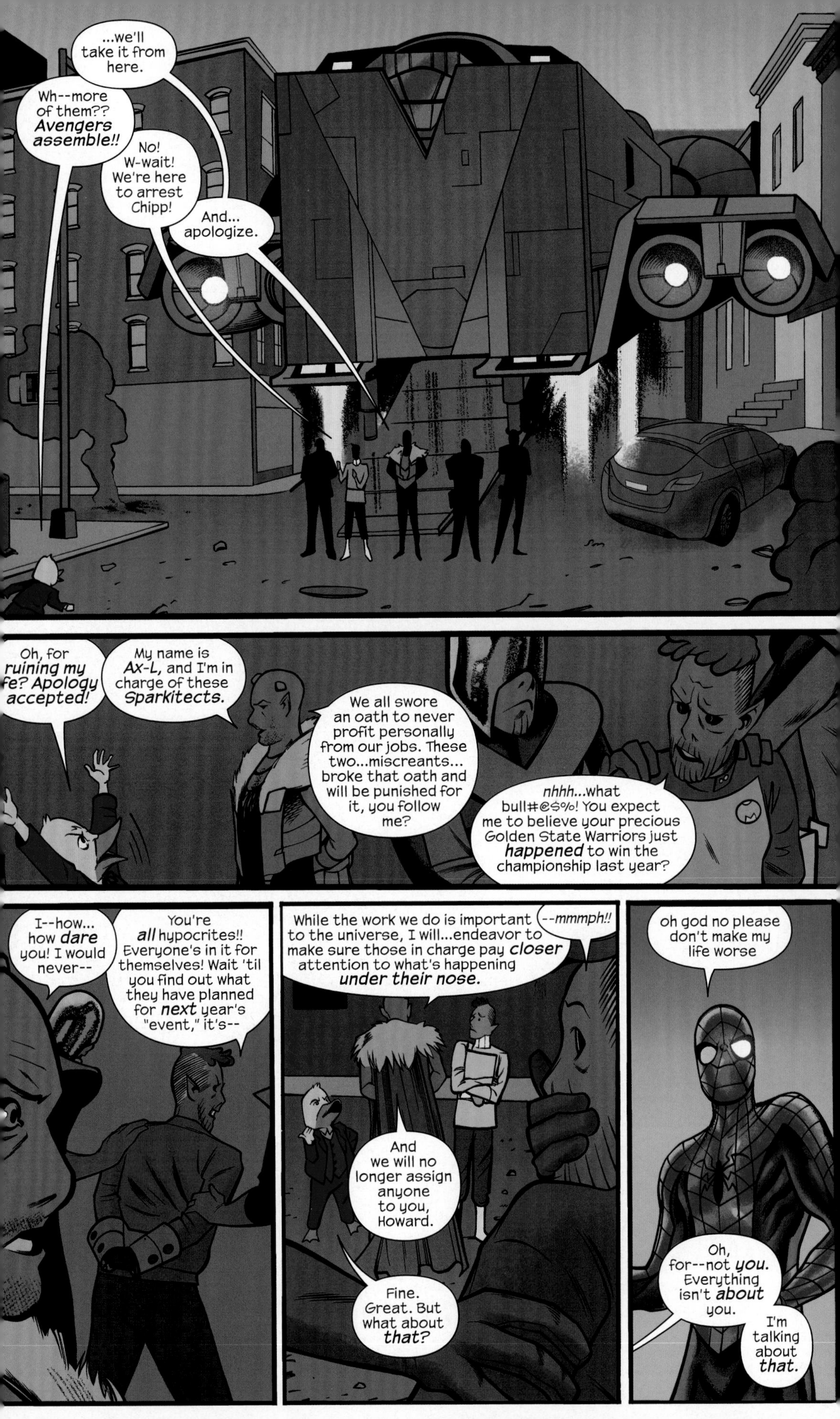
...we'll take it from here.
Wh--more of them?? Avengers assemble!!
No! W-wait! We're here to arrest Chipp!
And... apologize.
Oh, for ruining my life? Apology accepted!
My name is Ax-L, and I'm in charge of these Sparkitects.
We all swore an oath to never profit personally from our jobs. These two...miscreants... broke that oath and will be punished for it, you follow me?
nhhh...what bull#@$%! You expect me to believe your precious Golden State Warriors just happened to win the championship last year?
I--how... how dare you! I would never--
You're all hypocrites!! Everyone's in it for themselves! Wait 'til you find out what they have planned for next year's "event," it's--
While the work we do is important to the universe, I will...endeavor to make sure those in charge pay closer attention to what's happening under their nose.
--mmmph!!
And we will no longer assign anyone to you, Howard.
Fine. Great. But what about that?
oh god no please don't make my life worse
Oh, for--not you. Everything isn't about you.
I'm talking about that.

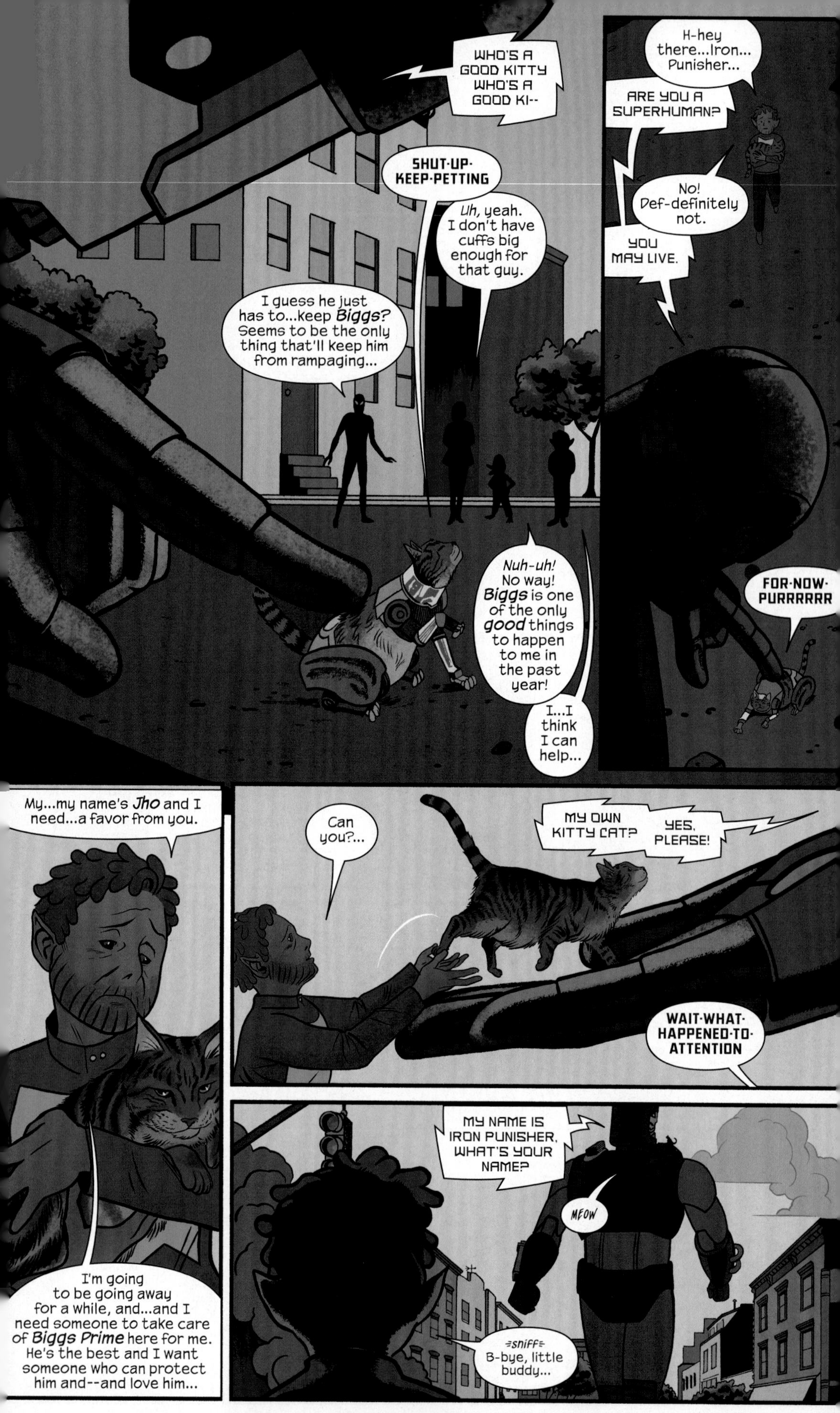
WHO'S A GOOD KITTY WHO'S A GOOD KI--
SHUT·UP· KEEP·PETTING
Uh, yeah. I don't have cuffs big enough for that guy.
I guess he just has to...keep Biggs? Seems to be the only thing that'll keep him from rampaging...
Nuh-uh! No way! Biggs is one of the only good things to happen to me in the past year!
I...I think I can help...
H-hey there...Iron... Punisher...
ARE YOU A SUPERHUMAN?
No! Def-definitely not.
YOU MAY LIVE.
FOR·NOW· PURRRRRR
My...my name's Jho and I need...a favor from you.
I'm going to be going away for a while, and...and I need someone to take care of Biggs Prime here for me. He's the best and I want someone who can protect him and--and love him...
Can you?...
MY OWN KITTY CAT?
YES, PLEASE!
WAIT·WHAT· HAPPENED·TO· ATTENTION
MY NAME IS IRON PUNISHER, WHAT'S YOUR NAME?
MEOW
=sniff= B-bye, little buddy...

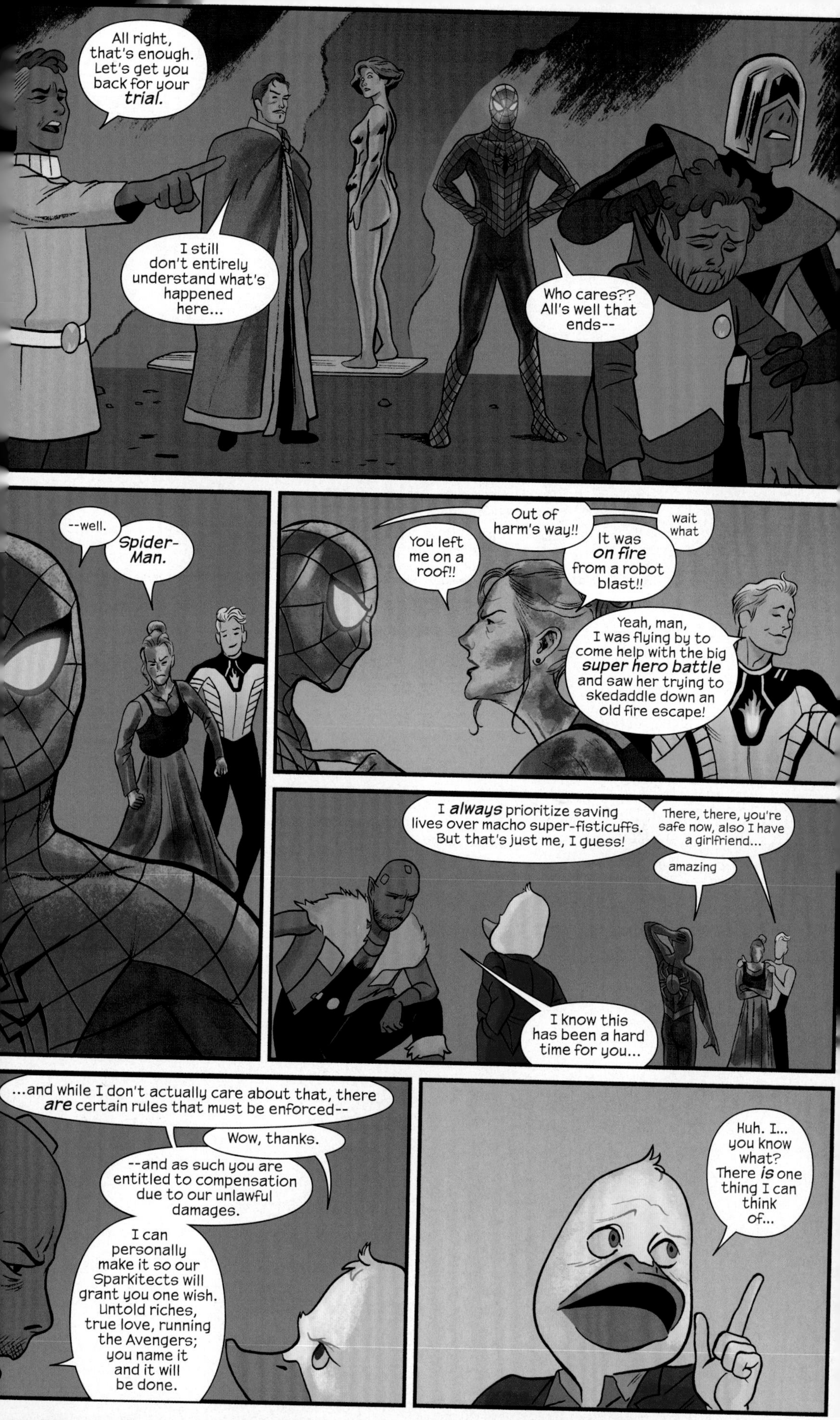

All right, that's enough. Let's get you back for your *trial.*
I still don't entirely understand what's happened here...
Who cares?? All's well that ends--
--well.
Spider-Man.
You left me on a roof!!
Out of harm's way!!
It was *on fire* from a robot blast!!
wait what
Yeah, man, I was flying by to come help with the big *super hero battle* and saw her trying to skedaddle down an old fire escape!
I *always* prioritize saving lives over macho super-fisticuffs. But that's just me, I guess!
There, there, you're safe now, also I have a girlfriend...
amazing
I know this has been a hard time for you...
...and while I don't actually care about that, there *are* certain rules that must be enforced--
Wow, thanks.
--and as such you are entitled to compensation due to our unlawful damages.
I can personally make it so our Sparkitects will grant you one wish. Untold riches, true love, running the Avengers; you name it and it will be done.
Huh. I... you know what? There *is* one thing I can think of...

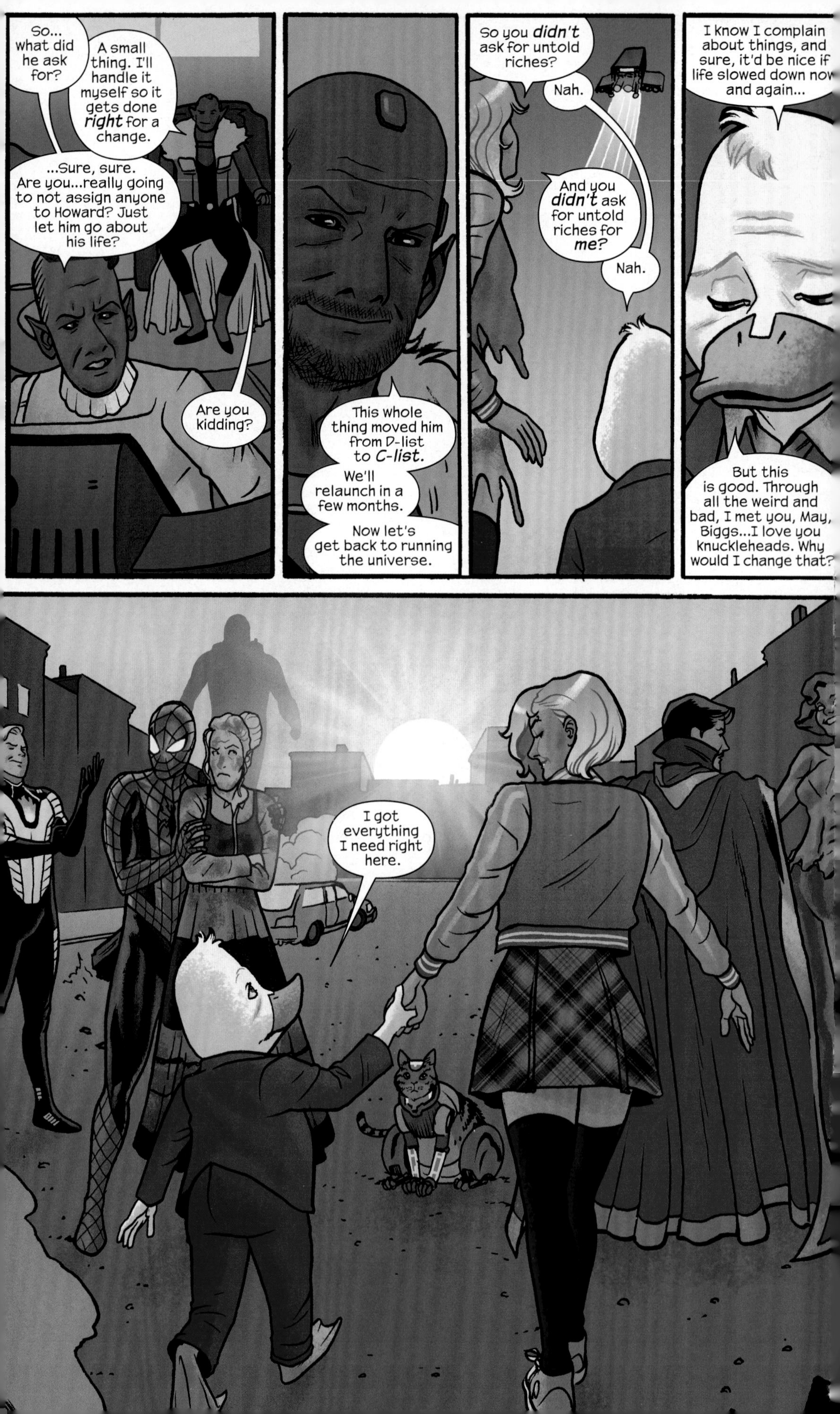
So... what did he ask for?
A small thing. I'll handle it myself so it gets done *right* for a change.
...Sure, sure. Are you...really going to not assign anyone to Howard? Just let him go about his life?
Are you kidding?
This whole thing moved him from D-list to *C-list.*
We'll relaunch in a few months.
Now let's get back to running the universe.
So you *didn't* ask for untold riches?
Nah.
And you *didn't* ask for untold riches for *me?*
Nah.
I know I complain about things, and sure, it'd be nice if life slowed down now and again...
But this is good. Through all the weird and bad, I met you, May, Biggs...I love you knuckleheads. Why would I change that?
I got everything I need right here.

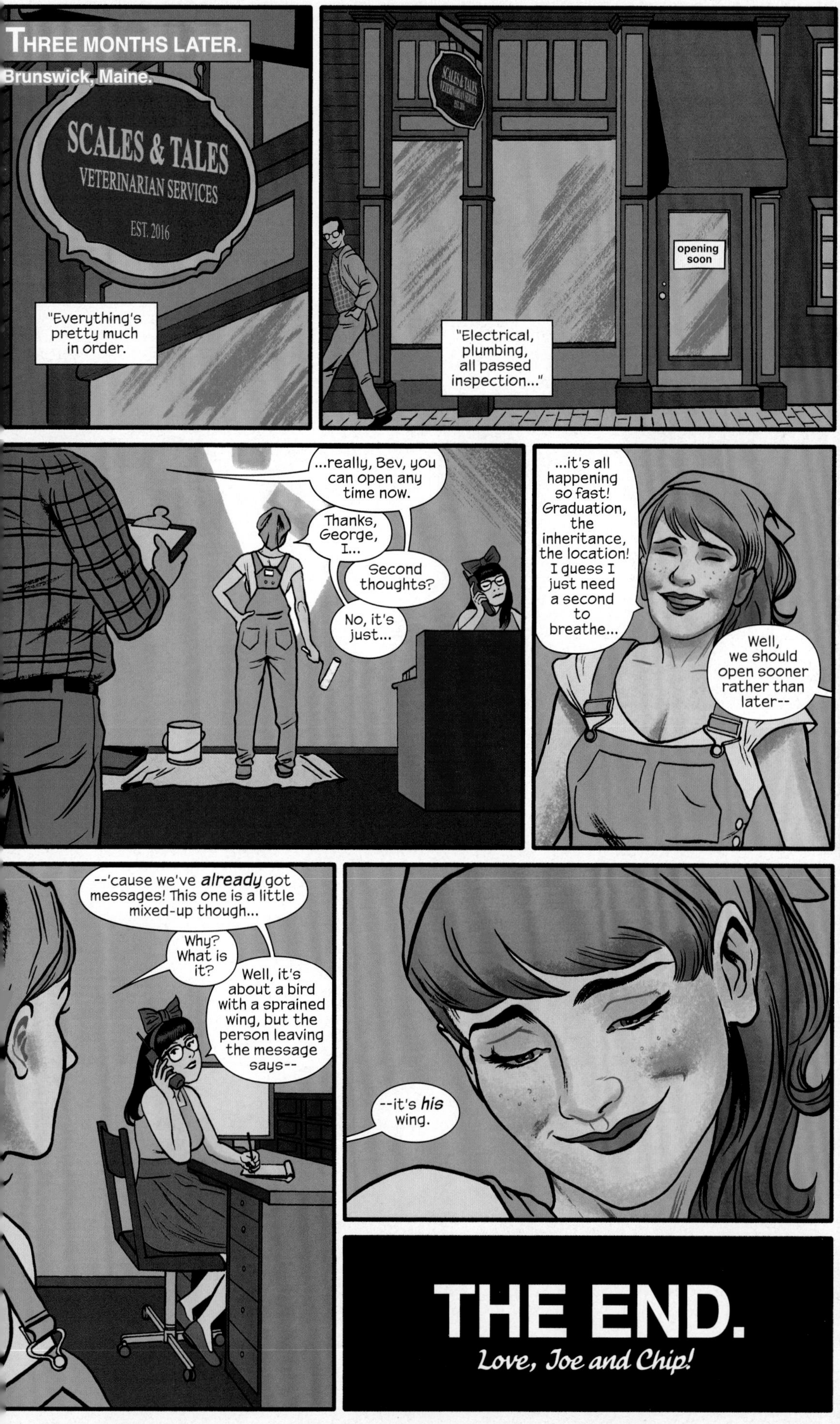
THREE MONTHS LATER.
Brunswick, Maine.
SCALES & TALES
VETERINARIAN SERVICES
EST. 2016
"Everything's pretty much in order.
opening soon
"Electrical, plumbing, all passed inspection..."
...really, Bev, you can open any time now.
Thanks, George, I...
Second thoughts?
No, it's just...
...it's all happening so fast! Graduation, the inheritance, the location! I guess I just need a second to breathe...
Well, we should open sooner rather than later--
--'cause we've *already* got messages! This one is a little mixed-up though...
Why? What is it?
Well, it's about a bird with a sprained wing, but the person leaving the message says--
--it's *his* wing.
THE END.
Love, Joe and Chip!

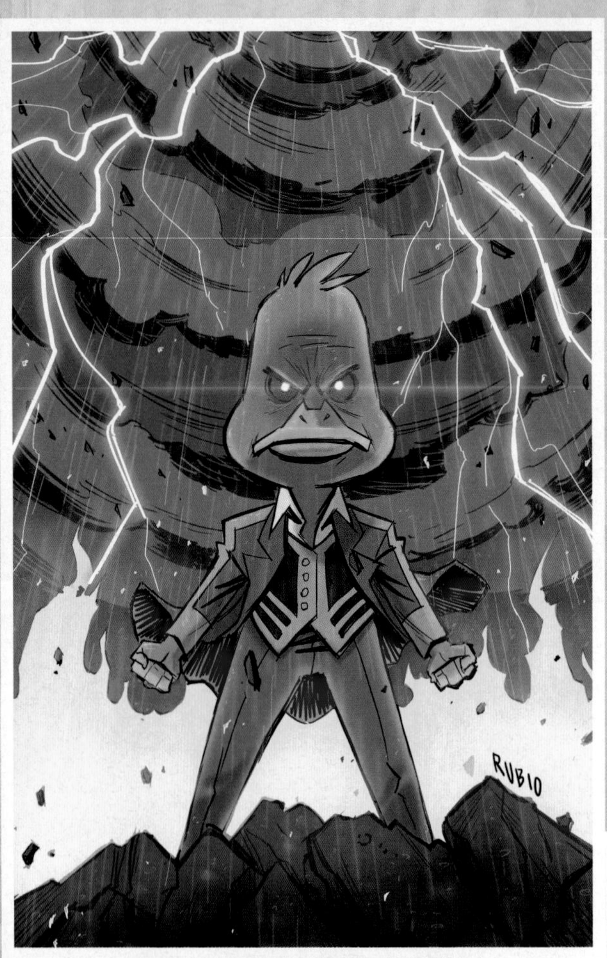
RUBIO

#7 AGE OF APOCALYPSE
VARIANT BY BOBBY RUBIO

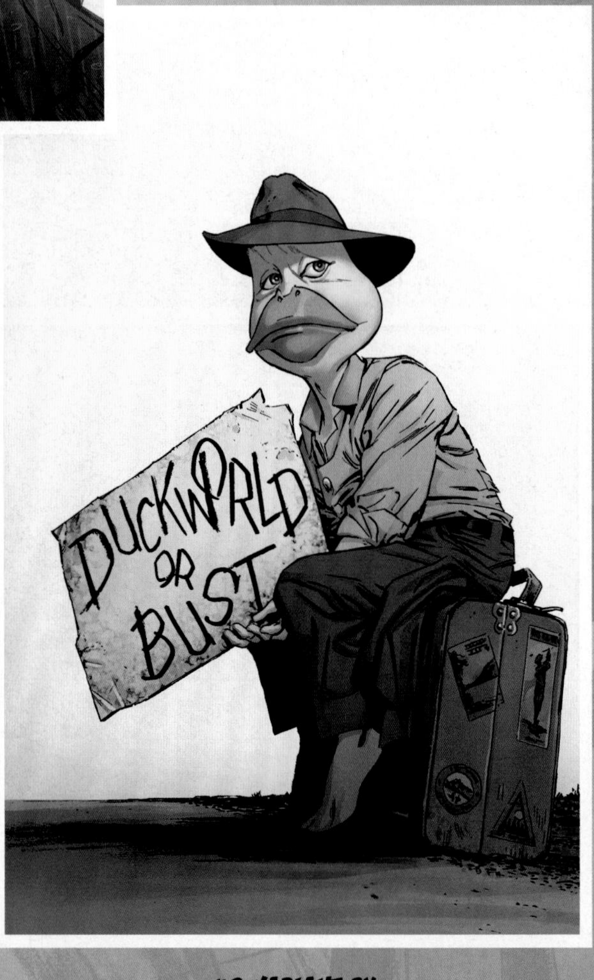
DUCKWORLD OR BUST

#8 VARIANT BY
BUTCH GUICE & FRANK D'ARMATA

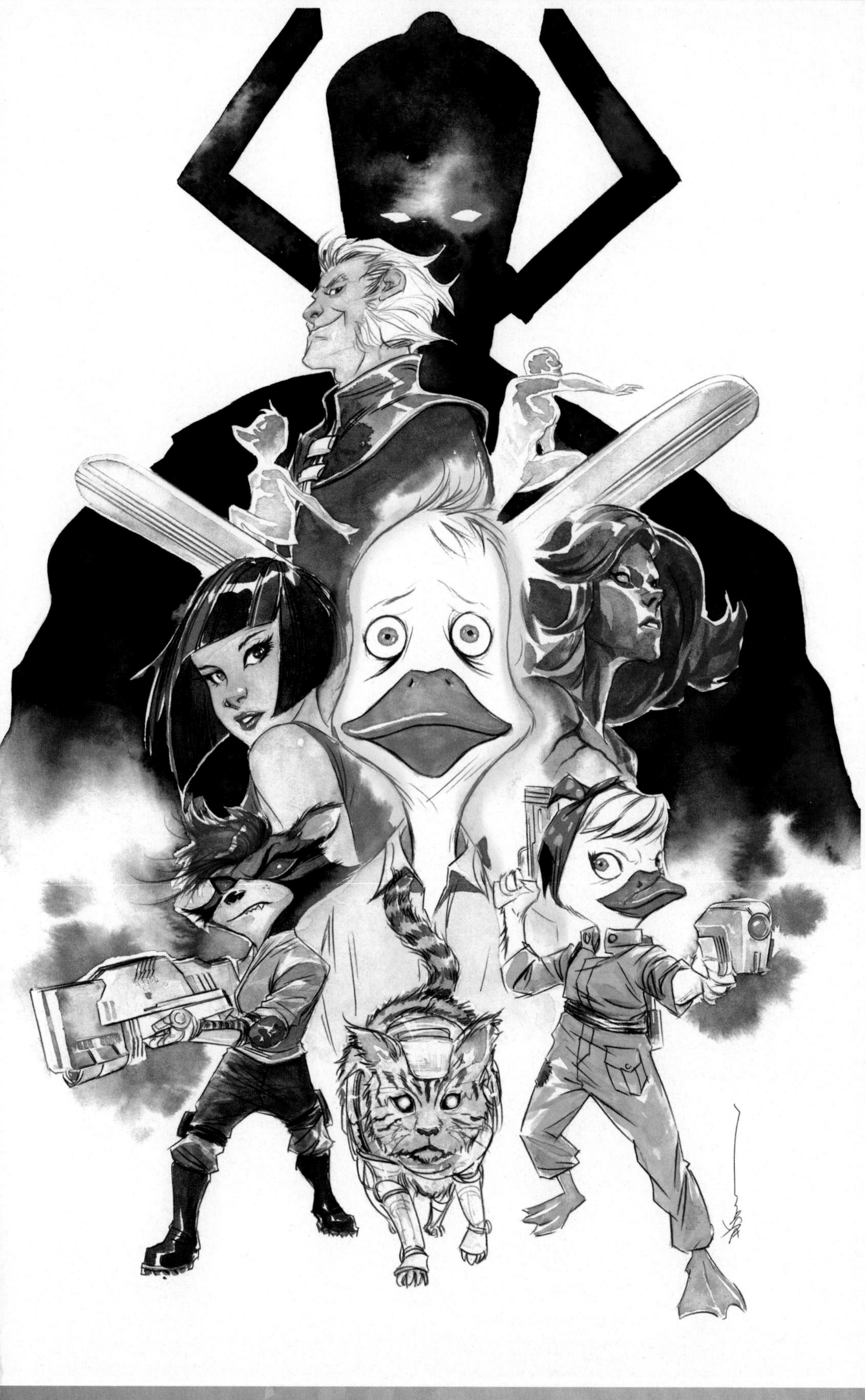

#8 STORY THIS FAR VARIANT BY DUSTIN NGUYEN

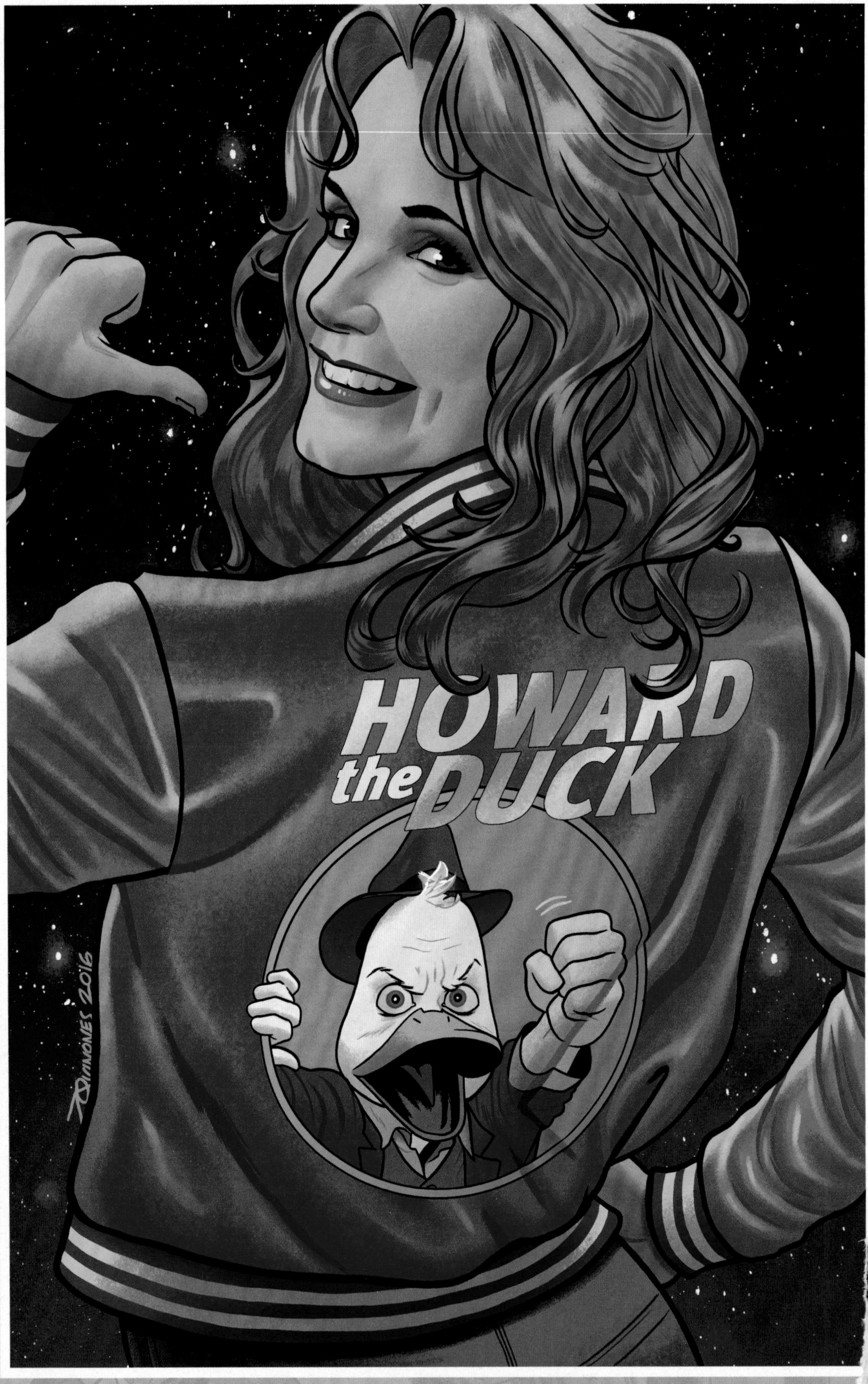
HOWARD the DUCK
QUINONES 2016

#9 VARIANT BY JOE QUINONES

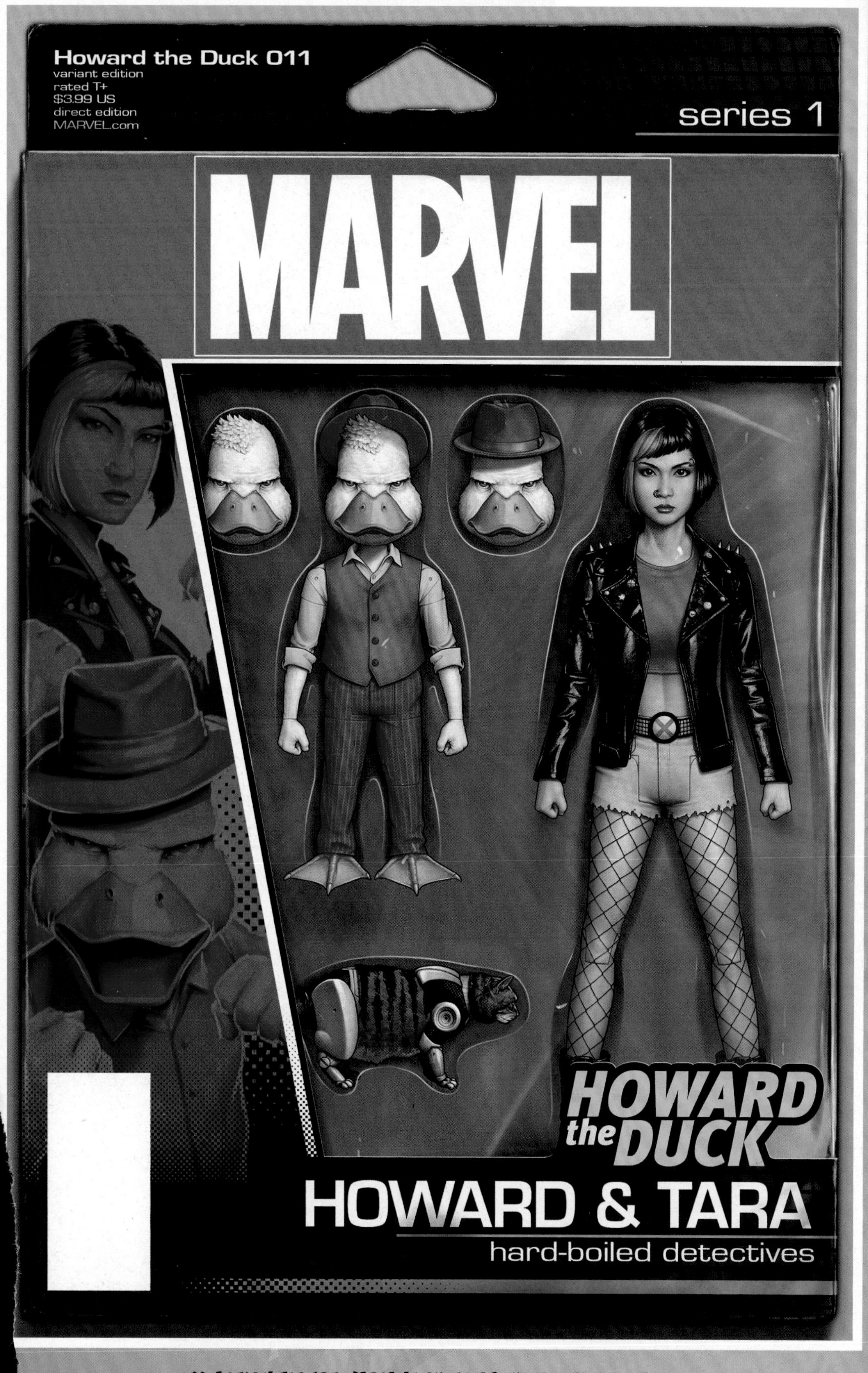
Howard the Duck 011
variant edition
rated T+
$3.99 US
direct edition
MARVEL.com
series 1
MARVEL
HOWARD the DUCK
HOWARD & TARA
hard-boiled detectives

#11 ACTION FIGURE VARIANT BY JOHN TYLER CHRISTOPHER

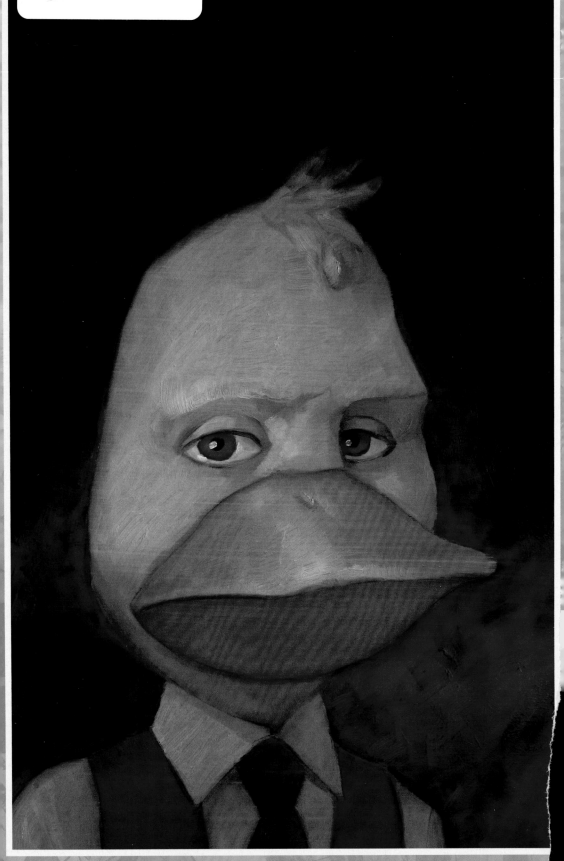

#11 VARIANT BY CHIP ZDARSKY